# Bi Lives
## Bisexual Women Tell Their Stories

## Kata Orndorff
### Editor

See Sharp Press ▼ Tucson, Arizona ▼ 1999

Orndorff, Kata, 1950-
    Bi lives : bisexual women tell their stories / Kata Orndorff. –
Tucson, AZ : See Sharp Press, c1999.
        252 p. ; 23 cm.
        Partial Contents: Safer sex / Rowan Frost – Resources / Robyn Ochs.
        ISBN: 1-884365-09-4
        1. Bisexual women - Interviews.  2. Bisexuality.  I. Title.
                306.765082

First Edition — June 1999

Cover design and illustration by Clifford Harper. Interior design by Chaz Bufe.
The cover and interior are typeset in Avant Garde and "Nebraska," a redesigned
version of Baskerville.

# Contents

*Introduction* . . . . . . . . . . . . . . . . . . . . . . . . . . . . . . . . . . 1

*Preface* . . . . . . . . . . . . . . . . . . . . . . . . . . . . . . . . . . . . . . . 7

*Acknowledgements* . . . . . . . . . . . . . . . . . . . . . . . . . . . 11

  1. Dannielle . . . . . . . . . . . . . . . . . . . . . . . . . . . . . . . . 13

  2. Anuhea . . . . . . . . . . . . . . . . . . . . . . . . . . . . . . . . . . 25

  3. Margarita . . . . . . . . . . . . . . . . . . . . . . . . . . . . . . . . 35

  4. Peg . . . . . . . . . . . . . . . . . . . . . . . . . . . . . . . . . . . . . 42

  5. Sonya . . . . . . . . . . . . . . . . . . . . . . . . . . . . . . . . . . . 56

  6. Rosa . . . . . . . . . . . . . . . . . . . . . . . . . . . . . . . . . . . . 66

  7. Mary . . . . . . . . . . . . . . . . . . . . . . . . . . . . . . . . . . . . 77

  8. Lani . . . . . . . . . . . . . . . . . . . . . . . . . . . . . . . . . . . . 98

  9. Susan . . . . . . . . . . . . . . . . . . . . . . . . . . . . . . . . . . 113

10. Vidya . . . . . . . . . . . . . . . . . . . . . . . . . . . . . . . . . . 126

11. Rachel . . . . . . . . . . . . . . . . . . . . . . . . . . . . . . . . . 133

12. Judy . . . . . . . . . . . . . . . . . . . . . . . . . . . . . . . . . . . 142

13. Carol . . . . . . . . . . . . . . . . . . . . . . . . . . . . . . . . . . 165

14. Michelle . . . . . . . . . . . . . . . . . . . . . . . . . . . . . . . . 180

15. Casey . . . . . . . . . . . . . . . . . . . . . . . . . . . . . . . . . . 190

16. Pamela . . . . . . . . . . . . . . . . . . . . . . . . . . . . . . . . . 207

17. Revi . . . . . . . . . . . . . . . . . . . . . . . . . . . . . . . . . . . 215

18. Diana . . . . . . . . . . . . . . . . . . . . . . . . . . . . . . . . . . 229

*Appendices*

  A. *Safer Sex* (by Rowan Frost) . . . . . . . . . . . . . . . . . 241

  B. *Resources for Bisexual Women* (by Robyn Ochs) . . . . . . . 248

  C. *Additional Resources* . . . . . . . . . . . . . . . . . . . . . . . . 252

# INTRODUCTION

*"In this culture everything's got to be yes/no, right/wrong, left/right, black/white. Nothing can be in the middle. To be bisexual means that you're not lesbian. You're not straight. You're somewhere where people have trouble dealing."*

—from Carol's interview

Bisexuality is the sexual orientation of a person who is attracted to people of both sexes. This does not mean that every bisexual person feels the need to be involved with both a man and a woman, or that they will have sex with anyone who is available to them. It does not mean, as some lesbians believe, that bisexual women are not serious about any relationship they have with a woman, because (they believe) bisexual women would place more importance on any relationship with a man. Yet these are some of the misconceptions that gay and straight people have about bisexuals. While there are bisexuals who fit these stereotypes, I have not found many of them.

I chose to do a book of interviews with bisexual women because our lives so clearly do not conform to these stereotypes. I wanted to illustrate the reality of several different women, all of whom happen to share the capacity to love and relate sexually to people of both sexes. Each woman's interview has been edited with the intention of communicating what is most important to her, and what is most unique and interesting about her life. Each interview is a personal portrait of the many ways that bisexual women live their lives.

Many bisexual women choose to be in monogamous relationships, knowing that their partner could be either sex. Other bisexual women are nonmonogamous—some specifically in order to be in simultaneous relationships with both a man and a woman, others to be open to whomever comes along. Most, but not all, nonmonogamous bisexual women I interviewed are involved in ongoing relationships.

Two of the interviewees are in a polyfidelitous relationship with a man. Polyfidelity is an intimate partnership in which three or more people are all primary partners with each other, are sexual only with these primary partners, and have a lifelong commitment to one another. Group marriage is another name for this type of relationship. People sometimes use the term "polyfidelity" to describe any nonmonogamous relationship, especially ones with a strong emotional component. The term "polyamorous" is now often used to describe these kinds of nonmonogamous relationships to distinguish them from polyfidelitous group marriages.

All of these are valid relationship options. It is important that every person choose a way of relating to other people that is right for them. It is equally important that each person be open and honest with any intimate partner as to what that choice is.

In our society, most people think monogamy is the only moral context for sexual relationships. As a result, many people who want to be sexual with more than one person are not honest about this with their primary partner(s). Being honest with ones intimate partner or partners is always an essential ingredient in a healthy relationship and in a life lived with integrity. In this book, several nonmonogamous women appear who are honest with their partners and have integrity in their relationships.

It is also essential to be able to be honest about your sexuality—both with yourself and with the people you are close to. This can be difficult for bisexual women. Many heterosexuals barely tolerate people being in same-sex relationships, while many lesbians are threatened by women who are able to be involved with them and with a man. There are straight people and lesbians who are truly comfortable with bisexual women, but the prospect of coming out, not knowing what people's reactions will be is frightening to many bisexual women.

I wish we lived in a society where the sex of a person's intimate partner did not matter—where, as Lani Ka'ahumanu says in her interview, we would just say that we were sexual and not be defined by the sex of the person we are with. However, we live in a society where heterosexuality is considered the norm. It is important for those who do not fit the heterosexual mold to define their sexuality in order to pressure mainstream society to include same-sex couples in their concept of possible human relationships. It also enables those who are not heterosexual to have a context for their own experience.

For many women, stepping outside the bounds of heterosexual

relationships initiates a consciousness-expanding process. It can become clear to a woman in this situation how much time and energy she has expended meeting a man's personal needs and his expectations of how she should be. She may never again be "male-defined," that is, seeing herself as someone who needs to be what a man thinks she should be.

In the second wave of feminism in the '70s, women who realized that they were attracted to women called themselves lesbian feminists, as a way of defining this orientation. It seemed to many of them that feminists who were still involved with men were missing a key ingredient of feminist consciousness, and they often viewed themselves as superior to straight feminists. There was no room in their political construct for bisexual feminists. For lesbian feminists, bisexuality was a figment of male imaginations—a fantasy based on the prurient interest of men who couldn't believe that all women weren't available to them.

During this time, feminist women were focusing on what it meant to be a woman outside the parameters of the patriarchal male definition of women. A political theory of lesbian feminism evolved based on where a woman chose to put her energy and focus. In this context, sexual desire was not what defined a lesbian; rejecting men and being committed primarily to other "woman-identified" women did.

Any woman who was a part of the lesbian feminist movement and then got involved with a man was considered to be a traitor, and was often ostracized. Lesbians who found themselves attracted to men had to choose between their real desires and their friends and community. Some women hid their relationships with men from their friends. Many thought of these attractions as a heterosexual phase they would eventually get over, because they were really lesbians.

This way of thinking was predicated on the idea that everyone is either gay or straight. Either you only want to be sexual with people of your own sex, or you only want to be sexual with people of the opposite sex. Because in our society most of us were raised with exposure only to heterosexual pairings, a woman could rationalize that she had been conditioned to be attracted to men. However, she really was a lesbian, because her feminist consciousness and commitment, as well as her attraction to other women, had not changed.

In the '80s some lesbians began to talk and write about desire and feminist erotica, issues that had previously been almost taboo because of the fear among feminists that, like pornography, erotica would be demeaning to women. Some lesbians voiced resentment about trying to fit their desires into what was acceptable to the lesbian feminist community. The idea was born that women's real desires needed to be incorporated into the dictates of feminism, and it became more acceptable to base one's sexuality on one's desires. In this context, more women were able to acknowledge that they were bisexual.

Several bisexual organizations and support groups formed in the '80s, such as the Boston Bisexual Women's Network, the Seattle Women's Bisexual Network, and San Francisco's BiPOL. These groups considered themselves to be a part of the larger queer community. This development met with a great deal of hostility from many lesbians and gay men. It still took a great deal of courage for bisexual women to come out to themselves, much less to others, particularly lesbians. There were women who continued to hide their attractions and even their relationships with men from their lesbian friends.

Bisexual organizing and visibility greatly expanded in the late '80s and '90s. It became much easier and more acceptable for women to identify as bisexual within the lesbian and gay movement. Many national and local gay groups started using the terms gay, lesbian and bisexual in their names. More lesbians became comfortable with bisexual women.

Many more straight people also became comfortable with gays and lesbians as well as bisexuals due to the work of queer activists. However, some straight people still believed that if a person is capable of being with either a man or a woman, they should choose to be with a person of the opposite sex, since this is a more acceptable option in this society. This line of thinking assumes that the only reason a woman would want to be with another woman is because she has no other choice!

Almost every woman I interviewed spoke of the greater emotional intimacy she experienced with other women. Several spoke of the pain they experienced when having to suppress an attraction to someone of either sex. I feel, and these interviews have reinforced this feeling, that when a person is able to connect with another person on a deep emotional and sexual level, that is a gift. To not allow that connection to happen because the person is not a certain sex is a major loss for both people.

# A NOTE ON SAFER SEX

I have addressed the issue of safer sex in this book because I think it is important. HIV (Human Immunodeficiency Virus), the virus that causes AIDS (Acquired Immune Deficiency Syndrome), is the scariest sexually transmitted disease (STD) because it is potentially life threatening. However, there are other STDs with serious consequences, such as hepatitis B and C which may cause liver damage, and herpes which can be painful and has no cure. For specific information on how to protect yourself from STDs see Appendix A on page 241. And, if you think you are safe from STDs because the people you are sexual with are not in a high-risk category, read Mary's interview on page 77.

Some people rely on knowing a potential partner's sexual history as a way of evaluating whether they need to engage in safer sex with them. This is only as reliable as the information we are given by that person. Carol, whose interview begins on page 165, was involved with a man she thought she knew very well. He identified as straight. Only after finding out that he was HIV-positive did he tell her that he also sometimes had sex with men.

There are women who think that they cannot get HIV from other women and therefore do not have to have safer sex with them. This is not true. There are women who have become infected with HIV by having sex with an HIV-positive woman.

Past or present injection drug users have the greatest likelihood of being HIV-positive. However, it is not always obvious that someone is or has been an injection drug user.

People have secrets when it comes to sex and drugs. It may be impossible to know if someone is being completely honest about their risk of infection. Also, merely because someone tells us what they know about their past sexual partners does not mean that those partners, seemingly at low risk, were not exposed to STDs from one of their past partners. When it comes to STDs, when we sleep with one person we are sleeping with every partner they have ever had, plus all their partner's partners, ad infinitum. For these reasons, some people only have safer sex, even with their primary partner.

## A Note on the Women in this Book

I've changed the names of all of the women I interviewed, and the people they mention, with the sole exception of those women who specifically asked that I use their real names.

I should also note that it has taken me several years to complete this project. In the interim some of the interviewee's lives have changed in ways they wanted me to acknowledge in this book. These women have added postcripts to their interviews briefly describing their current situation.

Other interviewees chose not to allow their interviews to be published at this time. The most common reasons were that they felt that what they had said at that time no longer reflected their lives, or they wanted to make changes in the interview but did not have the time to do so. Unfortunately, most of the women of color I inter-viewed decided not to have their interviews published. I regret this book does not have as many women of color represented as I would have liked. But it does include women of different ages and covers the range of relationship possibilities that I had hoped it would.

Bisexual women reading the interviews will undoubtedly find women they identify with and others whose experiences are very different from their own. I want this book to validate the lives of bisexual women, regardless of the choices they have made. I also want it to support women who are attracted to people of both sexes to acknowledge and embrace their bisexuality. To me, asserting our bisexuality is a truly feminist stance, because we are defining ourselves based on our real desires and insisting that these be taken seriously.

I hope that reading about the lives of women who have claimed their right to be their true selves allows more people to experience the freedom that comes from choosing a way of life that is right for them, while allowing others the right to choose a different way of living. Ultimately, I hope these interviews contribute to the acceptance and validation of all sexual orientations and relationship lifestyles in our society.

# PREFACE

Because this is a book in which I explore how different women came to know and accept their bisexuality, I will tell you about my own evolution as a bisexual woman.

I was born in Harrisburg, Pennsylvania in 1950, the second of five children in a white, working class, Catholic family. Making enough money to pay for our basic needs was always a struggle in my family.

From the ages of nine to eleven I was molested by a parish priest. At that time (the late '50s and early '60s) I knew that if I tried to tell anyone I was not likely to be believed, and if I was, I would be blamed for somehow enticing this respected and holy man. This is a terrible situation for any child to be in, and I lived for the day when I would be old enough to take care of myself, and therefore, be safe from people like this priest. I also assumed that I would fall in love with a man, get married and live happily ever after.

However, by the time I graduated from high school in 1968, the sexual revolution was well under way. I knew I did not want to emulate the unfulfilling kind of relationship my parents had in their marriage. So when I moved away from home, I started being sexually active with men, hoping that breaking free of the sexual constraints of my parents' generation would provide me with the kind of satisfying relationship I wanted. This did not happen.

I now recognize the sexism that existed in the sexual revolution of the '60s. While it was a positive step away from the repression of sexuality, it was still based on meeting men's sexual needs without any consideration for the sexual or emotional needs of women. Mine were certainly not met. As a woman, I also had to carry the burden of dealing with contraception, as men rarely took responsibility for it.

These were among the issues that brought me to my first feminist consciousness-raising group. It was exciting to be talking with women about what our lives were really like. It was also infuriating to realize our inferior position as women in society, and to recognize the demeaning way we were routinely treated by men.

Women all over the country were gathering in groups like the one I was in. We knew something major was happening. Then some women started falling in love with each other and feeling not just good about this, but liberated by it. An exuberant wave of sisterhood connected all of us who were a part of this phenomenon.

It was in this supportive environment that I fell in love with and had my first relationship with a woman. I believed then that the reason that my relationships with men had been so unfulfilling was that I had not really wanted to be with a man. I just needed a woman. I was sure that this would be the answer to everything that I had ever wanted in my life. For the first time I had a lover who considered my wants and needs, and who cared for me. She was aware of me when we made love, and making love was all new. There were no rules now. We could focus on what really felt good for each of us. And I was part of a community of women with common ideas and values. I was home.

I started talking about my experiences of being sexually abused as a child. I became a part of a self-help therapy group of women who were survivors of childhood sexual abuse. At this time there was little acknowledgement of how pervasive the sexual abuse of children was. This changed as feminist women started writing about the issue, and some of us came out about our own experiences of abuse. This was very empowering for me. I gained a realization of the personal strength which had enabled me to survive as an abused child, and felt a sense of peace in no longer having to keep the abuse a "shameful" secret. I received support and validation from other feminist women who recognized my strength in dealing openly with the issue.

But also at this time, the radical women's movement which gave me so much was developing a political stance that "real feminist women" were lesbians. The problem for me with this definition was that I kept experiencing attractions to men, and then found myself being involved sexually with a man again. I reluctantly concluded that I was bisexual, a category which at the time I felt would lose me the love and support of my sisters in the lesbian community.

Indeed, many lesbians had very negative feelings towards bisexual women. And many lesbians felt betrayed when women they thought were lesbians got involved with a man. It seemed to them that these women had taken the caring energy of women lovers and then fled back to the safe haven of being with a man. I had felt this way myself toward bisexual women. So I believed that somehow I was letting the lesbian community down by being involved with men again.

At the same time, it seemed to me that there was something very wrong with a movement for the liberation of women, lesbians and gays which would expect me to suppress a part of my sexuality. Wasn't the women's movement about supporting me to be who I was, and about having that acknowledged and respected in the world? Yet many lesbians did not accept or respect me if I loved a man, and many more who might still personally like me felt that I was no longer a part of the lesbian community. That hurt deeply, because it seemed to ignore the "woman-identified" focus I had in my life as well as my past and possibly future relationships with women. I already lived in a society which did not acknowledge or respect my relationships with women, and to have other women with whom I shared this shut me out was very painful.

However much I wanted them to, my attractions to men did not go away. I finally had to accept that I had the capacity to have deep loving relationships with both women and men, and that to not allow myself to be with someone because of their sex would negate my own true loving self. Furthermore, to hide my true sexual orientation from people I felt close to would lower my self-esteem and take away my peace of mind. So I felt compelled to be honest about being bisexual.

Coming to terms with my sexuality at that time meant that I needed to center my identity and worth in myself—not in the lesbian community which had been my home for many years. It forced me to challenge my ideas about the inherent superiority of lesbianism as an answer to sexism in our society. I came to believe that while it is essential for women's liberation that any woman be free to be in a sexual relationship with another woman—and the lesbian feminist movement has been responsible for making this more of a reality— this is only a truly freeing option if a woman is still allowed to choose whether to be involved with a woman or a man or to be celibate. It became clear to me that I wanted my feminism to be based on my commitment to all women having the freedom to be themselves and to choose a way of life that was right for them.

The focus of my life changed drastically nine years ago when I developed Multiple Chemical Sensitivity (MCS). This is an illness which causes me to react to the many toxic chemical products commonly used in our society as well as to the pollution in our environment. Because of this I live in the desert in Arizona. Most people I have contact with also have MCS. Many of us have little in common except the illness.

When the issue comes up, I am open about being bisexual. Many people, including members of my family, know that I am working on this book, but with few exceptions they cannot relate to it. I am very grateful for the people I feel connected to who do share my way of viewing the world.

This book project has been a way for me to focus on an issue that remains very important to me, and to reach out beyond my necessarily limited environment. Interviewing the women whose stories appear here, for whom coming to terms with their sexuality was often difficult, catalyzed my anger at the ways bisexuals are hurt by people who want to limit our options or punish us for being who we are. It finally enabled me to strongly and proudly ground myself in my identity as a bisexual woman. I am very grateful to the women I interviewed for this gift.

# ACKNOWLEDGEMENTS

I wish to thank the following people who helped to make this book possible. First, the women who allowed me to interview them, especially those who consented to having their interviews published in this book. Lynaea Search, for helping me come up with questions and ideas for interviewing women as well as help with editing. Lani Ka'ahumanu, for giving me support and encouragement throughout this project and for taking the time to give me feedback on my introduction. Faith Spaulding, Autumn Holder, and Kate Randall (of Antigone Books in Tucson, Arizona), for giving me feedback on my introduction and preface. Carol Orndorff, for giving me some very practical assistance at a crucial time in the process. Robyn Ochs, for providing excerpts from the *Bisexual Resource Guide 2000*. Rowan Frost, for allowing the information she presents in her safer sex workshops to be published in this book. And Chaz Bufe, of See Sharp Press, for putting up with the many hassles involved in preparing this book for publication.

# DEFINITIONS
## (AND A NOTE ON PRONOUNS)

I have used the terms "they" or "them" in the places in this book where such terms are appropriate in order to avoid being gender specific.

*Internalized oppression* means believing, often on an unconscious level, negative stereotypes about oneself as a woman, racial minority, or member of another oppressed group.

A *lesbian separatist* is a lesbian who only wants to be with other lesbians and does not want to give any of her time or energy to men or to women who relate to men.

*Queer*, a derogatory term when used by homophobes, is a reclaimed word in the gay community meaning other than heterosexual.

A *woman-identified woman* defines herself in terms of her commitment to and relationships with herself and other women, not by how men or patriarchal society view her.

# 1 ▼ Dannielle

*Dannielle Raymond McClintock is a 27-year-old drugstore clerk who lives in San Francisco. She is a "peer safer sex educator" and has been involved with the queer youth movement. Her mother is Lani Ka'ahumanu whose interview also appears in this book.*

**K:** Tell me a little bit about your family background, your class background, and your ethnic background. Were you raised with any religion?

**D:** My Dad came from a poor working-class family. My mother came from an upper-middle-class family. It was shocking for her when they first started dating, because the families were so different. So I got mixed class influence. I mostly identify with being working class, but in a lot of ways I'm very middle class.

Ethnically, I'm your basic mutt—mainly European, but my maternal grandmother was born in Japan and raised in Hawaii. She's European, Japanese, and Hawaiian, but mostly identifies as a Polynesian woman. So I was brought up with an awareness of various cultures and of how race impacts experience. Although it was very much a Euro-American culture. The schools I went to were very white. The neighborhood I lived in was mixed ethnically in that there were immigrants from different parts of Europe, but it was still white.

I was raised without a religion, and that was intentional on my parents' part. My mother was brought up Catholic. The story I always heard is that she was folding my diapers one day and decided she didn't want to go to church anymore, because she didn't want my brother and I to be raised with the kind of guilt feelings that she was raised with. So it was a conscious decision that she made when I was a baby. My Dad wasn't raised with much religion so it was easy for him to go along with our not being brought up in one.

This was in the '60s. There was a lot of change going on at that time—a lot of rejection of tradition and a lot of experimentation. My parents were very open to new ideas, and new ways of thinking and being and doing. So I grew up in that environment. I felt encouraged to explore who I was and to feel good about whoever I happened to be.

My parents divorced when I was seven years old, and my mother moved out. She lived in the same neighborhood for the first nine months, then she moved 20 miles away to San Francisco. She and I saw each other regularly and stayed in close contact, but I grew up with my dad. A couple of years after my mother moved out she came out as a lesbian.

**K:** How was that for you?

**D:** It was really hard. I was in the fifth grade when she came out, and I was still reeling from the divorce, which was probably the hardest thing that ever happened to me in my life. When my mother came out she wasn't subtle about it. She didn't just quietly tell her closest friends and family or have a discreet affair. She was marching in the streets and doing public speaking about it and feeling that it was really important to tell every single soul on the planet.

Approaching adolescence is a very difficult time anyway, but I felt like I had an extra stigma as the child of a homosexual. I felt like I had a big secret. So my first experience of homophobia and of being closeted was as the child of a lesbian. That was a big struggle. By the time I got into high school I was comfortable with my Mom's sexuality and I told everybody that she was a lesbian. How someone reacted to this information became a barometer of whether or not I wanted to be friends with them, because if they had any problem with it they were obviously somebody that I couldn't care about.

When I was in the eighth grade my mother figured out that she wasn't a lesbian, that she was really a bisexual. That was really hard for her, because at that time there was no such thing as a bisexual. By coming out as a bisexual woman she probably lost half her lesbian friends.

**K:** What enabled you to go from being closeted about your mother's sexuality to feeling comfortable with it?

**D:** Initially it wasn't my choice. I had this friend who I had been friends with since the first grade. My mother, being the kind of person that she is, thought of this friend as her friend too. Since she felt it was important to tell her friends that she was a lesbian, my mother came out to my friend. That was awful for me, because being 12 years old, in junior high school, is probably the worst time that anybody has. I felt that this friend used it against me in certain ways. Fortunately she moved, so after that I didn't have to worry about her telling everybody at school.

When I was in the eighth grade I met a woman who continues to be my best friend. She told me that my stepbrother had told her about my mom, and she was supportive. That meant a lot to me. She said, "It's fine. I know lesbians. A lesbian used to be my babysitter." I had met other kids who had lesbian mothers or gay fathers, but they were all in San Francisco; they weren't in the suburbs. They were two different worlds to me. So having one friend in the suburbs who was not just tolerant but supportive helped a lot.

I was also getting older with a stronger sense of myself and feeling less worried about peer approval. When you're approaching adolescence there's tremendous pressure to feel that you're just like everybody else whether or not you have a queer parent. I think just getting older and not worrying about being exactly like everybody else contributed to my being able to feel comfortable with my mother's sexuality.

I have always felt very comfortable with my mother. I always thought that her sexuality was fine. I didn't think there was anything wrong with it. What bothered me was that everybody else was so freaked out about it. I wasn't mad at her that she loved women. I was mad at the world for treating her as a pariah for loving women.

**K:** When were you first aware of sexual attractions and to which gender?

**D:** Having my mother come out when I was 10 made me hyper-aware of sexuality and sexual identity before I was ready to think about it. Not to say that sexual feelings didn't occur before then, but they were just part of sensual life. They were not conscious.

Because I had the stigma of having a queer parent, I censored my feelings towards girls. I remember in junior high school being attracted to my girlfriend and absolutely not showing it, not acting on it, not expressing anything remotely close to it, because I was so afraid of people calling me a lesbian. There're so many things to feel alienated about as an adolescent that if you're queer on top of it, or you think you might be, it's really hard. That's why the suicide rates are so high for young people who are attracted to people of the same sex. Also because I was a child of divorce and a child of a queer parent, I felt that the whole world was watching me to see how these things were going to affect me. I felt a lot of pressure to be the perfect child.

**K:** Did you date in high school and junior high?

**D:** I always had flirtations with boys. It was expected, but that's not the only reason why I was doing it. I'm a very sexual person so I started exploring sexually. I was kissing boys by late junior high school. Then in high school I seriously dated a number of boys and was sexual with them.

I began to identify as bisexual when I was in high school. It just felt natural to me to call myself bisexual, because I was attracted to men and I was attracted to women. My actual physical experiences were mostly with boys at the time, but I acknowledged to myself that I felt attracted to girls as well. It was very easy to find guys to date. It was very hard for me to find any women.

I would get crushes on women, and they would get totally freaked out if I tried to do anything about it, which I don't think is unusual. I tried a number of different times to expand my relationships with female friends in high school, and they were completely unresponsive. Some would get mad. I had a couple of women reciprocate interest but be too freaked out about the idea to actually do anything sexual with me.

When I got out of high school I kept trying to date women, and I kept having awful experiences while having successful relationships with men. When I was 20 years old it got to the point that I thought, "Maybe I'm not bisexual. Maybe I'm just fooling myself. Maybe I'm just doing this because my mother's bisexual, and I want to check it out."

Then I was in a relationship with a man for almost four years. When we broke up I was 24 years old, and I thought, "This is it. I'm single. I'm going to make my last ditch effort to be with a woman, and if it doesn't work out I'm going to drop this bisexual identity." I was not in a relationship with anyone for about a year, and in that time I was going out to the women's clubs and being where there were other women who liked to sleep with women.

Then I met Ann, the partner that I have right now. We've been together for over two years. We had this really fun flirtation for a little while, and then we went on a date. It was just like fireworks, and then a totally mad rush to spend time together and get to know each other. It was very intense.

**K:** Tell me about your current situation.

**D:** I'm living with my partner, Ann. We've been together for a little over two years. We're engaged to be married next summer, and we're planning our wedding. Everybody knows about it: my family, my dad, my stepmother, my mother, my extended step family and my extended queer family. Everybody is very supportive and very excited. I even got the approval of my best friend from the eighth grade, Dawn, which is great because she's never liked anybody I've dated. Nobody's ever been good enough, and Ann is.

**K:** Why did you decide to get married since this is not going to be legally recognized by the state?

**D:** For me marriage is only partially a legal relationship. For me a marriage is a public declaration of my love for the person I am marrying and my commitment to our relationship. I am gathering before my community, my friends, my family, and my God to make a public declaration of my commitment to this person for the rest of my life with the expectation of my community's support for this commitment. That's what it's all about. We can't get the legal protections and recognition that a heterosexual couple get, but we're going to do as much of that as we can through legal contracts. We're going to have power of attorney for each other and wills, but we can never fully duplicate what a differing-gender couple can get with one signature, $35 and a blood sample.

**K:** Are you and Ann monogamous?

**D:** Yes, we are monogamous.

**K:** Is the situation you're currently in with Ann your ideal in terms of what you want in a relationship?

**D:** For me it is. I don't think that it is for everybody, but I'm a very coupling kind of person. I don't feel like I'm dependent on being in a couple for my security and identity, but I find it very comfortable to be coupled. There's an intimacy that can be created over time. You could do this with somebody you're not monogamous with too, but I find just being with one person over a period of time you move into deeper layers of relating through getting to know each other, while you're getting to know yourself at the same time. That's just most comfortable for me in a couple.

**K:** Is Ann lesbian or bisexual?

**D:** Ann is lesbian.

**K:** How does she feel about your being bisexual?

**D:** She loves me, so I guess it's okay that I'm bisexual, but it definitely was an issue when we first got together. She had a lot of biphobia, a lot of misunderstanding, a lot of knee-jerk reaction about it. There's always the issue of, "If you're bisexual and we're living in a homophobic society, why would you choose to be with a woman?" Which to me is mind boggling because it's such a pleasure to be with her. Why would I not choose to do that?

**K:** How have you resolved this? Why is she with you, a bisexual woman?

**D:** Because I'm a wonderful person. Because we are really good for each other. We have a lot of fun together. We have a lot of similar interests. We live together really well. We enjoy each other's company. We find each other very endearing and interesting and comfortable.

**K:** What enabled her to be comfortable coupling with a bisexual woman?

**D:** I think just getting to know me. There are a lot of myths about bisexual women—like they can't choose; if they're with someone of one sex they're always going to want the other, or, like I just said, why would a bisexual woman choose a woman over a man in our homophobic society? Over time she came to see that those ideas were not really who I was.

**K:** Do you practice safer sex?

**D:** Not 100% of the time. We've both been tested for HIV, and we both were negative. Before Ann when I was single I was having totally safe sex.

**K:** What about Ann?

**D:** Ann was having almost safe sex. When we first got together we didn't have completely safe sex. At that time people weren't talking a lot about women needing to have safe sex. I think that if there had been a stronger message out in the community about women needing to have safe sex with each other, I might have behaved differently then.

We're monogamous so that's our form of safer sex now. Since we have decided to become safer sex educators, and are going out into the community and telling people that they should be having safer sex, we decided that we should go through the same struggles that everybody else is to have safer sex. So we started to try to be 100% safe.

**K:** What does it mean to be 100% safe?

**D:** Using safer sex 100% of the time means having no exchange of bodily fluids—blood, semen or vaginal fluids. So when Ann and I have digital vaginal sex we use gloves, and when we have oral sex we use a barrier of plastic wrap, since I don't like dental dams.

**K:** When you were being sexual with men what was safer sex?

**D:** In my last relationship with a man we started out having what we thought was safer sex at the time—which was condoms for intercourse--but we didn't use any protection for oral sex. Then after we were both tested, we didn't use anything.

**K:** What did you use for birth control?

**D:** I was on the Pill when I was with him. After we broke up I dated a man, and we had very safe sex. We used two condoms for intercourse, one condom on him for oral sex, and plastic wrap on me for oral sex.

**K:** Are you different in relationships with men and with women?

**D:** Because I've only had one relationship with a woman, it's very difficult for me to separate out how I am with Ann, the human being, and how I am with Ann because she's a woman. My relationship with Ann is significantly better than any other relationship I've had in terms of how well we're able to communicate, how consistently good the sex is, and how well we live and function in the world together. We socialize well together, our interests match up, and we get along with each other's friends. I am different in this relationship, but I don't know whether it's because of the person I'm with, or whether it's because I'm with a person who is a woman.

**K:** In this relationship with a woman, is there anything you miss sexually or emotionally about not being involved with a man?

**D:** No. I'm totally satisfied, which is really nice.

**K:** Do you feel differently about your body and about how attractive it is, with men and with women?

**D:** I grew up in an atmosphere that was always trying to bolster my body image. Although I've had struggles with my body image, I think it's definitely improved since I've been in a relationship with a woman. Making love to a body that's like your own gives you a different appreciation of it than you might otherwise get. I feel more comfortable with my body than I ever have, and even more appreciative of it—what it can feel, and what it does.

Actually what has been very influential in how I feel about my body is an accident I was in which just about destroyed my left leg. I spent a year rehabilitating it. I've always felt really strong and powerful in my body and able to do anything. I don't feel that way anymore. That's been a tremendous loss for me. I'm mourning the loss of my body as I've known it for 20 years or more. That's actually been more significant to me in terms of my body image than having sex with a woman.

**K:** Do you want to have children?

**D:** I'd like to have one child.

**K:** Do you have any plans about when that will happen?

**D:** I feel like I've got a decent time buffer, because I'm young still. I would like to be at least on my way to good financial stability when I have a child. I have a B.A. right now, and I'm planning on going to grad school. I would want to be far along in my graduate studies before having a child.

**K:** Why do you only want to have one child?

**D:** I would like to have the experience of being pregnant and giving birth and raising the child, but I don't feel like I need to do it more than once. I think there are plenty of kids in the world. I only need one to get what I want out of parenting.

**K:** Is Ann interested in being pregnant?

**D:** No, she's absolutely not interested in being pregnant or carrying a child. She figured out at a young age that she never wanted to bear a child. So she thought that meant that she was never going to raise a child. She never thought she was going to have anything to do with kids other than play auntie. Now that she's with a partner who wants to have a kid, she's adjusting to the idea of maybe being a mommy. She still has some trepidation about it.

**K:** How would you get pregnant?

**D:** I will make that decision when I come to that bridge. If I know somebody that I would like to have a sperm donation from at the time I'll do it that way. I may use a sperm bank. It really depends on what my life circumstances are at the time.

**K:** Would you consider sleeping with a man in order to get pregnant?

**D:** No, I couldn't do that, because that would break the commitment that I have in my relationship to my current partner.

**K:** Are you out to everyone? Does all your family know? Do your friends know?

**D:** Everybody knows. Absolutely everybody. Everybody I work with, everyone in my family, everyone who I'm friends with. Anybody who I meet on the street if it naturally comes up, knows. I think it's very important for me to continue to live my life the same way I did when I was in a relationship with a man. It's very important for people to see that I'm in a relationship with a person who happens to be another woman, but that I'm still just like them. I'm just a person in a relationship who has the same kind of relationship problems and the same kind of relationship fun as anyone else. I feel that it's really important not to modify my behavior just because I'm in a relationship with a woman. I'm just living my life, the same way I was living it before.

**K:** As a bisexual woman how is it for you dealing with lesbians?

**D:** Usually it's fine. Mostly that has to do with me feeling centered in my identity as a bisexual woman. I do hear a lot of biphobic attitudes from lesbians, while some of them tell me that I'm not like other bisexual women. When they say that I always ask them, "What does that mean? How many women in your life that you think are lesbian are bisexual but are afraid to tell you, because of these attitudes you're throwing around."

**K:** Since you are in a committed, monogamous, lifetime partnership with a woman, why bother to continue calling yourself bisexual?

**D:** Because I'm not a lesbian. That's the simple truth of it. I'm not a lesbian, because I'm attracted to men. There are times when if I wasn't in a relationship there's a possibility that something could develop with a man. If this relationship ended today and I finished the grieving, it is conceivable that I would end up in a relationship with a man. Even if I never have any sexual contact or am never in a serious relationship with a man again, it doesn't invalidate the fact that the attraction is there. For me my sexual identity is what's going on inside. It's not external behavior. It's not what's manifested in the world. It's what's going on inside me.

**K:** So how is it for you dealing with straight people as a bisexual woman?

**D:** It's fine. Most of the straight people that I interact with are my family, or people that I've known for a long time, or people who live in San Francisco where I live. Mostly they're used to being around gay people. I haven't had major homophobic reactions from straight people, but to some straight men it's like it's some kind of come-on. Their reaction is, "Can I watch?"

**K:** What is your response to men with that attitude?

**D:** I tell them to fuck off. It's inappropriate for them to think that my sexuality is for them.

**K:** How is it for you dealing with gay men as a bisexual woman?

**D:** It's usually fine. I actually have had a lot of strong friendships with gay men since I was a kid. In high school I was buddies with all the gay guys in my class. I was one of the few people who could validate who they were. The most negative reaction I've gotten from gay men is, "I just don't understand bisexuality."

I can't really establish any kind of pattern of interaction with any particular group. Probably because I approach people as individuals. I often don't know what their sexual identity is.

**K:** Are you a feminist?

**D:** Yes.

**K:** What is your definition of feminism?

**D:** I saw a T-shirt that I thought was really good. It said, "Feminism is the radical notion that women are people." I'm a feminist in the sense that I think that women are important, that women are significant, and that we haven't been treated that way. We should have the same rights and opportunities in the world as men. We should be equal partners with men in creating what the world is.

**K:** Do you feel that bisexuality has political implications?

**D:** Yes, I do. One of the implications is that the dichotomy that's been set up between homosexual and heterosexual is threatened.

Bisexuality is part of the gray area, so to speak, of the sexual dichotomy that has been promulgated over the years. When you acknowledge a gray area, it rocks the boat. It changes the way you perceive things. If you change the way you think about something it's going to change the way you do things. So bisexuality influences the way people think and act.

# 2 ▼ ANUHEA

*Anuhea is 44 years old and lives in San Francisco. She works in the AIDS field, particularly with women and children who are HIV infected.*

**K.** Tell me a little about how you grew up: your family, your ethnic background, your class background.

**A:** I was born in New York. Both of my parents are Filipino, and were born and raised in the Philippines. I have an older sister living here in the States and a younger brother who still lives in the Phillippines. He's developmentally disabled. I grew up on the Lower East Side of New York in the projects. My father was a bartender, and my mother was a traditional housewife.

My mother and father were both Catholic, and we were all brought up Catholic. My sister and I attended Catholic school when we went back to the Phillippines through elementary school. My mother was fairly devout, but my father was a non-practicing Catholic. Toward my mid 20s I started being a non-practicing Catholic. I was very devout up until that point.

**K:** When were you first aware of sexual attractions and to which gender?

**A:** I remember being acutely aware of sexual feelings and tensions when I was about nine or ten. I've always been attracted to both sexes, male and female. The pull can go either way for me.

**K:** Was that scary for you?

**A:** The thing that was scary for me was being attracted to women. By that time in my life I knew the words "homosexual" and "lesbian," but lesbian had a worse connotation than homosexual for some reason. I thought there must be something wrong with me that I was sexually attracted to women. I felt comfortable being sexually attracted to men.

That was the normal thing to do. To be attracted to women was abnormal. That part worried me.

**K:** When did you start dating?

**A:** I started dating boys when I was in my very early teens in New York. I had very close, very intimate relations with young women, but the dating was always with men. When you went out with your girlfriends they were girl friends. They were never "girlfriends," and they weren't dates. With young men you were dating, there was sexual tension. With women that wasn't supposed to be. I started dating teenaged men when I was in my early teens, very soon after I felt my awareness around sexuality.

**K:** When did you first become sexually active?

**A:** In my early teens, and it was with boys. Part of that had to do with growing up in New York and acting like an adult before your time. That's what you did, and that's what I did. But when I was 16 I came damn near close to having a sexual encounter with a woman.

It happened when my parents decided to move to California in 1964–65. I became friends with this young woman named Elizabeth and used to go over to her house. She wanted me to teach her how to slow dance. We slow danced, and from then on we would do this every time I would go over to her house. We'd shut the door, turn out the lights, and slow dance.

**K:** What happened from that point in terms of relationships?

**A:** They were still with boys. Throughout my high school years I had either a crush on a guy or a crush on a girl or both. It made me feel a little bit wacky, because I couldn't figure out what was going on. Why did I have this attraction to both, and where was it going, and what could I do about it? Therapy wasn't an option at that time. I couldn't go to my friends. They were all straight and Asian, and it was not within the realm of the Asian culture at that time to talk intimately about sexuality.

So it stayed inside me until one night a bunch of us went joyriding to the Chinese cemetery in Colma. It was stupid. The car got stuck, and we stayed there all night. I had a long coat, and both me and my friend, Elizabeth, were really cold. So I thought the thing to do was to open the coat and put her inside with me. My sister caught this and interpreted it as lesbianism.

After we got rescued and came home the next morning, my sister said to my mother, "I just want to let you know that your daughter's a lesbian," and I just about fainted. I said, "That's impossible. I couldn't possibly be a lesbian. I'm with this guy blah blah blah blah." My sister said, "Then there's a side of you that you need to look at, Anuhea." She was the one who put it out there.

When I got out of high school and started going to college and working, I had my first sexual relationship with a woman, someone I had met at work. We stayed together for about three or four years.

After that I could go either way. I began to feel very comfortable about this. Ironically, it only got oppressive when I entered the lesbian movement.

**K:** When was this?

**A:** About 1975–76.

**K:** When you were in your late 20s.

**A:** Yes. I started working at a woman's bookstore in Oakland, and I met all these people in the lesbian community. The word "bisexual" had the most incredible connotations there, and if you were one it was almost like you had leprosy. It was only when I started interacting with lesbians that I felt this incredible level of oppression—that you can't be bisexual. When I was by myself and interacting with the world I felt okay. Heterosexuals that I confided in about this thought it was unusual, but interesting.

**K:** So what did you do with that?

**A:** I did what I thought was best. I said, "Okay, fine, I'll be a lesbian." I did that until recently. All the while knowing that this is not really who I am.

One of the main issues that I've had struggles with lesbians about is bisexuality being tied to nonmonogamy. Many of them have the idea that bisexuals have relations with many men and women any time and any place. I have said, "There probably are bisexuals that have multiple relations, and I'm sure there are lesbians who have multiple relations. Being nonmonogamous is not limited to bisexuals. It's an issue that anyone of any sexual orientation can have." You can't make a generalization that all bisexuals are one way. There are certain things that hold us together. One of them being that we have the capacity and the capability to love, period, regardless of gender. Within that we choose at different points in time who our partner may be.

I started going with a bisexual woman named Pililani when I was still calling myself a lesbian. I got hell for this from the lesbians of color I knew. How could you go with a bisexual? And all this stuff about bisexuals giving you AIDS. Really the issue is more how could you go with a bisexual, because she's also into men. And she will leave you, and if she leaves you it's going to be for a man. That would be the worst thing in the world.

The worst thing in the world is that I was still in love with her and wanted a relationship, and she left, period. That's the worst thing she did, but we're still very good friends. That's the kind of reaction that I got from women of color who were close to me. They couldn't understand my being attracted to this woman who is bisexual.

K: During the time that you called yourself a lesbian were you ever sexual with a man?

A: Yes, in New York. I lived on the East Coast for a period of time in the mid '80s. I was only supposed to be in New York for about a year or two, and then was going to go back to Seattle. I met a man there who just knocked me off my feet. He was just wonderful to be with. He made me feel nice about myself. He asked me to stay. I think if I would have blinked one more time I probably would have stayed with him in New York.

K: So you were involved in a relationship with him?

A: Yes, I'm not gonna try to cut it in any other way. I was also in a relationship with a woman in Seattle. I chose her over him which was really stupid, because when I got back to Seattle the relationship fell apart. I often think about that guy, and what could have been between us.

K: How long were you involved with him?

**A:** For about six months. He was wonderful.

**K:** Did you tell any of your lesbian friends about this relationship?

**A:** They knew. They'd say, "Well this is sweet, Anuhea, but you're a lesbian."

**K:** Outside of that, between your late 20s and your early 40s, were you involved only in relationships with women?

**A:** Physical relationships with women only, yes; I was still very attracted to men, but never moved on it. Part of it is that I was in what they call my "dykey" years. The standard of beauty that men have for women, I didn't fit into. Although I had crushes on men I wasn't pursuing them, because they weren't returning my affections.

**K:** How many relationships with women were you in?

**A:** My relationships generally last for three to four years, and I've had six of them.

**K:** Tell me about your current situation.

**A:** A group of us were talking about this the other day. There are some of us who are single and miserable about that situation. There are some of us who are single and semi-happy and semi-looking, and there are some of us who are semi-single, semi-happy, and still semi-looking. Then the last category I think was semi-single, happy, semi-looking. That's where I fall in.

Pililani and I are still involved even though she lives with a man. She was living with him when we first met. She moved out and lived with me for almost four years, and then she moved back with him.

**K:** Was she involved with this man during the time she was living with you?

**A:** For about the first year. She would stay at their house up the block, and then we had an apartment. So maybe three nights a week she'd stay with me. I never thought I could do something like that, but it turned out to be actually okay.

**K:** What happened that she ended up moving back in with him?

**A:** That's her story. I know for me it was sad, but I felt that she needed to do what she needed to do, and that it would have an impact on our relationship if she continued to deny certain things. So she went back. We're very close. I never thought I would be able to do this, but it's not bad at all. It comes on the heels of my reclaiming my bisexuality. So it's been an incredible eye opener for me in terms of my own development.

**K:** What happened that you decided to reclaim the identity of bisexual?

**A:** I just simply got tired of denying to myself what was going on. Whether or not I decide to act on an attraction to a man is my choice, but I wanted to reclaim that part of me that was being denied.

**K:** Was it hard for you?

**A:** Yes, it was. When I finally came out publicly I was waiting for the reaction from lesbians. The tone of my voice was like, "This is what I am, and if you can't relate to it that's just too damned bad. I'm not going to sit here and struggle about my sexuality, because I'm very comfortable with it. That topic is closed. The struggle here is about you lifting yourself out of your little quagmire of stupidity. It's not with me." So I had an attitude of it's your problem, not mine.

The night that I reclaimed my identity I felt very at ease. The next day if somebody would have asked me, "So Anuhea, being a lesbian . . ." I would have said, "No, being a bisexual." It would have been that easy for me to say.

**K:** So, if you could have your ideal situation in terms of relationships, what would it be?

**A:** Probably something like I have right now with Pililani, where I am involved with someone but living by myself. I like living by myself.

**K:** Are you monogamous or nonmonogamous?

**A:** I have a tendency to be monogamous and have 35,000 crushes. Whether any one of them pan out is a whole other question. I have been nonmonogamous, and it's not been very good. That's why I'm looking at the relationship that I currently have with Pililani as testing the limits of what I can do in relationships. I never thought I could do this.

**K:** Do you practice safer sex?

**A:** Yes. I'm in the AIDS field. I've taken care of many people, who have died of AIDS. It's an awful way to die. I don't want to go that way.

**K:** What do you do for safer sex?

**A:** I don't use dental dams; I don't like them. They're too chalky and thick and they don't do anything. I use saran wrap. I think oral sex is probably the best part of sex this side of heaven. It's wonderful whether it's with a male or a female.

**K:** If you were involved with a man, what would safer sex be?

**A:** Condoms definitely for sexual intercourse.

**K:** What about oral sex?

**A:** I'd probably use a condom. I'd ask him to use saran wrap for me, because I want to be able to feel. But I would definitely insist on safe sex. Right now I'm not sexually active. That's another way of practicing safe sex—don't engage in it.

**K:** It's not a priority in your life to find a partner. Is that what you're saying?

**A:** No, it's not at all.

**K:** Do your parents know that you're bisexual?

**A:** My parents are dead. I told my mother that I was bisexual about a year before she died. My father always suspected, because his sister is a lesbian and has been with her lover or, as they say in the Phillippines, companion, for 35 years, and I'm very much like her.

**K:** Do other family members know that you're bisexual?

**A:** Yes. By this time I should have been married off and had 35,000 children and millions of grandchildren, as in most undeveloped countries. No one has ever said anything directly to my face.

**K:** Do all your friends and coworkers know that you're bisexual?

**A:** Yes, and now I think the entire Filipino community knows it, because I've written articles in the *Philippine News* about it.

**K:** How is it for you dealing with lesbians as a bisexual woman?

**A:** Sometimes it frightens me, and sometimes it doesn't. Sometimes I'm just so full of confidence, and other times I'm not. I don't know why that happens. I am getting more comfortable challenging lesbians' statements regarding bisexuals, and more comfortable raising the issue of bisexuality when it's not being raised.

**K:** How is it for you dealing with straight people as a bisexual woman?

**A:** They look at me and think I'm heterosexual. That's the impression I get. Instead of dealing with me as a person who's capable of loving both men and women, they view me as another heterosexual. I find it amusing. I find it very sad at the same time. To them it's as if bisexuals are carved down the middle and this part is heterosexual and this part is gay. They don't see the interconnectedness of it all, so choose only to deal with the side that's heterosexual.

**K:** How is it for you dealing with gay men as a bisexual woman?

**A:** I don't deal with men as a bisexual whether they're gay, straight, or bisexual. I deal with men as a woman, because I don't care if a man is gay, straight, or bi; he has one thing that unites him with other men: male privilege. It gets even worse when they have class or racial privilege as well.

**K:** In terms of how attractive you feel on a physical level, is it different with men and with women?

**A:** With men there's still this standard of beauty based on women being very small and petite. It's worse with Asian women, because in men's view Asian women are supposed to be small, petite, and demure. That disturbs me a lot. My body structure is not like that; I'm never going to be petite, I'm never going to be small. I may lose weight once in a while, but I'll never be a size two. With women there is also a tendency for that to be the standard of beauty, but I don't think it's as pronounced as it is with men.

**K:** Are you a feminist, and if so, what does that mean to you?

**A:** To me being a feminist is basically taking up the issues that pertain to women. To be a very strong feminist is to take up the issues of the most disenfranchised sectors of the women's community in a very strong and passionate way. The least protected sectors of the women's community being poor women, women of color, disabled women. They need the most fighting to be done on their behalf. I'm passionate about women's plight in this world. To me on one level it makes no difference if you're lesbian or bisexual or straight. It means everything in the world to me if you are poor, or if you're a single mother.

**K:** Tell me something about your politics?

**A:** I grew up in the antiracist movement, and that continues to shape my politics very strongly. I went on the first march with Martin Luther King in Washington, DC. The majority of my political interactions up to now have been basically around race. It's only been in the last two or three years that I've reinvolved myself in the women's movement. I'm not talking about the lesbian movement, I'm talking about the women's movement. That and AIDS are shaping my politics now. So I would say that I'm antifascist, antiracist, antisexist, and very inclusive of sexual orientations and gender identities. That's basically where I stand.

**K:** Do you feel that bisexuality has political implications?

**A:** Yes, I do think it has political implications, but I'm not all that clear as to what they are. I know that bisexuals have struggled in the gay and lesbian movement to be accepted as another sexual orientation. I think that probably in the next ten years it's going to be politically correct to be bisexual. That, ultimately, might be the way it does become socially acceptable.

**K:** What contribution do you think you have to make to the world as a bisexual woman?

**A:** Just being out there and not denying my sexuality. Just as gay and lesbian people came out of the closet and started a whole movement, I think it's really important that bisexual people come out when they feel they need to. I don't think there's an unwritten law that says that just because you're a bisexual you have to come out, though. It's when you feel the necessity to do it, and I feel that now.

When I came out as bisexual I felt as if another shackle had been taken off my shoulders. People see that. They see somebody who has arrived at a certain plateau and is willing to jump to the next one–whatever it is and however high it is. When people see other people coming out and taking very important stands around what they believe, hopefully it jars them and makes them step out of their boundaries and move one step higher themselves. Some of them might even begin to question their own sexuality.

**Postscript:** Pililani and I are no longer together, but we remain very close and loving friends. We are each with new partners—both women. I had a commitment ceremony with my partner last year.

# 3 ▼ Margarita

*Margarita is a 32-year-old painter and hair-dresser who lives in San Francisco. She is of German descent and has a blue-collar background; both of her parents worked in a factory.*

**K:** When were you first aware of sexual attractions, and to which gender?

**M:** I was attracted to my best friend when I was 14 or 15. We'd pretend we were playing Barbie and Ken. She would play Ken, and I would play Barbie, and we would kiss. That was the first time that I ever kissed a woman. We never discussed it. It was just part of the playing with the Barbie and Ken dolls.

**K:** What did you think of it?

**M:** I got a little scared, but we didn't go any farther than that.

**K:** When were you next aware of sexual attractions?

**M:** Probably my first boyfriend was shortly after that experience with my best friend. So I was about fifteen.

**K:** Did you consider yourself heterosexual then?

**M:** Definitely. I had never heard of lesbianism or attraction to women; it wasn't even in my vocabulary. I knew that I felt really comfortable being physical with women. I wanted to touch them and be touched, but I didn't think about it beyond that.

I am a very physical person. But I found that a lot of women weren't comfortable with me touching them. They didn't want to deal with a woman being physically open with them—just hugging or laying on their lap watching TV. I didn't understand that. I didn't acknowledge being attracted to women, until I fell in love with my best friend when I was 24.

**K:** Were you involved with other boys and men during that time?

**M:** I've pretty much always been involved with men. I'm someone whose always been in a relationship. I've always found myself wanting to be in a relationship.

**K:** And generally in a relationship with a man?

**M:** That's what I feel comfortable with, just because society says that's what's normal. I think if society was more open then I definitely would have had relationships with women along the way.

**K:** So what happened when you were 24?

**M:** I found that I didn't want to be separated from my best friend, Christine. I broke down one day crying on the phone with her, and told her that I was in love with her.

**K:** What was her response?

**M:** She said, "I know you are, and I'm in love with you, too," but at the time she wasn't comfortable being sexual at all. I was wanting to be with her sexually, but she wasn't feeling comfortable in her body. She hadn't actually had sex with anybody at that point.

**K:** When did you first get sexually involved with a woman?

**M:** I think acknowledging what was going on with me and Christine helped me to open up more to the possibility and be more comfortable about being with a woman. Shortly thereafter I started seeing this woman, Mary. She's also bisexual and so is Christine. I'm more comfortable being with a bisexual woman, because I'm not judged. I think the lesbian community is extremely judgmental of bisexuals—you're traitors. So I found myself being really comfortable with Mary, and we became sexual. It was my first full-on sexual experience with a woman. We could share a lot of our experiences about what it was like being bisexual.

**K:** Did you go through an identity crisis about being bisexual at some point?

**M:** Yes. When I was with Christine and acknowledging that I was in love with a woman, I knew all the derogatory words and connotations about lesbians. They made me feel like I was a bad person.

**K:** Tell me what some of those words were.

**M:** It gets confusing, because the lesbian community is reclaiming the word "dyke," but when I first heard that word it was really disgusting and dirty and perverse. I would think, oh my god, am I going to start being perverse? Is something wrong with me? But I just kept feeling it was correct for me, and finally I realized I was okay. A lot of it has to do with being in San Francisco, because San Francisco's a lot more open than upstate New York where I was when I was attracted to Christine. Being here allowed me to be more accepting of myself.

I'm still dealing with these feelings now, because of the societal pressures. I think it's beautiful that I can share myself sexually with a woman, and that she would want to be with me sexually. But I still feel pressures from outside that make me feel not so okay.

**K:** What are those pressures?

**M:** I don't really fit in. I don't fit in even with the lesbian community. I don't fit into the hetero community. I have felt isolated, except for when I was connected with Mary. I'm more in the hetero community than I am in the lesbian community right now. It's easier, because all of society's based on heterosexuality.

**K:** Tell me about your current situation.

**M:** At this point I'm living with a man named Ian. Before we moved in together I was seeing Mary and him both at the same time, separately. Everything was out in the open, and everybody knew what was going on. I saw both of them for about six months. I liked it a lot. It worked really well for me.

**K:** Why did you choose to move in with Ian?

**M:** Because we love each other. I like living with someone. It wasn't a choice between him and Mary. Mary doesn't want to live with anybody. I'm not seeing her anymore. When I moved in with Ian I told him that being bisexual I can't be monogamous; I told him I need to be able to have a relationship with a woman also.

**K:** Do you have any agreements such as that you won't get involved with another man?

**M:** Yes.

**K:** Is he free to get involved with other women?

**M:** He's not interested. He likes being monogamous.

**K:** How does he feel about the potential for you to get involved with other women?

**M:** He feels anxious and insecure about it. He totally respects my bisexuality, but he says he would prefer that I be the kind of bisexual that is monogamous with the person they are with at the time. He's not really into me having a need to be with a woman and him at the same time.

What feels correct for me though is to have a relationship with a man and a woman. I did it, and I really like it. I want to have separate relationships with them being friends where I can have her over to my house. That's what happened with Mary. It was very validating for me to have been in a relationship with both of them. Issues came up, but I was okay with that. I wanted to deal with issues that came up.

**K:** What came up?

**M:** It sounds funny but holidays like Valentine's Day came up. I had to be really grounded with both of them and very honest and open. Ian had a wedding he wanted me to go to on Valentine's Day. Of course Mary wanted to be with me. She and I planned on doing dinner Valentine's night, and Ian was upset, because the wedding wasn't going to be over yet. I would have had to leave early, and everybody would want to know where I went, and he'd have to say, "Well she's off to see her other lover." It would have been awkward.

Then Mary said, "Why don't we have brunch together." The night before Valentine's Day Mary and I spent together, and we had brunch in the morning. Then this was really sweet: Mary didn't have a car so

Ian drove her home, came back, got me and we went to the wedding. So it worked out. It was really cool.

**K:** What other issues came up at that point?

**M:** It went pretty smoothly other than just organizing time and working it out; if someone wasn't happy with what was up, we talked about it. The only other thing that was difficult for me is if I had a fight with both of them at the same time. Like one time I had a fight with Mary, and right after that a fight with Ian, and I was also sick. That was emotionally draining. On the plus side I got a lot of energy being with both of them, and there was a lot of love.

**K:** Were there issues of jealousy?

**M:** Yes, but it wasn't a horrible thing. A lot of it had to do with how grounded I was, and how willing I was to work on things. I know I was in a place where it was easy to have a fight with Ian and run to Mary, but that wouldn't have been the correct thing to do. It would have been misusing the situation and not a clean deal. There was a lot I needed to think about and process.

**K:** Why do you want to be involved with a woman even though you are in a satisfying relationship with Ian?

**M:** I feel empty not having an emotional bond happening with a woman. I think it's natural for me to be with both. I feel complete being able to express myself sexually with a man and a woman.

**K:** Do you practice safe sex?

**M:** I practice safe sex with men, but I didn't practice safe sex with women.

**K:** What are your safe sex practices with men?

**M:** Condoms for intercourse. Ian and I are both being very responsible. We had our AIDS test done, and we're both negative. So now we don't use condoms. I haven't slept with any other men. I don't feel that women are at high risk so I haven't bothered to practice safe sex with women.

**K:** Do your parents know that you're bisexual?

**M:** My mother asked me once when I was still living back East, because there was this woman I worked for, and we had a lot of sexual energy together, and my Mom's pretty keen. At the time I was in denial. I hadn't ever slept with a woman so I just said no, but I could tell my Mom today. She would probably just tell me it was a fad I was going through.

**K:** Do any other family members know?

**M:** No.

**K:** What about friends? Do people in your circle know that you're bisexual?

**M:** Yes.

**K:** How is it for you dealing with the straight world as a bisexual woman?

**M:** You know how some straight guys are about two women together. Sometimes it's weird. Most of my friends respect me though regardless of what they think. All of my friends respect my bisexuality. They think it's interesting. Some live vicariously through me when I talk about being involved with Mary and Ian at the same time. I think some of them think I'm brave for doing what I want to do in spite of societal mores.

**K:** How is it for you as a bisexual dealing with the lesbian community?

**M:** I have fear that I'm not going to be accepted.

**K:** How is it for you dealing with gay male friends as a bisexual woman?

**M:** Fine. I think that there's a commonality that we have, because we're attracted to the same sex. We can chat about that. Ian and I are really good friends with this one gay male couple. We hang out with them. They're great.

**K:** How is it for you with other bisexuals?

**M:** I feel really comfortable with other bisexuals.

**K:** Where do you meet the bisexual women you've gotten involved with?

**M:** Christine is one of my best friends. So it started out as best friends. I think I was always attracted to Mary, and I met her through friends. There's this other bisexual woman that I've been interested in getting to know. Again I met her through one of Ian's guy friends who was going out with her. So it's through friends.

**K:** Do you think you have a contribution to make to the world as a bisexual woman?

**M:** My contribution to the world is just me being true to who I am, feeling good about being bisexual and not being in the closet about it. All the hetero friends that I've discussed my lifestyle with have to think about it. It opens up another thought pattern with them if I talk about and feel good about being bisexual, which is hard to do with all the societal pressures.

**K:** What are the societal pressures that make it hard for you to feel good about being bisexual?

**M:** I don't know of any married couples where the woman is bisexual and having a relationship with her woman and her man. It's not the norm. I don't think I would ever have come out if I still lived in upstate New York. I would have been too inhibited, too scared to be judged. Maybe now having lived here I could go back and be out there, but I don't think I could have done it any time before this.

**K:** What would make it easier for you to feel good about yourself as a bisexual woman?

**M:** If more people came out. I think there are a lot of people who are bisexual. If a lot of people came out and just were who they are and didn't make a big deal out of it—just acted normal about it—it wouldn't be such an issue. I'd have role models. There are no role models other than the ones in the books I've been reading, though that has been validating—reading books that deal with bisexuality. I just wish people weren't so judgmental.

# 4 ▼ PEG

*Peg is a 40-year-old woman who lives in Arizona with her female partner, Brandie. She provides office support services for a therapeutic massage center.*

**K:** Tell me a little bit about your family, your class background, and your ethnic background.

**P:** I grew up in a large Midwestern city in a two-parent family with two younger brothers. We always considered ourselves to be the basic white, middle-class family. Probably we were lower-middle class, because while we were always comfortably fed and housed, we were always in debt.

I have a physical disability. Growing up I went to a school that wasn't in my own neighborhood. My neighborhood and my school were two different worlds. My neighborhood world included my family and a few friends. My school world was all kids with disabilities. Kids were brought from different parts of the city to my school, so I was exposed to a range of people from different socioeconomic and racial backgrounds there.

**K:** Were you raised in a religion?

**P:** We went to a Presbyterian church regularly when I was very young, and periodically as I grew up. My mother has always connected more to religion than my father. He just put up with it. I think ultimately he won out, in that we stopped going so much as I got older.

There's always been a spiritual component to me, probably because I got such a good grounding in God when I was a little kid—not just about going to church, but the idea that God or whatever you conceive the powerful being to be, is in your life, and there to call on and talk to about whatever your needs might be.

**K:** Tell me a little about your disability.

**P:** I have a neuromuscular disease which affects all my voluntary muscles. I've had it ever since I can remember. It's progressive, so I can do less physically now than I could when I was a kid. I've been in a wheelchair full time since I was eight years old.

The current result is that I'm dependent upon somebody else for all my basic care: getting in and out of bed, getting dressed, meal preparation, housekeeping. I hire people to do most of that, and my partner does some of it. Ideally I prefer her to be able to choose when to help me rather than having to do it, but it doesn't always work that way. I get some assistance through the state's long-term care program to pay for people to help me, because my income does not permit me to pay for all the care I need.

**K:** So when were you first aware of sexual attractions, and to which sex?

**P:** I was first aware of attraction to males in late elementary school. When I think back about that time, I don't recall ever knowing any lesbians or gay men, let alone bisexual people. Nor do I remember ever hearing gays being talked about or acknowledged.

I remember being attracted to boys, and I remember that being really important, because disabled people are perceived as nonsexual beings. Part of what we want to show the world is that we can relate like other people, that we can have intimate relationships with the opposite sex, too. That's probably another factor in my not even thinking early on about my feelings about women. Looking back now, I remember having feelings for certain girls that, had I been open to them, I probably would have acknowledged were deeper than the feelings I had for most of my friends. But being romantic with girls wasn't an option, so I didn't even entertain it.

**K:** Did you date? Were you involved with anyone during your adolescent and teenage years?

**P:** I didn't date much because it was logistically difficult. I had a boyfriend for about two weeks in junior high, but then he went back to his other girlfriend. I dated a little bit in high school.

My first real relationship was in my senior year of high school. I met a man who was quite a bit older than me, and he asked me out. My parents were worried about him being an older man, but nonetheless they were excited that I was going out with him. My grandma especially was ecstatic, because she always wanted me to find a man to take care of me.

**K:** What was your relationship history from that point to the present?

**P:** I was with this man for about a year and a half. Then I went away to college, and during that first semester I realized that there was a huge world out there that I needed to explore. The man realized how far apart we were in age and in where we were at in our lives. So we mutually decided to end the relationship.

I didn't really have another significant relationship with somebody until a year and a half after that. I had a few crushes in the meantime, mostly on guys, but there was at least one woman who I remember having strong feelings for. I worried about that; I liked her so much it occurred to me that maybe I was having feelings that I shouldn't be having, at least not according to the narrow Christian path I was following at the time.

Then I got into a very intense relationship. We almost got engaged, but I decided that I wasn't ready to get married right away. I wanted to stay focused on school, because even though I thought that I was in love with this guy, I really did not want to just be somebody's wife. I wanted to have my own life, and I knew that the only way I was going to do that was to get an education, because I couldn't do any physical kinds of jobs. Ultimately, the guy started seeing my roommate so that ended the relationship anyway.

I had my first sexual experience with this guy. We actually had intercourse only once, because I was focused on the "I don't want to have sex till I get married" thing.

I wasn't sexual again for three or four years. I had short relationships with a little bit of messing around in them, but nothing real intense.

During my senior year at college my primary attendant was a young woman who was bisexual. She was very open about her life and her philosophy, and she had a lot of ideas that I secretly shared with her. But at that time I was doing the "fear of God" thing. So while I maintained a good friendship with her, I kept an arm's length between us. She was one of the best attendants I ever had.

I had been an activist in college around the issue of accessibility for folks with disabilities. After I graduated I started working in the field of independent living. I began as a volunteer, but then I got an assistantship at a local independent living center. I was able to continue my education in counseling while working at the center. Relationships floated in and out of my life during that time, but there weren't any significant, long-term relationships. Most of the men that I dated during that time had disabilities, which was new to me. Before, I had mostly dated able-bodied people.

Then, my blind friend, Kris, moved into my apartment building. People at school talked about both of us a lot, because we were so fiercely independent compared to most other disabled students. So we had some real camaraderie.

We had always wanted to get to know each other better, but had never done much about it. We were both quite busy. It turns out that the reason she moved into my building was because she'd broken up with her woman partner and had to move. She was in the midst of despair, because she didn't want to break up with this woman.

I knew that she had been living with a woman, but I didn't know about their relationship. At the time I had been involved for about two years in a religious organization that was incredibly conservative and charismatic. So while they said that ultimately what was important was your connection with God and the Holy Spirit, it was clear what kind of sexual orientation they thought was permissible, and what kind wasn't. I was involved with this group, because I really thought that these people knew God better than I did.

So here was my friend, Kris, telling me that she'd just broken up with her woman lover of four years and she's devastated. And here I was, wanting to be supportive of her, but knowing that what I was really supposed to be doing was getting her to go to this church. In the midst of all this I found out that a woman she knew had just had a baby together with her lesbian partner. I was horrified. Still, against my pastor's counsel, I continued to be friends with Kris.

That summer I was having trouble finding and keeping attendants (as I always have). So Kris asked me if I thought she would be able to do attendant care for me. I didn't see why not. So we decided to try it.

The first shift that she ever did for me was a morning shift with a shower, which is complicated, but since I was used to giving directions it wasn't hard to give them in more detail. The normal time for something like that would be three hours at the most. It took us five hours, but we did it. So she decided that she'd be my attendant part-time. She got to be as quick as anybody else.

At this time I had an opportunity to go to a state university to focus my counseling degree on rehabilitation counseling. We decided that Kris would go to the new college with me and be my attendant there.

So, off we went to this university, her with her guide dog, and me with a service dog and all my equipment. They put us in a little dorm room about the size of a closet, which wasn't accessible enough. So we found somewhere else to live in that town during the week. We also both kept our apartments in the town we had been living in, traveling to the university town by train. It was a great experience for us to be able to travel independently back and forth between these two towns.

It was during this time that we started having strong feelings for each other, although I was denying them big time. Then I got very sick, so I couldn't finish the semester and we ended up going back home. We spent a lot of time sitting in my hospital bed watching TV together. We started talking about the feelings after she kissed me one night.

That was the start of a difficult but really wonderful time for me. I not only had to acknowledge my feelings, but also my personal belief that they were okay, even though everybody in my social life at that time—which was the church—was saying, "You can't do this." I started being sexual with Kris. There were about two months when I was feeling really happy, but really guilty, because I continued to go to church and act like the good little follower that I was supposed to be, while inside I was feeling that this wasn't right for me.

Ultimately I wrote a letter to my pastor telling him what was going on in my life and that I needed to leave the church, because I knew that this was not okay with what he taught. He came over to my house and gave me a lecture. Then he wanted me to repent. I told him, "All I can do is say, God, if I'm doing something wrong, show me, because I don't think I am." The people in the church also tried to get me to come back, but I knew that it wasn't ever going to be okay for me to be there again.

When I was better and went back to school, Kris and I ended up moving to the other city. I had faded out of the church. I still saw a few of the people from it, because some of them were bold enough to disobey the pastor and visit me. Kris hadn't had much of a social network after college anyway. So we decided that we would just make a new life in this other town.

We lived there for about a year, but we had incredible housing problems in this town. Finally we just said, "This isn't going to work."

I decided to quit the program I was in at school, because I realized that what they were teaching me to do wasn't relevant to independent living. I decided that I would take what I had learned and use it to do what I was already doing working in independent living.

So we went back to the town we had lived in previously. We started establishing connections with the women's community, and also with a church there that was supportive of people with different kinds of lifestyles. That church addressed a big void I felt after I left the conservative church.

I had always kept a connection with a spiritual community. Over the years I had been involved in several different christian denominations. After I left the conservative church for a while I didn't go to any church and felt unsupported spiritually. The new church helped me feel okay about exploring different forms of spirituality, to accept that which rings true for me and not to go along with that which doesn't. It was really an important experience for me.

Kris and I were in a relationship for seven years. It was very wonderful in lots of ways, but hard in others, because much of the time she was uncomfortable with intimacy. So while I was very much in love with her, I wasn't happy with the relationship. Ultimately I ended it.

During the time that I was getting ready to break up with her, I had an affair with a guy named Richard. I met him when he contacted the AIDS service organization I worked for. He does body work and psychic work, and wanted to make his services known to my clients. I was real fascinated with what he did and the way he thought.

We got to be friends and started spending some time together, partly because I was looking for ways to get away from my home situation. He believes in open relationships, and I needed some nurturing, so we were sexually intimate. I was honest with Kris about this. I told her I was attracted to him and needed to check it out.

In the midst of all this, Kris and I were going to counseling together to decide what was going to happen with our relationship. Ultimately I said I needed to be free. Her perception was that I wanted to leave her to be with Richard, which wasn't true. I was having fun with him, but we considered each other playmates; we weren't in a "relationship."

It was shortly after Kris and I broke up that Brandie and I started seeing each other. We had been flirting for several months before that, but we were both in a relationship, so we just flirted and saw each other at church. After our relationships ended we decided to start spending time together. That time increased. Shortly into the relationship with her, I told Richard, "I love you a lot. I've had a great time with you, but I really want to be committed and exclusive with this woman. I found something that is what I've wanted in my life for a long time."

Brandie moved in with me a few months after we started dating, then moved back out after a month, saying that she had to finish up some things with her former lover. She needed time to sort out her feelings, wrap up some loose ends, and figure out what was going to happen. During that period we saw each other on weekends. For me it was a very difficult time, because I knew that I was very deeply in love with her, and I wanted to be with her. She was telling me that she was in love with me, but at the same time she was still being with this other woman.

After about three months of this I had had enough. One night I had somebody drive me to her place to talk to her. I told her she had to make a decision to either be with me or with the other woman. She came back with me that night. We have lived together since then.

**K:** How long have you two been together?

**P:** Four and a half years. I know this is what I want in my life. Not that I couldn't be connected with a man again, but I feel that while I'm in this relationship this is all I want. If Brandie were to leave me or if for whatever reason we decided it was not right for us to be together anymore, I don't know if I would be with a man or a woman. I do know that a relationship would be based on the person, not on what gender they are.

**K:** If you could have your ideal relationship, what kind of situation would it be?

**P:** I think that I'm almost there. I went through a time when I was messing around with somebody while being in a relationship with somebody else. It was fun for a while, but it wasn't what I really wanted. I'm really a one-lover person. A primary relationship is really important to me. So my ideal would be to be with a person that I'm deeply in love with, that we be compatible not only emotionally and sexually, but have some common interests and shared life goals, that my partner enjoy being intimate as much as I do, and that we be able to live together.

**K:** Do you have any children?

**P:** No. I've always wanted to have children. When I was younger I thought that I'd like to at least have one child. I was told that it would be possible, but very difficult. But it's hard enough to care for my own physical being. To have the responsibility of caring for a kid would probably be more than I could do. I've thought in more recent years that I want to find some creative ways to have children in my life.

**K:** In the situation that you're currently in, being involved only with a woman, is there anything that you miss emotionally or sexually about being with a man?

**P:** I don't miss anything, because I relate to people as individuals rather than as a member of their sex. Any physical or emotional feelings that I can get being with a man I can also experience with a woman; you just go about it in different ways. The same kind of sexual fulfillment can be there; you're just using different body parts.

**K:** In situations where you've only been involved with a man, is there anything you missed sexually or emotionally about being with a woman?

**P:** In most of my relationships with men I haven't felt as emotionally connected or as much on the same wave length, as in most of my relationships with women.

**K:** Do you feel differently with men and with women about your body and how attractive you feel?

**P:** Not different, but it's always a wonderful surprise to me when I find a partner who feels good about my body and how I look. Because I feel fat, and I feel unattractive because I don't move well. In my current relationship I feel more attractive than I've ever felt in my life. Really it comes down to the person I'm with, and how they relate to me, not what their sex is.

**K:** Do you identify as either butch or femme?

**P:** Sometimes one, sometimes the other. I'm really comfortable being in a frilly dress and having my hair fixed up. I'm also very comfortable being in my jeans and checking out the tools at Sears, or being grubby in the backyard. It's important to me to be how I want to be at the moment and for that to be okay.

**K:** Do you practice safer sex, or have you practiced safer sex?

**P:** Brandie and I don't. Although because of working at an AIDS organization, it's always in the back of my mind. I've educated a lot of people about condoms and rubber gloves and dental dams.

When I was first intimate with Richard we had a long discussion about it after making love. I said, "I feel really bad about this. Here I am, I've been doing this job at an AIDS organization, and we didn't use any protection last night." Of course we talked about trusting each other, but then I said, "I don't know who you've been with, and you don't know who I've been with."

I have been tested for HIV a couple of times, just to make sure. At one point Brandie got involved with somebody else, so I do have some concerns about her HIV status. Sometimes I think we should be safer than we are. Most of our intimate activity doesn't put us at a lot of risk. When Brandie's doing attendant care for me she wears gloves. We do a lot of very intimate activities, but not a lot which involve body fluids. We do a lot of caressing and a lot of petting, but not a lot of oral sex. I suppose there are times when I should say, "Maybe you should be wearing a glove," but she hasn't so far.

**K:** And has Brandie ever been tested for HIV?

**P:** Not since we've been together. We've talked about it, but we just haven't done it.

**K:** So, do your parents know that you are bisexual?

**P:** My father died before I was in my first relationship with a woman. I don't know if my mother knows that I consider myself bisexual, but she does know that I'm in a relationship with a woman. It was very hard for her at the beginning. She still has some of the "what did I do wrong" stuff in the back of her head, but mostly she's okay with it.

**K:** Do other family members know that you're bisexual?

**P:** My brothers know, and are pretty cool about it. My oldest brother, who is three years younger than me, had some trouble when I had my first relationship with a woman. At the time he was with a woman who was very much against it. She had two daughters and didn't want us to be around them. But I've always been really close to my brothers. That has helped them to accept me now.

I think that a lot of my extended family knows, but they don't deal with it. On my dad's side, I have a lot of family that I spent time with growing up. I've only seen them a few times over the last ten years, but a couple of those times, like at my cousin's wedding, I was with Brandie, and the two of us were affectionate. So I'm sure people talked about that.

**K:** What was their reaction?

**P:** Nobody has treated me any differently that I can tell. Most of them think that I'm "asexual" anyway, because of my disability. But one aunt and uncle came out here and stayed with me once, and they were terrific. No one talked about it, but Brandie and I slept in the same bed, and I don't think that they're that naive.

**K:** Do other people in your life know that you're bisexual?

**P:** I think most people in my life right now perceive me as a lesbian.

**K:** How is it for you as a bisexual woman dealing with lesbians and the lesbian community?

**P:** Mostly I don't talk about being bisexual with lesbians. Although when I feel it's important I do say that I am bisexual. I've never had any major negative repercussions for doing that. There have been a few women who think it's not okay, or not a real possibility, but then I don't let the discussion go any further.

**K:** How is it for you dealing with the straight world as a bisexual woman?

**P:** Mostly, the straight world sees that I'm in a relationship with a woman and they have a hard enough time with that, so that's usually as far as we get—if they even see it at all. Most people don't know me well because they distance themselves from me because I'm disabled. People who are part of my life to some significant degree know about my being with Brandie and are okay with it, or we wouldn't be significantly connected.

One of my biggest challenges is needing attendants. I have to hire people to come into our home and provide care for me, knowing that Brandie and I have an intimate relationship. Sometimes people are just not comfortable with it. So in the initial interview I'm open about the relationship, and say, "If this is not okay with you, we can stop right now. We don't need to go on." Some people have said that it was okay but it really wasn't, and eventually we had to part ways.

**K:** How is it for you as a bisexual woman dealing with gay men?

**P:** When the subject has come up either they say that they're bisexual too, or else they say that don't get it, but it's okay. I haven't had any extremely negative conversations about bisexuality with gay men.

Actually I think that our own attitude about our sexual orientation, our lifestyle, our disabilities, whatever, sets the stage for other people's responses. Not that there aren't people who are going to be bigoted, because they are out there. But my experience has been that with most of the people I want to connect with if I feel okay about me, they do okay with me. If I feel uncomfortable about myself, they have a harder time accepting me.

**K:** How is it for you as a bisexual woman dealing with other bisexuals?

**P:** I don't often have an opportunity to be with other bisexuals, because I don't know very many—or at least don't know very many who admit they are bisexual. One time a woman at the AIDS organization I worked for made a reference to an article in a bisexual woman's newsletter. I had never seen a bisexual publication before. I was so excited to see that there are other people who think that it's okay to be bisexual. That you don't have to be one or the other.

**K:** Do you feel pressure to be one or the other?

**P:** I have at times. I don't right now. Partly that's because a lot of people don't know I'm bisexual. Partly it's because I'm comfortable with who I am, which helps other people to be comfortable with me.

**K:** How would you say your disability has affected your sexuality and your relationships?

**P:** It's a little bit of a physical hassle. You have to be creative and use what works. Because I don't have a lot of independent physical movement, many intimate activities require the cooperation and help of my partner. I have issues about if I'm contributing my part, because there's a lot that I can't do.

**K:** Do you think it has been more of a challenge for you to find people to be in relationships with because of your disability?

**P:** I think there is probably a narrower range of candidates, either because of people's attitudes about disability or their fears, or their feeling that I probably can't do what they would need or want.

**K:** Are you a feminist?

**P:** Yes.

**K:** What does feminism mean to you?

**P:** To me, feminism is about equal opportunity and equal ability. It is the idea that women are just as good as men at doing whatever we want to do, and that we should have the opportunity to do what we want to do.

Feminism also is a way of thinking that contradicts American society, where the men basically determine what's going to happen, and the women just go along with it. It's a different way of looking at things. The traditional mind set is that things are either right or wrong, black or white; that one person is the leader and everybody else follows.

Feminist thinking in my perception is more "let's work this out together. Let's hear everybody's viewpoint, because they're all important, and try to come to a solution together. There's much more than black and white to things. Let's look at all the possibilities. No one way is always right. There are a lot of options, and a lot of ways to resolve an issue." Feminism is a lot more freeing and a lot more respectful of the individual than our society at large is. It points to a way for people to come together and accomplish something without leaving anyone out of the process.

**K:** Do you think that bisexuality has political implications?

**P:** Unfortunately, yes. I don't think that it should have. Actually, it's the misperception of what bisexuality is that has the political implications. People believe that bisexual people are sexual with many people simultaneously. So, of course that has implications for our social structure, which is based on the nuclear family.

I'm sure there are some bisexual people who have multiple sexual partners. Individuals need to have the right to choose their lifestyle, whatever that is, with an understanding of the ramifications it will have. If I as a person in a significant relationship with a woman decide that I also need to have an intimate relationship with a man, I have to recognize that I will be risking the relationship I've already got. For me, if the potential loss of my current relationship wasn't a big deal, I probably wouldn't be in it in the first place.

**K:** Do you think there are political implications to your being a disabled bisexual woman?

**P:** There are political implications to everything. There are political implications to being disabled if you have any kind of life other than staying in a nursing home being a good little crip. If you don't do that you're saying, "I can survive, I can contribute to my community. If you don't like it, don't look—but it's going to happen."

Because people with disabilities have been and often still are perceived as asexual, there's a lot of pressure on a person with a disability to be seen as normal sexually—normal being, of course, heterosexual. When I started coming out in my first relationship with a woman, a lot of my friends with disabilities had a very hard time with that.

**K:** Do you think you have a contribution to make to the world as a disabled bisexual woman?

**P:** I think I have a lot of contributions to make. I've always felt like my life had a purpose or a mission, plus a lot of little missions along the way. Part of just living life as who I am is an important contribution to the world. And that contribution happens most effectively one person at a time.

Individuals who really take the time to get to know me for who I am, both as a person with a disabilty and as a person in an alternative sexual lifestyle, are enriched; they can then hopefully pass on to others the message that disabled people and bisexual people are okay. The more true I am to myself and the more other people see that, the more we know about one other and the more we can ultimately all be the family we're supposed to be.

I also have some tangible contributions to make. Right now I'm working on a housing and attendant care project where disabled people can live cooperatively. This will be a place where we will be in control of our living situation, and choose the people who will be caring for us. A lot of the time disabled people don't get the opportunity to make those choices. So part of my role around my disability is to help disabled people be more independent and more in control of their lives.

My role in the disability community in terms of my bisexuality is to say let's acknowledge the full range of who we are and not be afraid of that. To the able-bodied community I am saying, if you're thinking of me as asexual, look at this: I can do both.

**K:** Is there anything else you want to add?

**P:** It took me a while to be okay about saying I'm bisexual, because when I first got involved with a woman bisexuality was not an option. I thought I must really be lesbian and just didn't know it before. It took a while for me to admit that while I was happy being with a woman, I had also been happy being with a man. Politically I do identify with lesbians a lot and will use that term in reference to myself, because I am in a relationship with a woman. At the same time I don't want to deny my bisexuality. I'm in a lesbian relationship right now, but that's not all of who I am.

Connecting with other women and experiencing the camaraderie of sharing similar political and spiritual ideals has all happened for me in the lesbian community. I want to continue to learn and grow in that community. There have been times in the lesbian community when I've talked about being bisexual, and I haven't been excluded because of that. My ultimate hope is that I can be who I am, and yet still be a part of all that I believe in and value about the lesbian community.

# 5 ▼ SONYA

*Sonya is a 41-year-old legal worker who lives in San Francisco. She has two children.*

**K:** Tell me a little bit about how you grew up. What your family was like, your class background?

**S:** I come from a progressive, middle class, Jewish family. My parents were teachers. I have one sister who is three years younger than me. I grew up on Long Island, and had a normal, happy, healthy childhood.

**K:** When were you first aware of sexual attractions and to which gender?

**S:** My first attractions were to boys, although my best friends were always girls. I remember a particular guy in seventh grade. I liked what he looked like.

**K:** Were you only attracted to boys throughout high school?

**S:** Yes, but I didn't go out in high school, because it was hippie time, and we all just hung out together. I guess I had attractions, but they never went anywhere. We were all "buddies." We didn't really date. I don't know if I've ever really dated, because I think you only do that in high school.

**K:** When you first got involved in sexual relationships, was it with men or women?

**S:** It was with men when I was 18. It happened between high school and college and then in college. I lived with one boyfriend who I was involved with for two years, and I slept with a couple of others.

But when I was in college, in '73 or '74 in Burlington, Vermont, it was beginning to feel uncomfortable to be straight in the women's community; it almost felt politically incorrect to sleep with men. We had a support group for straight women. I'm sure we knew about bisexuality, but that wasn't included. Most, if not all of us, have come out since, but it was interesting that at that time we needed to validate that it was okay to be straight.

There were two years in college when I lived with my best friend. I remember thinking and possibly saying to her that I could go on like this, just having women roommates and having men come and go, because really security is found more with your women friends.

It wasn't until the end of college that I realized I was attracted to a woman. She was interested in me first for a long time before I realized what was going on. I didn't sleep with her then, but that was the first time that I was aware that I could feel attracted to a woman.

**K:** Did you go through an identity crisis then about your sexuality?

**S:** Not really. After I graduated from college I took off traveling. I visited a hippie commune out West for a weekend, and in the course of the four days there I decided I was interested in both a man and a woman who lived there. I decided to move into the commune, but by the time I actually did that, the woman had flipped out and was in a mental hospital. So I got involved with the man.

But it was a hippie commune. It was very "everybody sleeps with everybody." So I got interested in another woman, and I actually propositioned her. I don't remember an identity crisis. It was in the context of a hippie commune. It was like, why not? It didn't seem like a big deal.

After I left the commune, I lived in Palo Alto for a while and then moved to San Francisco. I was working in a halfway house, and this guy called and said he was going to kill himself and then hung up. I freaked out and called my boyfriend at the time, who was a very politically correct, sensitive man. I said, "I can't believe what just happened to me." He didn't know how to respond; he didn't know how to give me support. I felt like no woman would have responded that way. I decided to give up on men for a while because of that.

I felt then that I had gone through many years of only being interested in men, basically for most of my adult life. I also felt that it was too much to be open to everybody. I wanted some time to just focus on women. So for about eight years I just saw women, and I called myself a lesbian, because in my mind I was. I'm not sure I ever said I would never sleep with a man again, but I did throw away my diaphragm.

**K:** What was going on during that time in terms of your relationships?

**S:** Serial monogamy they call it, right?

**K:** Yes. Did you have any long-term relationships?

**S:** My average even with men has been more or less four to six months. I don't consider that short term, but I don't consider that long term either. I think of it as long enough to know that the relationship is not going to work.

**K:** When did you start opening up to men again, and why did you do that?

**S:** I left the city and moved to Mendocino County, where I was around mostly women. I was in a lesbian community, but nothing was happening for me. It was probably one of the longest periods of celibacy I ever had, about a year.

I think that just out of frustration I became interested in this guy. I practically propositioned him, but didn't. That was the first time in many years that I realized that I would have slept with a man. Although when I moved up to Mendocino County, before I became attracted to that guy I must have known that I was bisexual, because I got fitted for a cervical cap.

When I moved back down to San Francisco ten years ago I was still in the period of celibacy. I ran into this guy who I had known when I had lived in the city previously, when I was a dyke. It had never occurred to me before to be interested in him. He was the first man I slept with in eight years. It lasted less than a month. After him I had one brief affair with a woman.

None of my relationships were working, so I propositioned an old friend of mine, named Josh, who I'd never been particularly attracted to. I didn't think I'd fall in love with him, but I did. Then I told him I wanted to have a kid with him, and we did. I married him because he wanted me to, and there didn't seem to be any good reason not to; it also made sense for me to be covered by his health insurance.

When I started seeing him, I made it clear to him that I wasn't giving up women for the rest of my life. We didn't talk about my giving up other men, but it was very clear that I wasn't saying goodbye to women.

**K:** What was his reaction to that?

**S:** Fine, because he's bisexual, too. Later on in our marriage, when I realized that I was still bisexual—which meant that I was still attracted to other men as well—he didn't like that. Our agreement at that point was that I could sleep with women, but not with men. We never discussed nonmonogamy again after the first six months of the relationship. After we got married I think he had some changed assumptions that I didn't have.

**K:** So he was assuming you were going to be monogamous, and you were assuming that you didn't have to be?

**S:** The discrepancy seemed to be whether I could sleep with other men. I think he knew that I was going to sleep with women at some point, but I think he assumed that I wasn't going to sleep with other men. The marriage ended a little more than a year ago. Nonmonogamy wasn't really the issue. The whole time we were together we were only monogamous because other relationships just weren't happening.

**K:** Tell me about your current situation.

**S:** I've had two lovers since the end of my marriage. The first one was the guy that I had been in love with on the hippie commune. So I reconnected with a lover I had sixteen years ago. I was really in love with this guy when I was 24, but this time it didn't last very long, and the sex was lousy. It always was, and always will be. In fact I think he's a repressed queer, a recovering Catholic. I saw him for a couple of months.

While I was still in the marriage I was getting closer to this dyke, Beth, I work with. We got tight talking about nonmonogamy. I didn't know that what was happening was that I was falling for her. At the time she was in a relationship that was eight years old and that had always been nonmonagamous; she seems to have made nonmonagamy work for her.

When I was still married to Josh I told Beth that I was interested in her. At the time she said she wasn't interested. I was a little hurt, but it wasn't that big a deal, because I saw it from her point of view: that she would be the secondary relationship to my primary one.

Then I broke up with Josh. Four months after the end of the marriage, Beth and I traveled together out of town for work. We shared a bed in a hotel. I thought we were going to be platonic, but we weren't. Now I'm in love with her, and it can't work because she is in a primary relationship.

K: Because you want to be in a primary relationship with her as well?

S: My druthers would be that.

K: If you could have your ideal situation, what would it be?

S: To be with Beth right now. I don't think she's my partner for life. I don't know if I'd miss men.

K: Do you have more of a long-term vision than that?

S: I'd probably like another life partner. If the person had kids it would be easier.

My kids have always known gay people. After Josh and I broke up, my son said to me, "Daddy said that someday you're going to bring home a boyfriend or a girlfriend, and he's going to bring home a boyfriend or a girlfriend." And I said, "Right."

K: Would you say that you are a monogamous or a nonmonogamous person?

S: I think I'm a serially monogamous person. I like being someone's favorite.

K: Do you practice safe sex?

S: Not with women. With men, yes.

K: What is safe sex with men for you?

**S:** Condoms for oral sex and intercourse.

**K:** Why do you not practice safe sex with women?

**S:** I'm still not totally convinced it's necessary, and it's a drag. It ruins the whole point, if you ask me.

**K:** When you've been involved in a relationship with a man, what have you missed most sexually and emotionally about not being with a woman?

**S:** My husband used to say that he could hear a difference in my voice when I talked on the telephone to my close women friends. He could tell that I was different—more relaxed and spontaneous—with my women friends than I was with him.

**K:** Is there anything sexually you missed about not being involved with a woman?

**S:** A woman's body.

**K:** When you've been involved with a woman in a relationship, what did you miss sexually and emotionally about not being with a man?

**S:** I don't think I missed a man's body. In terms of penetration, which I always liked, I had one woman lover who used a dildo. Probably if I had a very long-term woman lover I might want to use a dildo some, but I don't remember particularly missing penetration with women.

**K:** Did you miss anything emotionally about not being with a man?

**S:** No, I guess that's why I thought I was a lesbian.

**K:** Do your parents know that you're bisexual?

**S:** Yes.

**K:** How do they feel about it?

**S:** I came out to them when I had given up men. They cried and thought they had done something wrong. Then they adjusted and decided that I was fine. They met a couple of my women lovers. Then my mother assumed that I was sleeping with all my women friends, because she mistakenly thought that if you're going to sleep with one woman you're close to, you'll sleep with all of the women that you are close to. I don't think I told her about the one man I slept with before I was with Josh, because I didn't want to get her hopes up.

The high point of my parents accepting my sexuality was when I was in New York for one of the Gay Day parades. They went with me. We stood on the sidelines so that the marchers could see us. My mother held a sign saying, "We love our lesbian daughter." Our picture was in *The New York Times!*

**K:** What was that like for your parents?

**S:** They were proud. They were actually very proud. The ironic thing is that they were proud to have their name in print in *The New York Times.* But then when I got together with Josh they were thrilled, just thrilled.

I recently had lunch with my mother. She asked me, "Is there anybody." I said, "Yes, I just slept with Beth." She said, "Wouldn't that be hard on the kids?" I said, "But that's who I am, and they'll have to get used to it." I think she feels conflicted about my sexuality. She asked me again this year about it, and I emphatically told her that I am bisexual. She would prefer that I was straight.

**K:** Where is your father in all this?

**S:** He doesn't really discuss any discomfort that he has. We're really tight; he loves me and accepts me, but he will probably never understand it.

**K:** Do other family members know?

**S:** Yes, my sister and her husband know. My sister was pregnant when she got married. I met her brother-in-law for the first time at the wedding. I said to my mother, "I think he's queer. I'm going to ask Judy if he's queer." My mother said, "I think he might be, too, but don't ask Judy, because it would upset her to think that there might be gay people on both sides of the family, because her baby might come out gay." I said, "Mom, I don't think it works that way, and I'm going to ask her." I asked her, and she said she thinks he is, but he's totally closeted; he'll never come out. I saw him again. He'll be single forever; it's really sad.

**K:** Do all your friends know that you are bisexual?

**S:** I think all my friends know.

**K:** How is it for you dealing with lesbians as a bisexual woman?

**S:** For women who have know me for a long time, it's not a problem. It might become a problem with lesbians who I'm getting to know for the first time, since they would probably assume that I'm a dyke until they find out that I have this sordid past.

**K:** How is it for you dealing with the straight world as a bisexual woman?

**S:** Work is mostly a straight world. Because they've all known me for a long time, I don't fear not being accepted.

**K:** Is there any other situation where you deal with the straight world?

**S:** The kids' school; they don't know that I'm bisexual. Someday they might find out that I have a girlfriend.

**K:** How does that feel to you?

**S:** There could be some weirdness—not from the directors of the school because, though they probably wouldn't understand it, they'd accept it. But I'm a little aloof from the rest of the parents. I don't know how it would be if they found out I was bisexual, or whether the kids will talk about my being involved with women in school; that's yet to be seen.

**K:** How is it for you dealing with gay male friends as a bisexual woman?

**S:** Most if not all of my gay male friends have only known me during and after my marriage. I don't know if any of them knew me when I was a dyke. I don't think it matters to them.

**K:** How is it for you dealing with other bisexuals?

**S:** It's not an issue with bisexual people. These days these categories are getting a little bit more fluid. I think more people are identifying as bisexual now than there were ten years ago. I think once you've enjoyed sleeping with a partner of the same sex, you're always queer. I don't think anybody can ever go back to being straight, if they've enjoyed being queer once.

**K:** Are you a feminist?

**S:** Yes.

**K:** What does it mean to you to be a feminist?

**S:** It means understanding women's oppression and trying to change it. I'm sure there are more times that I should call men on sexism than I do. I really don't do it very often. Luckily I'm not around assholes very often. I can't stand men who talk too much and dominate, who take up all the space.

**K:** Do you think that bisexuality has political implications?

**S:** Sleeping with a same-sex partner has political implications. For a woman sleeping with another woman is a refusal to accept male power as necessary for our happiness.

**K:** Do you think you have a contribution to make to the world as a bisexual woman?

**S:** Maybe my contribution is just to my kids. They are freer than I was growing up, and hopefully won't be oppressed by rigid rules. I want my daughter to know that she has lots of options that are not defined by men.

**K:** Is there anything else that you want to say in the interview?

**S:** I'm more wary of being objectified by men than by women. When I first started sleeping with Josh I felt it. I think he objectified me sexually in a way that I've never experienced with a woman. On some level seeing somebody as a sexual being is objectifying them. There's a way that when you sleep with anybody that's what's going on, but there's something different when a man does it than when a woman does it.

I'm 41 and newly single, with two kids who I nursed for a long time, so my breasts sag. Recently I was in a hot tub with a male friend and his male roommate. My female roommate was there, too. She's a lot younger than me, and her breasts don't sag. It was the first time that I picked up the feeling that aging breasts are not attractive. I am also aware that I don't think a woman would be as concerned with how my breasts look as men are. It was one of these times that I felt oppression as a woman based on how men judge my physical appearance. I realize that now I'm going to have to deal with what getting older means for my body image.

# 6 ▼ ROSA

*Rosa is a 30-year-old Latina performance artist who works in a woman-owned retail sex store, and lives in San Francisco.*

**K:** Tell me a little about how you grew up.

**R:** My parents' first language was Spanish. They grew up going to a school that had a white line down the center of the playground—on one side were the European kids, and on the other side were the Black kids and the Latin kids and the Native American kids. The side with the European-Americans had grass and play equipment, and the other side was just dirt and old tires. This was in the United States in the '40s and the '50s.

So I was raised with an emphasis on assimilation. I'm the youngest of six kids. My parents made sure that we all spoke English perfectly, without an accent, and that we assimilated into the culture. They didn't want us to have the same hardships they had, and they wanted us to get an education. Now I'm really sad that I don't speak Spanish fluently. I didn't even get to talk to my grandparents as I was growing up, because they only spoke Spanish.

I grew up in San Joaquin, California, which is 40 miles west of Fresno in the Central Valley. It was a town of about 1,000 people. When I was a senior in high school my parents moved to Fresno. Most of my family still lives in the Central Valley.

**K:** When were you first aware of sexual attractions, and to which gender?

**R:** I think I've always been a romantic, though I was sexually abused as a child. I have been innocent most of my life about what I would call the gruesome parts of sexuality; instead I was interested in the spiritual romanticism of sexuality from an early age. I've always been falling in love with someone.

I had a late start with sex. I had my first kiss from a boy when I was about 12, but I didn't date anyone until I was out of high school, when I was around 19. I didn't actually touch myself until I was 19. I didn't have any of the natural adolescent masturbation fantasies, or have a boyfriend, or even hold hands with anyone until I was into my 20s.

I got married to the first man I fell in love with when I was 21, and it was a very romantic and spiritual union. Our relationship was sexual, but it was sexual more in the spiritual realm than in the animal realm. We were married for four years.

About the end of that time, I had my first experience of infatuation with a woman. It was a natural transition for me from being "straight" to being bisexual; I really didn't think about it. I was just attracted to this one particular person who happened to be a woman, so it was easy for me to cross that gender line and want to be romantically involved with her. She was very wary about getting involved with me though, because she had what she called "broken in" women before, and it had been a very traumatic experience for her. So she wasn't willing to go for it with me sexually, but we were very sweet and romantic with each other. We're still really good friends.

After that I didn't necessarily identify as bisexual, but then I had never really identified as heterosexual either. It took me about four years of being with both men and women to finally state publicly that I was bisexual. Because I'm an artist and in the public eye frequently, it became an issue.

When I first started being in the lesbian community, I had some lesbian friends who said, "Don't tell any woman that you're interested in that you're bisexual. They'll be afraid of you, because bisexual women will always leave a woman for a man."

But a woman I was attracted to early on said to me, "I heard you were bisexual—that you're with men, and you're with women." I said, "Yes, that's true. How does that feel to you?" I was expecting her to give me some sort of rant about how she doesn't trust bisexual women, but she said, "I think it's great. I would be with men if I could be, but I just can't. I'm not really attracted to men. I find men's bodies erotic, but I'm not really attracted to men themselves." She had no problem with it, but I have known someone since then who said she didn't feel that she could come out to her lesbian friends as bisexual. I thought it was just twisted not to be able to come out as a sexual minority within a group of sexual minorities.

**K:** When were you sexually abused as a child, and was it continuous?

**R:** I'm still uncovering it. I believe that it was a one-time incident of my father masturbating in front of me when I was about nine. I completely blocked the memory of it until I was 20, about the time that I started being sexual. I realized at that time that I had to deal with it, so I embarked on individual and group therapy as an incest survivor, which was hard for me. I wanted to minimize it, because it was a one-time event. I wasn't penetrated; I wasn't raped; but it definitely affected the way that I saw sex, especially coming from a strict Catholic upbringing.

When I was a kid I wanted to be a nun. That was my fantasy, because I was very spiritual and in touch with God energy. Having God as my husband seemed a good alternative to growing up in the sexual world.

**K:** You said when you were married that you had a very strong spiritual connection. Was that around a particular religion?

**R:** No, it was having a personal vision and meeting somebody who could fit that vision, feeling ecstatic with this person and thinking, "This is it. It can't get any better." That's why we got married, because it just seemed that it couldn't get any better. By the end of the marriage I had started expanding in a lot of different ways that I didn't think the marriage could sustain: becoming more radical, doing performance art, becoming bisexual, being nonmonogamous, confronting my incest.

**K:** Did you go through an identity crisis at that point about being bisexual?

**R:** No, I didn't. I put on the identity of bisexuality like a coat or a label; it doesn't really explain my being. It explains that I am a part of several communities. I'm really involved in the lesbian/dyke community and the gay community, also the straight art community. I'm also involved to some degree in the anarchist pagan community, the S/M community, the incest survivors' community, and the Latina community. I belong to all these different groups of people, and I interact with all of them. And I'm out almost everywhere as a bisexual.

I haven't come out to my family yet, but I also haven't come out to them about the incest and a big part of my art. Somehow it seems like a big ball of string—that once I come out as bisexual I'll have to unravel the whole thing for them to see and accept. I think I'm about to embark on that journey. I've asked my mom to come and spend some time with me alone, and I think I'm going to come out to her about everything at that time. She's very open and accepting, and I think our relationship will survive.

**K:** Tell me about your current situation. Are you involved with anyone?

**R:** I've recently come out of a nonmonogamous relationship with a man who moved out of town. Right now I have multiple flirtations, and I have a woman friend who I have a very sweet, romantic relationship with. We're both really busy with our lives. We see each other maybe once a week, or once every two weeks. It's always really great when we get together; we have a very easy, romantic relationship.

**K:** Is it a sexual relationship as well?

**R:** Yes, it's a sexual relationship. I don't know exactly how to explain it, except we're both 30, we're both artists, and we both have a lot to do. So we have a very special connection. We don't have a mundane connection.

Right now I don't really want a mundane relationship with anybody, because I am married to my art. I work with a group of performance artists, and we're getting ready to go to Taipei and Hong Kong in November. So my practical life is getting that together with them. With my lovers I like it to be more sparse, but to have really intimate, intense contact when we get together.

Right now my relationship with men is mostly involved with dominating them. I do S/M (sado-masochistic) play with them. I seem to have an inclination for dominating men. I have two slaves right now who are both really wonderful, creative men. We set up a magical space where we work together with S/M play. We're doing a lot of work combining ecstasy with S/M: ecstatic states through breath and awareness and conscious touch, along with the S/M world of role playing, sensation play, and bondage.

**K:** Do you consider yourself in a relationship with these two men?

**R:** I am. I'm in a mistress/slave relationship with them.

**K:** Would you say it is a sexual relationship that you have with these men?

**R:** We do have sexual contact. I would say it's a sexual relationship, but it's not a partnering relationship; we're not partners. One of the men I'm involved with is in a nine-year relationship with another woman, who is completely supportive of our play together. It's just been an amazing gift to be with this person and explore that side of myself—to put some of my creative energy around sex into an actual scene. Interspersing meditation and conscious states and play acting and sexual contact—that's my preferred way to be in a relationship with men right now, aside from the friendships that I have with them. I don't know that I'll ever go back to a romantic model with men. I reserve that for women right at this moment. I haven't yet dominated any women, but that's not to say that I won't.

**K:** How are you different in relating to women and to men?

**R:** I'm a romantic by nature, so I'm romantic with both, but my relationship to men right now is around power dynamics. There's this thing happening right now with men wanting to experiment with powerful women, and that's what's happening between me and men.

With women I have much more classically romantic relationships. I go through more courting rituals. I have more process around dating, kissing, holding and love-making. They fit into my mind a little bit differently.

This is new for me, though. At times I've made less of a distinction between men and women. Men have sometimes been my primary partners, and women have been more like the muses in my life. Although right now I don't have a primary partner, I see myself as more likely to strike up a partnership with a woman than with a man. With men I can explore these intense dynamics, and receive a lot of love and admiration from them, but I don't feel the attachment that I once had for them. I'm more emotionally attached to women.

**K:** Are you nonmonogamous, or are you also open to being in a monogamous relationship?

**R:** I'm not opposed to being monogamous if I were in a primary relationship that needed to be monogamous for a period of time to revamp the relationship, or because my partner wanted us to be monogamous. But there are so many different ways to define what being monogamous is. Is it emotional intimacy with only one partner? Is it not getting excited about somebody else? Is it not fucking somebody else? Is it not tongue kissing somebody else, or is it just not kissing somebody else? Is it not sharing an ecstatic state with somebody else? Is it not looking into somebody else's eyes? Is it not sharing your soul with somebody else?

I had a really terrible time with this in my last relationship. I was incredibly jealous the whole time. I think that I don't want to live with a partner—even a primary partner—at this point in my life. I do feel that the way people are in relationships is undergoing some sort of revolution right now, and the possibilities are wide open. So I don't want to be limited by a traditional model at this point.

Sometimes I do think it would be really nice to have somebody special to care about. The truth is I have a lot of people to care about, and I have a lot of people who care about me. Right now I'm in a state where I need to care about myself and make sure that I get fed, cleaned, showered, rested. When I'm involved with somebody, I'm always taking care of them. It's important for me not to do that, so I can move into a place of more independence. I love being my own person at this point and living on my own, being able to come and go as I please.

**K:** Tell me more about how you reach ecstatic states with other people, and how that fits in with doing S/M.

**R:** People do S/M for different reasons. S/M is not always accompanied by sex. Some people do it because they like to experiment with different places around sensation and what that does to the mind and body. Some people really fly when being whipped or clothes-pinned or needled or burnt or even with feathers or light fingertip sensation. What happens for them is that they get beyond their minds and move to different realms within their souls.

But there are all kinds of ways to reach ecstatic states. Some people do it through specific exercises, like Tantric or Taoist exercises. Other people find that it just happens—that thing that happens when you fall in love with somebody, and just being next to them puts you in a wonderfully blissful state. That's what it is to reach ecstatic states with somebody.

I believe that we create that within ourselves, and that somehow it's released when we meet somebody who fits the idea in our psyche of who we want to be with in that way. I think that it's an energy that we have access to at all times. When we can get in touch with that, and we're with somebody else who is willing to go to that place, it's possible to go there together.

You can reach ecstatic states by doing simple things like looking at somebody and breathing with them while at the same time doing what I would call "conscious touch," which is putting your consciousness in your hands or in your body where you're touching somebody. As a society we're so starved for real intimate touch—just somebody saying, "I care about you" in the way that they touch you. It's not just about sex. It's about loving. It's not necessarily about being in love with somebody, although that can accompany this state. It's more about being in love with yourself, and being in love with the world, and seeing those oases in the world where you can go and receive that ecstatic pleasure.

I think that sex is really a sacred act. That's a missing component right now in the way our culture views sex. For me, S/M is a sacred, role-playing space, and there's a lot of responsibility inherent in that. Entering that space with a completely loving mind and conscious body, with conscious awareness of the other person's state of being, is really important for me. It's a practice. It's like a meditation; it's a path.

When I do S/M play with somebody I enter into a sacred space with them. I create a physical space that's separate from ordinary reality for us to step into. Once we step into that space we leave our ordinary reality behind: getting up in the morning, going to work, dealing with people, writing letters, and fixing dinner. All of that isn't relevant any more. There's something special about really giving yourself up to somebody that you trust and that you know will respect that gift.

When I dominate, I'm a guide. I see this person, and I use my intuition and my power over them to guide them to a place they haven't been before. I help them to surrender to their highest place of being.

To give yourself over to somebody and let go of control can lead you into some surprising places. Basically what happens is that we take a journey together in our minds and in our bodies. We don't know where we're going to end up. It's an experience that people don't allow themselves to have on a mundane level. So we create a space to get there. Some people get it through watching sports. Some people get it through having children. I don't like to watch sports, and I don't want to have any kids. So I create my own ways to obtain important insightful revelations in my life.

**K:** If you could have your ideal situation in terms of relationships and how you express your sexuality, what would it be?

**R:** I think that's really tricky, because if you were to have asked me five years ago, I would have said that I want to be with somebody who's perfect, and who completely loves me, and is completely devoted to me and gives me everything I want. If you asked me two years ago, I would have said that I want a primary relationship which is monogamous, and I want to be nonmonogamous. I want to be sexual with anybody I want, and I want my partner not to be jealous at all.

If you would ask me today, I would have to say I have no idea what I want, because I don't know what I am capable of. It would be nice to develop an intimate, sustainable sexual relationship with somebody. By that I mean a relationship that allows both of us to keep our independence and that won't tear us up emotionally. Also, that it can change with the way that my life and that person's life might change.

A part of me still wants that one person who I can call my very own to love and cuddle. I think, though, that that person really is myself. I'm still trying to have a loving, sexual relationship with myself. That's my goal for this year. Then I'll expand to relating to other people.

**K:** Are you saying that next year you will be able to talk about what you want in terms of relationships, but you don't know at this point what they will look like?

**R:** Yes, because five years ago I couldn't have imagined that I would be capable of sustaining several ongoing nonmonogamous contacts with different lovers.

**K:** Do you practice safe sex?

**R:** All the time.

**K:** Since it means different things to different people what is safe sex for you?

R: Safe sex to me means using barriers when there is contact with the genital region. If I am doing hand to cunt play with a woman, I'll use a glove. If I'm massaging a man's genitals, I'll use a glove. If I'm going down on somebody I'll use plastic wrap or a latex barrier. If I'm fucking someone either with a dildo or with a man's dick, I'll use a condom. I will touch people's bodies with my body and with my hands, but I will not have genital contact without a barrier. Because I'm having multiple relationships, it's really important to practice safe sex. I also let people know that I am relating sexually to other people.

K: If you're only in a sexual relationship with a man, what do you miss sexually or emotionally about not being involved with a woman?

R: There's definitely a more relaxed state around sexuality with women. I don't have as many issues about my body come up with women. Even though the men I'm with completely love and accept my body, I still find that I have a lot more self-judgment come up about my body with men than with women. Also because of my abuse being perpetrated by a man, I have abuse issues come up when I'm with men. So being with a woman is less complicated.

I usually turn men into lesbian lovers. I play with sex toys with them, and I show them what I need to reach orgasm, if that's what I'm interested in. I often do butt play with them. I know about different massage techniques for genital/anal stimulation. There has to be a lot of physical play with the anus before entering. So I work up to entering my male lovers. I fuck most of the men I play with. I teach them how to fuck with dildos and with their hands. I don't emphasize that they have to maintain an erection for me. I disengage sex from intercourse. That opens up a place for men where they can surrender and get to know the woman's body as if they were a woman.

K: When you're only involved in a relationship with a woman what do you miss sexually and/or emotionally about not being involved with a man?

R: There's a place in my psyche that only men fill for me, in the same way that there's a place in my psyche that only women fill for me. My upbringing conditioned me to be with men. So a lot of my emotional, romantic reflexes have to do with the image of a man, and I'm able to play those out more readily with a man than I am with a woman. I get a lot emotionally and mentally from being with a man.

I can't say that men are more rigorous than women, because usually I find that men are much lazier than women in bed. And I can't say that men are more intellectually stimulating, because that hasn't been the case. There's some sort of connection for me that both men and women fill. Maybe it's that I can then connect with both the male and female sides of myself.

**K:** How "out" are you as a bisexual to friends and to colleagues?

**R:** I'm really "out" in my everyday life. All the friends that I have day-to-day contact with know that I'm bisexual, by virtue of knowing about my romantic shenanigans. If I go to a lesbian space, probably a lot of women there assume I'm lesbian. I don't usually wear something that will identify me as bisexual. But the people I have contact with on a day-to-day basis know I'm bisexual. It's not a problem where I work.

**K:** Do any of your family members know?

**R:** No, but I think my mom suspects. She has told me stories about people she's met who are gay, and she thinks they're really nice. Then she says something like, "When I was growing up in the '50s, being gay was worse than doing drugs." Since I've done drugs and I am bisexual, I'm out on both accounts.

I think that some members of my family suspect that I might be a lesbian because I don't have a boyfriend, I live in San Francisco, I shave my head, and I don't seem to care that much about makeup. But at this point nobody in my family is aware that I'm bisexual. I think it would be easier for my family to accept that I was a lesbian than that I was a bisexual, because bisexuality probably would imply to them that I would have more than one partner.

**K:** How is it for you dealing with the lesbian community as a bisexual woman?

**R:** I feel like I am a part of the lesbian community, but I know that I'm not a lesbian. I do know women who identify as lesbians who sleep with men. I could probably do that if I wanted to, but it just seems to me that it's more clear to say I'm a bisexual. Even if I were a lesbian I don't know if I would identify with the lesbian community much differently than I now do, because I have so many different sides to myself that it seems limiting to identify with only one particular group.

**K:** How is it for you dealing with the straight world as a bisexual woman?

**R:** I definitely have a bias against straight people at this point. If I go to a party that's all straight people, it seems boring to me for some reason. The exclusively straight culture feels really limiting to me. So I'm hardly ever in a completely straight environment anymore, except when I visit my family. Then I have other things to deal with. The straight world is not my world. The world I move in is really mixed, and the straight people that are in my world are very inclusive of gay culture.

**K:** Are you a feminist?

**R:** It seems to me that almost any woman alive today should be a feminist, because being feminist is linked to a movement that has given us the basic human rights we have today. All women need to own that heritage. If a woman doesn't want to call herself a feminist, that's her business, but I would like all women to recognize the role that feminism has played in their lives and be thankful for it.

**K:** Do you feel that bisexuality has political implications?

**R:** I think it must. A lot of people see bisexuals as the bridge between the gays and the straights. I think in some way it is, because it brings in a third possibility. I think that there's a consciousness coming about right now that is getting away from the black and white dichotomy and coming to a place of seeing that there's a variety of types of people. I think also that it's important that bisexuals are joining the struggle for their rights along with gays and lesbians. Straight people are also joining the struggle for gay and lesbian rights. Hopefully it will turn into this big pot of "give everybody human rights." Everybody deserves human rights—that's the bottom line, but there's so much resistance to that.

# 7 ▼ MARY

*Mary is a 42-year-old, HIV-positive woman who lives in Southern California. She is self-employed. Her husband died of AIDS.*

**K:** Tell me about your background. How you grew up, your class background, and what race you are.

**M:** I'm of Italian heritage, and I'm the oldest of three. My parents divorced when I was seven years old, and I grew up mostly in Southern California. We were middle class. My mother raised me until I was ten, and then my father got custody of my brothers and me. I left home when I was 21.

**K:** Were you raised in any particular religion?

**M:** I was raised Catholic. My father still went to church and ushered and acted like a devout Catholic, when in fact he had been excommunicated, because of the divorce. He just snubbed his nose at that and still practiced his faith. He still practices it. I do not at this time.

Some people raised Catholic are afraid to sexually explore, but I don't think my religious upbringing impacted my sexuality. I didn't have an Elizabethan upbringing about sex, but we didn't talk about it a whole lot either. My father said, "Don't let any boy ever put his hand on your knee, because that means he wants something." That's all I can remember him saying to me about sex.

**K:** When were you first aware of sexual attractions, and to which sex?

**M:** I remember I had my first crush on a neighbor boy when I was 14. I used to spy on him. I was really jealous thinking of him being with other girls. That was my first feeling of jealousy and desire.

I wasn't attracted to women until the mid '80s. That was mostly due to watching x-rated movies and being curious. My boyfriend at the time picked up on that and created a scenario that would fulfill my fantasy.

**K:** Can you give me a brief sexual history?

**M:** I had one boyfriend from age 16 to 19. We didn't "go all the way" —remember that expression?—until I was almost 18, and we had been going together for a couple years. I can barely remember that experience. I remember I didn't like oral sex a whole lot. To tell you the truth, I don't remember the actual act. I didn't know what the big deal was—I didn't have orgasms. In fact, I didn't have an orgasm probably until my mid-20s. It's amazing, because I usually dated older men. How that never came to be, I don't know. I broke that relationship off, because he wanted to get married, and I knew that I wasn't ready for marriage. I needed to date more.

I moved out of the house when I was 21, moved to another city, and reunited with a high school boyfriend. I lived with him for about ten months. I was out on my own for a short while and then got another boyfriend. I was with him a couple of years. I'm usually in a relation-ship with one person.

Then I met my first husband, Eddie. I dated him for three years before marrying him. That marriage lasted six-and-a-half years. After the breakup, I met my late husband, Dan. We were together for five years. Currently I'm in a relationship that is a few months old. Between the death of my second husband, Dan, and my current boyfriend I've had one relationship that lasted a little over a year with a bisexual HIV-positive man.

**K:** When did you start being attracted to women?

**M:** The year before our divorce, Eddie and I got involved in an open lifestyle, because I thought our marriage needed some spice. I tried an encounter with a woman at that time, and it just didn't work. I wasn't emotionally present, and it felt very awkward. I felt like I was "doing" her, and she wasn't really responding to me. I have realized since then that women have to connect with each other and like each other to have it work. So arranging encounters for me with women I didn't know didn't work.

**K:** I assume that you have also had good sexual encounters with women. What were those?

**M:** When Dan and I were on vacation, there was a single woman on vacation by herself, and we went up to her hotel room. She and I connected once we were together. In fact, so much so that we didn't want him around. Then later on she came to visit, and I basically shut the bedroom door on Dan. I just wanted her for myself. He was a little bent out of shape about that. But that situation was short-lived, because she lived out of town.

My other encounters have been with girlfriends of mine; they have been extensions of our friendship and our feelings towards each other. We haven't had ongoing sexual relationships, but at some point in time there was some touching or some stroking or some masturbating—nothing ongoing. No expectations for the future. It just happened. I think a lot of that had to do with their knowing how sexually open I am, and wanting to experiment. Some of the women had not been with women before.

The other experiences I've had with women have been in open lifestyle party situations. They were okay; they weren't bad. I'm usually the doer; I don't receive as easily. I like to please. That's been fun.

**K:** Was your husband's death sudden?

**M:** No. It was due to AIDS. I was with him for five years, and we knew for four of those five that he was HIV-positive.

**K:** How was that for you and your relationship?

**M:** That's a whole book in itself. When Dan found out that he was HIV-positive he was very angry, because he had an open lifestyle before we met. All his friends were into that lifestyle. Anything social he did was with the open lifestyle community. Being new to this community, it was fun and exciting for me at first, but it was also very empty. Really what I wanted was to just be with him and occasionally maybe play the field, but it wasn't something I needed in my life. He needed it, though, to feel fulfilled and desired, and for his ego.

So when we found out we were positive, he was quite angry that a lot of what he was doing had to stop. We'd still go to the parties, but we wouldn't play.* I didn't really want to go, but he wanted to hoping he would change my mind and coerce me into playing, using condoms, but not telling anybody we were infected. I couldn't do that. Very rarely at those parties did anyone use condoms, and it infuriated me. Here I was sitting with this news that was devastating to me, and these people were having unprotected sex like there was no AIDS in the world.

**K:** How did you find out that you were HIV positive?

**M:** We were both divorcing at the same time. That's what brought us together, because we found comfort in sharing our pain. He was dating to camouflage his pain. I wasn't. About six months after our separations from our spouses, I made him choose. If you want me like you say you do, then I have to be the only one.

Six months later I decided on a whim to get tested for HIV, because I'm a responsible person in terms of getting my car tuned up, the oil changed on a regular basis, going to the dentist, and I knew that this test existed. I didn't even tell Dan. I was going to surprise him. They took the blood. It takes two weeks to get the results. When I went back to get my results they told me I was positive.

I was shocked. In fact my first reaction was, "I'm not a prostitute, I'm not a drug addict. You guys must have mixed up my blood. You've got to take it again." They agreed with me, because I didn't seem to fit the profile. So we took it again. At that point I had my boyfriend be there for the results, and we found then that in fact I was positive. Then they took his blood and found out he was also positive. That definitely changed out lives. It also affected our sex life, because his sex drive diminished. Mine never changed, but he felt dirty and unclean. I never felt that way.

When we were going through our divorces and getting together as a couple, I didn't expect to be with him the rest of my life. When we found out we were both positive, it became the glue that kept us together. We thought we were the only heterosexuals in this county that were infected, and we'd better stick together because nobody else would want us. That was difficult, because as in any relationship we had to work out our problems and differences. He hadn't been my

---

* At open lifestyle parties, "playing" is the term used for having sexual encounters with other people.

choice for the long term, and now he was. It's like dating somebody, and then all of a sudden you're married to them.

But over the years as the disease stripped him of his ego, I fell in love with the real man. He had always loved me, had always said that, and I'd loved him, but I fell in love with him all over again through this process. It was basically the disease that humbled him enough that he could be real and authentic with his feelings—to just be the sensitive guy that he really was. That was special.

**K:** How was it for you when he died?

**M:** He died on my birthday. It was one of my biggest fears that that would happen, but I think I have dealt with it in a healthy manner. Birthdays to me are very special. I refuse to give up my birthday to his death, but I acknowledge it.

This last year is the first year I haven't acknowledged his death on my birthday. In years past I'd always light a candle, and I'd bring out pictures and music we used to listen to, and I'd cry for a couple of hours. Then I'd let it be, and the rest of the day would be mine.

This year I didn't have time, or I didn't make time. It was a turning point for me. I think I have grieved enough over the years that I've let it go. It's in the past, and I'm moving on. I'm in a relationship now, too, and that helps. I probably still will do the ritual on his birthday.

When he died I had a lot of different emotions. He was in a coma, on morphine, so he didn't know what was happening to him. It was a relief for me after attending to him and trying to figure out what he needed or wanted, for him finally to let go.

I also felt like I was out of a job. I didn't know what to do with myself, because my whole life was consumed with his health care. People were worried about me, but I was real healthy at the time. The last thing I worried about was me. He required a lot of care. He was like a little boy, and I was his mommy.

**K:** Because he got so ill?

**M:** Yes, and he was scared. I just took control. I'm a take-charge type of person anyway, and he allowed me to do that. As he got weaker and more depressed, I tried to keep his spirits up. I had people come and visit. I had him feed the dogs and do some chores. One of the things I didn't do was give myself much of a break. The only thing I did was to go once a week to a support group for caregivers. Then I'd come right back home. Other than that I was with him constantly, because I did the best job, of course.

I did all of the home care. He had a catheter in his chest for drugs and for infusions. He was also on liquid nutrition through the vein, which I prepared and gave him every night. It was quite an ordeal; I felt like a nurse.

**K:** How many years ago was this?

**M:** Four.

**K:** Tell me about your current relationships and your health?

**M:** This year has been the toughest year for me health wise. I've been positive for eight years now. It's only this year that my HIV status has hit me in the face. It's scary. I've lost so many people to this disease. I've personally known about a dozen women, a few from the open lifestyle I was in, who have died—strong women, mothers with a reason to live, who couldn't make it. Sometimes I'm not sure why I'm still here, but I thank God all the time. My health has definitely taken a drop this year big time, and it scares me. I feel fine, but my blood work says I'm in dire straits. I have almost no immune system left, which is really shocking. I feel very vulnerable.

It's the best and worst times of my life happening all at once. I'm in a relationship with a HIV-negative man who has known since day one about my status. He has been there supporting and nurturing me through all the trials and tribulations of this year. He's new to this; he has never experienced illness like this, much less HIV. So it's been an education for him. I believe he's hanging in there for the duration.

**K:** How long have you been together?

**M:** Nine months now. It's not an easy relationship. We're still working out the standard communication stuff that takes some effort. I think we both love each other so we're not going to bail. I've wanted to many times. I've tried pushing him away, because of my health situation. I don't want to drag him down, but that's not for me to say. He's deciding what he wants to do.

**K:** What have you worked out in terms of safer sex?

**M:** We do practice that. Definitely condoms for intercourse, saran wrap for oral sex. He works in construction so sometimes he has cuts on his hands. He doesn't seem to be concerned about it. I tell him if he has cuts to please be careful touching my vaginal secretions. I don't have sex on my period. That's a rule of mine. We do deep kiss. I don't floss my teeth when I'm going to see him. I floss when I know I'm not going to see him so that my gums have time to heal.

**K:** How was it for him and for you when you told him you were positive?

**M:** I've been rejected. I'm one of the few women that are positive that are out there dating. A lot of women give it up, because they got infected through sex, or they have addictive behaviors, and they don't want to get involved sexually because that creates that addictive scenario for them again. But I feel very normal. I blend into society very well, and I refuse to give up relationships.

I did go with a guy who was also HIV-positive for over a year. I've been with a few negative men—all of them knowing that I'm positive. I wouldn't deep kiss anyone without telling them first.

I told my boyfriend I was positive when I could tell things were starting to cook, and I wanted to kiss him. It was very scary, because I feared rejection. I know what guys go through now. I just blurted it out somehow. His reaction was really refreshing. He said, "If it was that easy to get I'd think we'd all have it." Then he said, "What about kissing?" I didn't want to give him the answer, because I wanted him to find the answer himself.

People tend to think I know everything, because I'm infected. I have information, but I don't want to influence what anyone else will do, because I have my own way of looking at things. So I always want people to go get information themselves. Call the Center For Disease Control.

He didn't buy that. He kept pushing me on the question of kissing. I told him my philosophy on that—that as long as there's no blood, no cuts, no sores, saliva is not going to infect you. It's the blood in the saliva that will infect you. As long as your mouth is okay then there's no problem, and that's about communicating with each other. With that he raised my chin up and kissed me, and to make a long story short, I spent the night with him. He had his own condoms which really impressed me, because a lot of men I have been with didn't know anything about condoms, and I had to educate them.

I'm sure I've educated everyone I've come in contact with. I have one friend who didn't know that lambskin condoms were not good for HIV protection. That's all he had been using. Now he's using latex. I point blank ask my friends, if they are going out with someone, "Did you use protection?" I don't mean to be their conscience, but I'm living this, and I don't wish it on anybody.

**K:** Are you assuming that your boyfriend is HIV-negative? Has he been tested? Do you use protection with him for oral sex?

**M:** He got tested a month after we started dating, and he will continue to get tested every six months. That's our agreement. He has been negative. I do believe that he is negative, so I do not use protection to give him oral sex, and that's a choice we've made. It's very rare that I could infect him through oral sex. If anything, he can reinfect me if he was HIV-positive.

**K:** Is it possible for an HIV-positive person to become reinfected?

**M:** Yes. There are 200 or more different types of HIV viruses. Especially when I was dating my HIV-positive boyfriend, reinfection was a concern, because I didn't want to get his virus. He may have a different type of virus than I have.

**K:** What do you say to people, particularly women, about safer sex?

**M:** There's an HIV and Women conference coming up here in September, and I'm going to be doing a safer sex workshop for women there. I'm going to talk about different sized condoms. That maybe you should have magnums and regulars, so that if you do engage in sex with someone and the condoms aren't fitting properly, you can put a larger one on. I teach women to put condoms on with their mouth for oral sex and different lubrications and flavorings that can enhance oral sex. I have a panty wrap that I've designed out of saran wrap for oral sex on a woman. I have handouts that talk about massage and body rubbing. There are other ways of having sex and still being pleased. Fantasizing. Role playing. Reading to each other.

Watching movies. Masturbating. Watching each other masturbate. Taking a shower together. It's all about being creative. We can have fun with sex while taking into account the risks involved.

I did one of these workshops at an open lifestyle convention. It was a real challenge for me to teach these women who are out there partying their rear ends off about safer sex. Twenty women showed up, and I was thrilled. They did not know that my husband and I used to be in "the lifestyle," or that my husband died of AIDS, or that I was HIV-positive. I just stood up there and showed them how to have fun with safer sex. Basically, it's all about a little bit of planning and empowering yourself to take charge—carrying your own condoms, not assuming that the man's going to have them.

In terms of woman-to-woman sex there's a lot of denial still. I have gone to the lesbian safer sex workshops here in town, and quite frankly they were boring. I got up there and showed those women a few things and got them laughing. A lot of women, especially in the lesbian community aren't comfortable talking openly about sex. I talked about vibrators and dildos and latex gloves and finger cots.

Now there is a latex mask called the "oradam" you can buy that goes over your mouth and has a protrusion for your tongue so your tongue is covered in latex. It goes all the way around the back of your head. It's pretty bizarre, and I thought it was funny when I first saw it. But since I presented it in a workshop last year at an HIV retreat, I take it more seriously. One of the gals was intrigued by this thing. She said, "That's something my husband could use." Her husband was negative, and she was positive. I realized at that point that I shouldn't make fun of the safer sex toys that are out there, because they might save somebody's marriage or relationship.

**K:** Do you encourage women to use latex gloves? How important do you think that is?

**M:** Here's what I suggest to people in my workshops. If you have any doubts about your hands, there are ways that you can test whether you have cuts on your hands that you're not aware of: put lemon juice, alcohol or vinegar on your hands. You will know immediately if you have any paper cuts, hangnails, any openings that might be of concern. Then you can make your decision about whether you want to use a glove, a finger cot, or nothing.

For ass play I always use a finger cot. It's just easier for me that way, and cleaner. Plus I have nails, so I feel more comfortable that I'm not hurting my partner. That's a personal choice again.

We have to have peace of mind. That's worth a lot. If our heads aren't comfortable in the bedroom, our sex is not going to be good. I'm empowering women to take charge a little bit in the bedroom, because men are going to try to talk you out of using condoms. They're going to try to talk you into doing what they know best, and that's just getting on with it and not using protection. I'm trying to help women take care of themselves.

In 1987 HIV was a gay disease. At that point in time I had no clue that I was living at risk. In looking back I think I should have known better but, as my therapist points out, at that time they were not saying that heterosexuals—or women for that matter—were at risk of getting this disease. It's one of those things that just happens to some of us. Why that is I really don't know, because I know there are people living at risk all the time, and they feel immune to it. Someday, somewhere it's going to touch their lives, whether it's personally or through someone they know.

I know my life has touched all my friends. I've gotten them involved in some of the work that I do, because I want them to see what it's like for me living with this so that they can educate others. That's what it's all about. I'm a gardener; I'm planting seeds so that these people can educate others, and they have. It's been really wonderful. I have girlfriends say, "I wish you'd talk to this girl at work. I told her about you. I tell her to be careful, but she just doesn't want to use condoms. She doesn't like the way they feel." I'm thinking she obviously hasn't been at an AIDS clinic and seen some of the women in wheelchairs, or been at the Women and Children's Center and seen the mothers who have lost their husbands, or that are feeling too ill to take care of their kids. Some people need to see what's real before they get the message.

There are many implications to being HIV-positive. You can't be a donor. It bothered me taking that little sticker off my driver's license, because I took pride in thinking I take care of my body, and if I die prematurely I can let someone else live. Now I can't do that. Having children is not important to me, but that choice has been taken away. That bugs me, because I want to have the power to choose.

K: Are you monogamous at this point?

**M:** We are monogamous. My boyfriend knows about my past. He knows that I was bisexual. He also knows I was in an open relationship, and that is not his thing whatsoever. I did mention that if I ever was with a woman I would like to share her with him, to include him. But whether that ever happens or not, who knows?

Currently I have some medical problems that have prevented us from having intercourse for five months now. I'm really chomping at the bit until all my infections get cleared up and we can have regular sex again. My boyfriend has really been a saint in all of this. We still manage to meet our needs. It's just that sex as we know it is different.

**K:** If you could have your ideal situation in terms of relationships what would it be?

**M:** I don't have a problem with monogamy. I'm basically very traditional at my core, but occasionally it'd be fun to experiment or to play with a third party, mainly a woman. My attraction to women has not been emotional as much as it's been physical or sexual. I've been in bisexual women's groups, and I feel awkward at times, because a lot of the women will be talking about their breakup with their last girlfriend, or that they're still in love with this woman—all this relationship-based stuff. I'm sitting there thinking I've never really been in love with a woman, or in a one-on-one relationship with a woman. It's always been a sexual, one-night stand type of thing, although we had to like each other, like I said before. But I didn't have a consuming relationship with a woman. It would be intriguing to experience that, but I'm primarily heterosexual.

**K:** Do your parents know that you are bisexual, and/or that you're HIV-positive?

**M:** Both parents know I'm HIV-positive. I think my stepmother knows I'm bisexual, because I said something about a bisexual conference that I was involved in. I don't know if she told my father. Being bisexual is not something I need to tell my parents. I know that for some people it's a part of them, and they need to tell people who they are. My bisexuality is more of a sexual thing, and I don't need to tell my parents what I'm into sexually.

**K:** How are they with you about your being HIV-positive?

**M:** I don't think they know what to do. My father and stepmother live back east. My father calls me periodically and wants to know about my T-cells. That's all he can ask me. He doesn't know much more than that. I told him what my numbers were, and he says, "Oh, they went up." I said, "No, Dad. They went down." It bothers me that he isn't more informed. He says, "I read everything I can in the newspaper and watch what's on the TV." Well, those sources are so skewed and so narrow minded. Granted they give you a little bit of information, but the real information is at an AIDS resource center.

My mother, who lives here, has done some things with me on a very small scale regarding HIV. She's not involved in the HIV community like some parents are, but she calls me all the time and tells me how special I am. She tells me she loves me and wants me to take care of myself and take my vitamins, like a Mom. I think she prays a lot.

**K:** Do you have siblings, and do they know that you're bisexual and HIV-positive, and do other relatives know?

**M:** Nobody else knows about my bisexuality in my family. But everyone in my immediate family knows my HIV status, and I believe an aunt knows, and that's about it. My grandparents don't know.

**K:** How many siblings do you have?

**M:** I have two brothers and one half-brother and two half-sisters.

**K:** How are they dealing with you in this situation?

**M:** I get periodic phone calls. One brother calls me quite often to check on me, because I've made some crisis calls to him at times. He wants to make sure I'm eating and taking my vitamins and all that. So he's being a big brother. Really everyone calls and checks on me. One sister has been putting out some energy to me, checking on me, because I've finally taken off my mask.

For almost eight years I've been wearing a mask saying I'm fine. Now I'm taking it off and saying things aren't so hot, and I'm scared. I'm letting people in on the real story now. What I go through. I don't know if I've been trying to protect everybody, or if I've just been in denial. I'm scared and I'm concerned about my future. I'm not going to pretend any more.

**K:** How are things not fine?

**M:** I've had two surgeries in the last four months, unrelated to HIV. I had a tumor in my labia that I had removed, and because I'm HIV-positive I haven't healed. Consequently I've got an infection going on that I've had for months. It's very frustrating for me. In the process of all this I'm not supposed to take my HIV drug, because my doctor says he thinks that it impairs healing. Now I've convinced him that I've been doing it his way for months and I haven't healed anyway, so can I start my HIV drug again?

I'm getting worried. My T-cells have dropped drastically. Even though I feel fine, my numbers are not good. So I'm to the point of starting up my HIV drugs again. I've been on every experimental drug there is to see if anything slows it down, and nothing seems to do the trick. I've had fevers. I've had some weight loss, and I've gained the weight back. It's been the roller coaster.

I'm not used to this. I'm not used to being sick. I'm used to feeling normal for most of my life, even being positive. That's what I say when I speak. I don't feel my disease; I feel like you. But a doctor's telling me that my blood is infected. It's really hard to get it into my head that I have this serious, life-threatening disease, when I don't feel it.

Now this year I have started to feel it. I feel fatigued and have loss of appetite. I'm depressed, because of the roller coaster of my health. I'm not a real good sick person; I have too many things I have to do. I look around this house and all the projects and commitments I've made, and I get overwhelmed, because there are days when I just don't feel like doing anything. I couldn't imagine having a regular job. There are nights that I don't sleep well, when I have a bout with a fever. I take an aspirin, and I sweat, and then I'm up. I recently had a bout with diarrhea, and I didn't know what that was about. Then it went away for some unknown reason. There are a lot of things that come and go. It wears you out emotionally and physically.

I'm having a real struggle right now. I need to start talking to other long-term survivors, because I'm considered to be one. A long-term survivor is anyone who has been HIV-positive for over seven years. I qualify there. Or having an AIDS diagnosis for three years. This year I am now deemed to have an AIDS diagnosis. It's difficult for me to say that. I prided myself on the fact that I was just HIV-positive. I just had the virus. Now because my T-cells have dropped, according to the Centers For Disease Control I have "AIDS."

**K:** How does that feel?

**M:** It's devastating. It's scary. It makes me think I'm going to die. I don't want to buy into that fear, and there's no reason for me to, because there are people I know personally that have been around 15 years after becoming HIV-positive. But I've seen so much death, you see, and I've lived through my husband's death. So I have all this information in my head that does a number on me. Everything you read and hear says you're going to die, and then you see death around you that supports that. Then there're the few who are still here after 15, 20 years and are doing okay.

**K:** Mary, do your friends know about your HIV status, and do they know that you're bisexual?

**M:** A small group of friends in the bisexual community know I'm bisexual. Some of my other friends know that I'm bi. When I tell straight women, it opens them up. In fact I just had a girlfriend tell me at lunch, "Now don't take this wrong, but I've just recently started fantasizing about women." I think knowing I'm bi opens women friends up to being a little freer about their own sexuality.

Most of my friends can talk to me about anything, because I am open about things. If you're a good friend of mine you're going to know about all the things that are going on with me. I have a large circle of friends actually, and I haven't had any negative feedback regarding my HIV status. I've had a lot of support from my friends.

**K:** So they all know that you're HIV-positive?

**M:** Pretty much everybody, because I can't dance around the truth. This is my life, and if you're a good friend of mine you're going to know, but I am selective about who else I tell.

**K:** How do you decide who to tell?

**M:** It depends on the circumstance. One gal that was in this dance group that I'm involved in worked at a college, and I was going to speak about HIV at this college. I was concerned that she might see me on this panel, and I didn't want her to find out that way. So I had her over to my house. We sat here on the couch and I told her, and she was so grateful that I opened up to her. As it turned out she had a brother who died of AIDS. It touches everybody in different ways.

Sometimes I'll just be talking with a friend, and I'll feel this urge to tell them, because we're sharing, or I've been thinking about it for a long time and I want that person to understand me a little better. That's when I make a judgment call about deciding to tell them. I've told people in different ways, but it's always face to face. Never on the phone, because I want them to see me. A phone is too impersonal for this issue. I want eye contact.

**K:** What kind of responses have you gotten?

**M:** Sadness. Love. Support. It gets people to think about what they're doing. That happened with a girlfriend of mine. When I first met her we went out for coffee, and for some reason I just told her point blank. We hardly knew each other, but I felt like telling her. She was shocked that I was telling her this. What it brought up for her was her fear about getting tested for AIDS; she'd been wanting to get tested, but she hadn't. Meeting me reaffirmed for her that she needed to do this. We've just been dear friends ever since. That happens a lot of times when I tell people. It's a little bit like being gay, because I live in a closet and I come out when I feel the need to.

**K:** How is it for you with gay men as a bisexual and HIV-positive woman?

**M:** I have some wonderful gay friends that are really supportive and call me when they know I'm not feeling well. A lot of gay men are surprised that I'm infected. I'm still meeting men who say, "You're the first woman I've ever met that's HIV-positive." I say, "Well, there's a lot of us out here. Over 100 in this city." I'm going to a retreat for people who are dealing with HIV. I hope there's going to be about a dozen women there this year. I've always tried to recruit more women for them. I remember at last year's retreat, sitting at the dinner table and mentioning something about myself. One of the guys looked at me and said, "You mean you're positive!" I said, "Yeah, eight years." He was just floored.

When I used to go to the AIDS support groups in the early days, I was the only woman with all these men. The way I dealt with that was to tell myself that we were all human beings fighting to stay alive and dealing with this disease. So it didn't matter to me that I was the only woman. A lot of the men thought I was a nurse, a caregiver, or a counselor—there in some kind of capacity other than infected myself. In fact I played a game one time at a Christmas party that was primarily for HIV people. I sat in a circle and I said, "Okay, you guys, why do you think I'm here?" They went all the way around saying, "You're going to school, you're a nurse, you're this, you're that." Nobody guessed that I was infected.

**K:** How is it for you as an HIV-positive bisexual woman dealing with straight people and the straight world?

**M:** The denial in the straight and open lifestyle community regarding HIV infuriates me. Heterosexuals often point out that only three percent of them have HIV, and they feel that's a small percentage. Well, when it happens to you it's a big percentage.

I have to admit that I don't want to beat my head against the wall either. So now I've sat back and said, "You know what? It's out there in the news. If they're not doing something about it, that's their problem. I can't save everybody." I was on this crusade in the early days, and now I'm to the point where I'm tired, and I need to worry about my own health first.

Yes, if someone wants me to speak or do a workshop I will do it. I have been asked to speak in many college classes, and I've educated many college girls. I've shown them some tricks to help them take hold of their sexual prowess and not let guys talk them into anything. Straight guys could be infected; it's very easy to have happen. There is closeted bisexuality, especially in the open lifestyle community. There's a couple of women I know who have gotten HIV from their bisexual boyfriends. They could just kick themselves now, but at the time they didn't think about it.

**K:** How is it for you as an HIV-positive bisexual woman relating to other bisexuals?

**M:** I used to go to a bisexual group in this area. I came out to that group. In fact three of us came out—two men and me.

**K:** You came out as HIV-positive?

**M:** Right. To educate the group, because nobody ever talked about it. We talked about all the other issues around bisexuality, bur nobody ever talked about AIDS and safer sex. It was a biggie for us to do this, because these were our peers. I don't lose anything when I talk in front of strangers, but we're talking about people you chit chat with on a monthly or a weekly basis. I had a handful of friends who already knew, and I asked them to make sure they would be at the group that night to support me. A guy I was dating in the group was one of the ones who came out as positive, and one other guy. The other guy has since died. We got a good response; perhaps we touched some people's lives, and shocked some people into taking care of themselves.

**K:** How does it feel to you to be with other bisexuals?

**M:** Good. It feels very open. It's better than with lesbians, because they're down on men. I like men, I'm sorry. So being with other bisexual women is fine with me. There's a bond, and it's like the girl's club for the most part.

**K:** How are you different in relationships with men and with women?

**M:** Women are nurturing. We talk about the love we share and how special our friendships are. I get told all the time how glad they are that I'm in their life. I'm very thankful that I have some really dear friendships. A lot of them are with women, and they're not on a sexual level. They all know about me. They tease me about my being with a gal.

**K:** How are you different in intimate relationships or situations with men and with women?

**M:** In the past with men I've tended to lose myself in the relationship. I'm not doing that this time. I think because I'm so consumed with my health right now, I'm a little more selfish than normally I would be.

**K:** You mentioned that you got emotionally involved with men and you didn't get emotionally involved with women.

**M:** When I say emotionally involved with women I mean in terms of a committed relationship. I'm emotional with my girlfriends, and affectionate. Hugs and kisses or rubbing on their neck—but I haven't been in a committed relationship with a woman; that's the difference. But I think I'm much the same with most of my friends. I'm affectionate and straightforward and funny and witty with both sexes. I don't act differently because they're men or women.

**K:** Do you identify as either butch or femme?

**M:** I don't. What I'm attracted to though in women is feminine women just like me. So I'm attracted to femmes. I'm not attracted to butch women whatsoever.

**K:** Being involved only with a man, is there anything that you have missed sexually or emotionally about not being involved with a woman?

**M:** I don't feel a void or a sense of loss at all. Not at this point anyway. I've had a lot of freedom for the last couple years before I got into a committed relationship; I could do what I wanted and be free floating, go with the flow. So wherever I was I could be what I wanted to be. In this relationship so far my bisexuality hasn't been an issue.

**K:** How was it for you during the couple of years you were single?

**M:** I liked being solo. I felt in control. I could go to a party by myself and not know where the night was going to lead. If I chose to go dancing with a group of people, I could do it. I wasn't "with" anyone. I liked the idea of not considering anyone else. It was nice to have that sense of freedom.

**K:** Is the way you feel about your body different with men and with women?

**M:** I have worked on that in the last couple of years. My body image has not been that great, especially around men. I haven't been naked around women as much, but how I feel about it depends on the woman. If she looks better than I do, I may develop a body image problem due to that comparison. I've lost some weight, so right now

I feel good about my body. I used to have saddlebags on my legs. I've lost that, probably due to HIV. I like the way I look now, and the way I look naked. Before I used to have more cellulite, and didn't like to be naked.

**K:** Would you call yourself a feminist?

**M:** I used to call myself a female chauvinist when I was younger. I like to be treated like a lady, have doors opened for me. Over time I've changed a little bit, but I am still very traditional; when I'm dressed up I like the door opened for me on a date with my boyfriend. I had to tell him that, because we're so used to jumping in a car and going. When I'm dressed up and we're going out on the town I want it to be special, and in order for that to happen I need to be pampered by having the door opened for me. I'm a kid of the '50s.

I don't think I consider myself a "feminist." I have an opinion and I like to be heard. Don't choose for me; ask me what it is I'd like to do or what I want. I'm not really clear on what the word feminist means, because I think everybody has their own interpretation. I do believe in empowering women and taking charge.

My generation grew up at the crossroads of the bra burning and the traditional. The "Leave It To Beaver" family, then the love-ins. I was told as a child that I could be a secretary or a nurse or a teacher. Those were the three possibilities for a girl when she grew up. I wasn't going to be a doctor or dentist. My brothers were going to be the doctor and the lawyer. I bought into that for a while and then I rejected it, because I didn't want to be a secretary. As it turned out I was a secretary, and I resented it. I didn't like being in a subservient role. I'm a strong woman in the sense that I have a hard time taking orders.

I want to be respected, and I want to be asked what my thoughts are on different issues. I want to be a partner in any decision that's being made with someone. I'm not very political, but I do believe in women having choices. I believe in equal pay for equal work. I think women are as capable as men.

**K:** Do you think you have a contribution to make to the world as a bisexual woman who is HIV-positive?

**M:** I don't tell people when I speak that I'm bisexual. As an HIV-positive woman, I do feel I have something to contribute, and I think I have contributed quite a bit to the community, being positive and being a woman.

**K:** What do you see as your contribution?

**M:** Educating people. Making them aware that it can happen to them. Sharing my story. Impacting people—and I do believe I have. After I speak to college classes, I've asked the professor to have the students write to tell me how what they've heard from me has impacted their lives. I can't tell you how many kids get tested after hearing me; how many people start using condoms.

So my contribution is making people aware that HIV is out there, and that it can happen to them. These college students, they look at me, and they don't know how old I am; I look young. I say, "I could be sitting here in this classroom with you. You wouldn't know I'm positive. You can't see it. I could be dating any one of you guys, but unless I tell you I'm positive you wouldn't know it. So, if you guys think you can't get infected by a woman, then it's okay for you to go to bed with me unprotected. Right?" Then I just leave it for them to think about.

Would I listen if it was reversed? I hope I would listen. Until it touches you personally, or until it impacts your life, you're not going to get it. Some of us have to learn the hard way. That's a fact of life I think for a lot of people; they don't want to change or adapt. They like their sex the way it is. Especially men. Men have to get their hard-on. I realize that. That's a real issue about being with a man. He's got his hard-on, and then you want to use a condom, then he loses his erection by saying, "I can't use condoms—I lose my erection." Then the woman feels responsible for ruining their sexual encounter. What I say to that is then you can do other things. Get off the issue of his hard-on. You can have him work on you. Sex isn't just about copulation. It's other things as well. You find out about your partner. Really.

**K:** What do you find out?

**M:** If you're asking them to use a condom and they're resisting, what's that really about? Why aren't they being more responsible? What are they afraid of? Why aren't they willing to meet you on this? The whole dialogue that goes on tells you something about that person. How willing are they to compromise with you or to respect your wishes? The bottom line is you shouldn't be having sex with someone that you can't discuss safer sex with.

**Postscript:** Since this interview, my health has made a recovery. My problems from a simple surgery resulted in a colostomy for a year and then a reverse colostomy. I am now "back to normal." My T-cells are up, and my viral load is very low. I continue as a free-lance HIV speaker, promoting and conducting safer sex workshops for women and creating art sculptures. Three years ago, a friend and I started a long-term survivors support group.

My relationship has continued with the same HIV-negative man for three-and-a-half years. Eleven years after I tested positive for HIV, I'm still here living and loving life! Please remember my advice: "test and protect."

# 8 ▼ LANI

*Lani Ka'ahumanu is a bisexual activist who lives in San Francisco. With Loraine Hutchins, she edited the book* Bi Any Other Name: Bisexual People Speak Out *(Alyson Publications, 1991). At the time of this interview, she was 50 years old and working as the coordinator of an HIV-prevention project targeting high risk lesbian and bisexual women; she was also serving on the Lesbian, Gay, Bisexual, Trans-gender Advisory Committee to the San Francisco Human Rights Commission. She is of mixed heritage: Hawaiian, Japanese, Irish, and Polish-Jew.*

**K:** Tell me about how you grew up, your family background, and your class background.

**L:** My mother was an immigrant. She was born in Japan and moved to Hawaii when she was 12 years old. She married my dad in Hawaii, where I was conceived. I was born in Canada. My dad was stationed there during World War II. We settled into San Francisco before I was a year old. Then we moved south of San Francisco when I was around four. I grew up on the San Francisco peninsula when it was still countryside.

I'm the oldest of four girls. My parents raised us Catholic, although they had both been married and divorced really young, so were excommunicated from the church. I went to a Catholic elementary school. I remember praying that my parents would get into heaven. My mother was a full-time housewife. My father owned various construction companies. Some of them went under.

As a kid I was friends with boys and girls, although I didn't like playing house; I liked playing sports with the boys. I was a tomboy. When the boys picked teams I was one of the first picked to be on the team. My father always hired the boys, my friends, to work for him, but I was never allowed to work, even though I wanted to and would ask. Puberty ended my athletic career, because I was supposed to have a boyfriend, not compete with boys anymore. I guess the competition changed to competing with other girls for the boys' attention.

**K:** When were you first aware of sexual attractions, and to which gender?

**L:** I was raised Catholic in the '40s and '50s. No one in my family ever talked about sex. So I never had the words, but knew I was different. In high school my best girlfriend and I would always talk about how women were more interesting to look at than men, but we had boyfriends. I knew I was attracted to women and that I might be a lesbian, but I couldn't even find out what a lesbian was! Throughout high school I'd talk to girls about boys, the so-called normal thing to do, but I also talked to boys about girls.

When the captain of the football team and I fell in love, it put me onto the fast track to become a housewife and a mother. The first time I actually had sexual intercourse was when I was 16 with him, my future husband. I don't even remember it, because I was so terrified about going to confession afterwards. We worked up to sex gradually over a six-month period. I guess I didn't want to admit that I'd crossed that line. I remember the day I admitted it to my best friend, and then she confessed to me that she had also had sex.

My godparents had given me a statue of the Blessed Virgin Mary for my first Holy Communion. It was a really old statue that my aunt had when she was a little girl. I went to bed holding it the night I admitted being sexual to my friend. I cried myself to sleep. In the middle of the night Mary fell out of bed, and her head broke off. I thought, "This is it. I'm going to hell." I glued the head back on. Nine months later, I went to confession.

**K:** Were you still sexually active at that time?

**L:** Yes, but I was guilt ridden. I loved sex. It was fun, and I loved my boyfriend a lot. We were really good friends, and we were going to get married, which we did eventually—three years later when I was 19.

**K:** What did you do for birth control?

**L:** Coitus interruptus. I was Catholic; I couldn't deal with birth control. We tried a condom only once, because it was like admitting we were being sexual. If you're Catholic, the whole point of intercourse is getting pregnant. So from our honeymoon night on, we tried to get pregnant. I got pregnant three months later. Sex was for procreation. Period. In my marriage, we abstained and we practiced the rhythm method for a while, too.

Before we got married I went to confession and told the priest I wasn't a virgin. I asked him if it was all right for me to buy a white dress for my wedding. I look back at who I was and how I sincerely believed I could not wear a white dress for my own wedding. I remember the tone in the priest's voice. He couldn't believe what I was asking him and told me that of course I could wear a white dress. That's how intense being a Catholic was for me.

I married a good person. We were married 11 years. But I was still attracted to and anxious about women and thinking that I might be a lesbian. I remember talking to my husband about it. Never mind that I was having great sex with him. I didn't think there was such a thing as bisexuality. You either were this or that. So if I had these feelings it meant I might be a lesbian.

I was a full-time housewife and Little League mom, who baked cupcakes and went to the PTA. I had two kids, a son, and two years later a daughter. By the time I was 23 I had done everything that I had been raised to do. That was depressing.

About six months after my daughter was born I left the Catholic Church. It was Holy Saturday, the night before Easter Sunday. A friend and I were hiding Easter eggs and talking. I said under my breath, "I don't want to go to church tomorrow." He looked at me and said, "Don't go." It was like I needed permission—for somebody to just say out loud that I didn't have to go. I never went back. I never looked back. It cracks me up that it was that simple.

Leaving the church was a relief. I felt less guilty. There was a sense of freedom. I realized I didn't want to raise my kids with all the shame and guilt I was raised with in the Catholic Church.

This was around '67 or '68 when the political scene was getting heavy with the Vietnam War. I got involved with Another Mother for Peace and was picketing the Safeway store for the United Farm Workers grape boycott. I was looking at life differently. Instead of giving my power away to a church and having total faith without thinking, I started thinking for myself and making decisions for myself. I felt for the first time like I could make a difference.

I really loved being a mother, but it drove me crazy, because I was so isolated. I was doing exactly what I was programmed to do. I had a perfect husband and two wonderful kids. We owned our home, and my husband taught at the high school where we met. He was a wonderful man who came home at 3:30 in the afternoon. We had an organic garden in the backyard, and life was perfect. Except I wasn't happy and I was crying all the time.

I couldn't put my finger on it, but I knew that there had to be more. I had never in my whole life done anything just for myself. Everything I ever did was for my husband or kids.

My husband didn't have that mind set. If I said I wanted to go away for a weekend he'd say, "Sure," and he would take care of the kids. But I was so programmed that I would have all the meals lined up and labeled. I would have their clothes all lined up and washed. I would even take my sewing machine and material and make clothes while I was visiting a friend.

**K:** What finally broke up your marriage?

**L:** The shortest answer is I didn't come home one night. I was with friends, and one of my friends had a flashback about being raped. It was clear to me that I needed to be with her. So I called my husband and said I wasn't coming home for dinner. Then I called back later and said I was staying overnight with her, which made sense to me. I knew my family could take care of themselves.

The next day I called my husband at work, and we made a date to go for a walk on the beach. On the walk he said, "I figured it out. You need to leave." As soon as I heard that, I knew he was right. He said, "You've never had a life of your own. You've never held a job. When I went away to college, I had a chance to explore, but you've never had that." He went on, "I don't want to be alone. I want the kids, and with what you need to do, it doesn't make sense for you to have them." I was gone in less than six weeks.

**K:** Where did you go?

**L:** I got an apartment about a mile away, and instead of being the volunteer mom at school I became the paid teacher's aide. I was higher than a kite. I couldn't believe it. It was very exciting and fun, but my new life was also hard. I cried myself to sleep every night. I was terrified to sleep alone. I had been married for 11 years. I was 31 years old, and all I'd ever done was be a housewife and mom.

I also cried because I was leaving my kids. That was a big, heart-wrenching deal. They were little; it was just before their eighth and tenth birthdays. Some people ask me if I would have had kids later on if I hadn't had them so young, or would I just never have had kids. I would have had kids, but I would have lived my life a lot more before I had them.

Something else that was hard was that my husband and I seemed to have the perfect marriage. Many people we knew stayed together even though they often fought and treated each other badly, so when we separated it was very threatening to them.

I started coming out as a lesbian in 1975, but then I had an affair with a man. I still called myself a lesbian though. In the '70s many women who thought they were lesbians but still found themselves attracted to men said things like, "I'm just working something out; I have some unfinished business with men."

By then my feminist politics were getting radical. I was understanding patriarchy for the first time. What being in a male-dominated society means, what sexism is, and what being a second-class citizen means. I was raised to be a housewife and mother, and was never allowed to work. I also saw my father as a victim of sexism: he died of a heart attack when he was 46.

I started going to school at San Francisco State. My best friend from San Mateo had left her husband a year before, and she was in the process of coming out as a lesbian. We hung out together a lot. She took me to her women's studies classes, and I started meeting amazing women who had incredible lives. In these classes they would talk about women in the suburbs. They were developing feminist theory based on lives like my own. I was encouraged to write and to talk about my experiences.

**K:** Were you open with other lesbians in the community about being with men?

**L:** Yes—we were all sisters and part of each other's lives. It was distressing to them when I was with a man, but it wasn't like they would kick me out of the community for it. For the most part we were all in the process of coming out as lesbians. There was no room for bisexuality anywhere in that process. I didn't think bisexuals even existed, and I was vocal about that.

There was one bisexual woman who used to hang out at the women's bars. She was very "out" about being a bisexual. I used to hate it when she was there, because I thought she didn't belong. I was always "outing" her as bisexual. I was really obnoxious, but nobody saw it as obnoxious. Letting other lesbians know that this woman was bisexual was considered helpful information.

**K:** Were you involved in relationships with women during this time?

**L:** They were more affairs than relationships. We were all figuring out what it meant to be with a woman. Everybody was sleeping with everybody. My husband and I had been married for eleven years, and had gone steady for three and a half years before that. So I was just coming out of a 14-plus-year monogamous relationship, and there was no way I wanted to be coupled with anyone. I was getting to know myself. Women were falling in love and having relationships, but I wasn't in a position to be in a serious relationship with anybody. I was independent, and that's how I liked my life. I didn't have a committed relationship for six years.

**K:** Did you go through an identity crisis when you were first involved with women?

**L:** No. I felt like I had come home. Finally, this explained my whole life since I was a little girl. Once in a while, maybe every year or two, there'd be chemistry with a man, and I'd explore the situation. It never lasted long, because sexism was in bed with us. I wasn't one to avoid challenging that.

I graduated in Women's Studies in 1979, and needed a break from the city and my activism. So I got a job at a heterosexual New Age resort in Mendocino County called The Village Oz. I was the out-lesbian chef; I was the only lesbian and the only highly verbal self-proclaimed feminist at this resort.

About a month into my second summer season at Oz a young man came hitch-hiking through. The first thing he said to me was, "Have you ever read *Of Woman Born* by Adrienne Rich? I said, "Yes. Why?" He said, "I read it, and I got my mom to read it, but she doesn't identify as a feminist, and I do. I've always wanted to talk to somebody about it, because I think it's one of the most important books ever written."

We ended up having amazing conversations—similar to the most radical conversations I'd have with my lesbian friends. He was involved in antisexist work in the Bay Area. He challenged ideas I had about men. He was also one of the smartest people I'd ever met. He nurtured my intelligence in a way that no one ever had. Needless to say, we fell madly in love.

He identified as bisexual, and he kept saying to me, "You're a bisexual." I would cry and say, "No, I'm not. There is no such thing. I can't go back to my lesbian community and say I'm a bisexual. I can't do that."

But of course, I went back to my lesbian community after this wonderful summer in the country. He enrolled in the Women's Studies Department at San Francisco State. And I came out as a bisexual in the lesbian community. It sounds simple, but it wasn't. I've always been an organizer and a rabble rouser, so I couldn't be a closeted bisexual. My politics hadn't changed. I simply was in an incredibly healthy and clear relationship with a man.

**K:** What happened with your lesbian friends?

**L:** Well, I found out who my real friends were. I can say that philosophically now, but it was devastating at the time.

I had joined Mothertongue Feminist Readers Theater collective in 1976. Mothertongue was a feminist collective, not a lesbian collective, but there was an intense lesbian assumption among the women in it. These women had been my support group. They were my lesbian family of friends, but they were not there for me when I came out as a bisexual. Predictably the separatists were the most vicious. Many of them would make very biphobic remarks to my face and to the woman sitting next to me. They were very rude.

**K:** Tell me about the "lesbian assumption" in that group. What exactly does that mean?

**L:** Lesbians talked as if there were only lesbians in the room. They put down women who slept with men. They made biphobic remarks and didn't even hear it. This wasn't purposeful, but the fact is they were making an assumption that none of the women in the room had loving relationships or friendships with men, that we're all lesbians. It's just like being in a room full of heterosexuals, and everybody assumes everyone is heterosexual and going to meet a man, settle down and get married someday. It makes you invisible.

Now I realize I also didn't know what to do with myself in the lesbian community at that time. Really good friends would have parties, and I wouldn't get invited, because they were afraid I was going to bring my boyfriend. Like I would forget this was a woman-only party! There was no etiquette; nobody, especially the lesbian feminists, knew what to do. Plus I had my own issues of feeling I didn't deserve to be there, because I was involved with a man. That was my own internalized biphobia, my belief that on some level being bi was less than being a lesbian. I had a lot of internalized lesbian chauvinism.

**K:** What is lesbian chauvinism?

**L:** Many lesbians see themselves as better than other women—that you're a better feminist if you're a lesbian. I felt that way when I was a lesbian. It was a badge of honor, coming out lesbian, in the '70s especially. It was very empowering. I always felt strong and proud when I said I was a dyke or a lesbian. When I said I was bisexual it was not empowering; it didn't feel good. And of course when you said you were bisexual after having identified as a lesbian, you weren't coming out into a community. You were coming out to yourself and one or two other people. You were losing a community, and you were losing friends. You were losing respect. You knew women were talking behind your back.

But my phone rang all the time. Women were calling saying, "I can't believe it, but I'm attracted to a man," or "Somebody gave me your number, and I don't know who else I can talk to about this. I'm having an affair with a man, and I don't know what to do. I can't be a bisexual. I don't want to be!" I became the underground hotline for lesbian-identified women who were sleeping with men. Gay men also called me, but not as often. This included people in leadership positions in the gay and lesbian community.

**K:** Tell me about your current situation.

**L:** Politically I'm involved in many different areas. Everything from the Lesbian Gay Bisexual Transgender Advisory Committee to the Human Rights Commission, here in San Francisco, to National Coordinator for BiNet USA. I was responsible for the inclusion of Bisexuals in the title of the SF advisory committee.

I'm in a relationship with a lesbian woman that's still really new. It's only been happening for four months. She has always wanted to be monogamous with her lovers, and settle down and get married, but it's never, ever worked for her. After her last relationship she started reassessing everything. So she's trying nonmonogamy. Most of my women lovers have been lesbians.

And I have had an on-going relationship with a man from Boston for a couple of years. He comes out here on business three or four times a year. That relationship is very fun. He's a writer and an activist. He is in a 20 plus year polyamorous relationship with a woman. They own a home together. I know her. His relationship is a role model for me of what's possible. Their situation is unique in some ways, because they both travel in their jobs, and they both have other relationships.

**K:** If you could have your ideal situation in terms of relationships, what would it be?

**L:** I like what I share with the man from Boston. I like that we are clear about what it is and what it isn't. I know I don't want to live with anybody. I really don't. I would like to keep what I have with him for however long it's going to be. So any relationship that I have with someone here in San Francisco or elsewhere would be nonmonogamous. Committed nonmonogamy is what I want.

I have a lot of very close friends. I have a whole snuggle network of women and men so my nurturing is taken care of. I can always call somebody up and have them come over or go over and sleep with them.

**K:** Do you mean you sleep with them nonsexually?

**L:** Right. It's very sensual. Every once in a while I'm sexual with one of them, but this doesn't happen very often. I know other bisexual people in my network of friends that also have that setup in their lives. That's really important for me.

**K:** Do you feel differently with men and with women in terms of your body and how attractive you are?

**L:** It's easier to be around women than men; I don't feel objectified. Among feminist women there's a level of respect and admiration for aging women like me who are really out there. I don't see myself ever not being out there. I get a lot of good energy back for that.

On the other hand, in the world at large I'm being looked at and treated differently now by men, because I'm old. In general I'm not even flirted with anymore.

**K:** Do you practice safer sex?

**L:** Yes, I do. I've been talking about safer sex with partners since '86. With men there is always a condom. In the past I would bring up safer sex with women, and they'd say, "You're the one that's more at risk than me." Back then I thought lesbians were not at risk, so I went along with them, because I didn't really want to be safe with women lovers either.

Then I went out with this woman who, when I brought it up, said she had never used latex. She had never been sexual with men, and she felt comfortable not being safe. I said, "Well, the truth is that I'm committed to figuring out how to make safer sex fun. So I want to do it just to figure out how to make it fun." So we were semi-safe. Sometimes we'd slip, but it wasn't a big deal. We'd end up just laughing sometimes, because it was so ridiculous that we would give up. So we playfully tried to be safe.

When I brought up safer sex with my current woman lover, there was a level of seriousness about it that had never happened before. She works at the women's health clinic where I work, plus she had made the choice to be nonmonogamous, so she wanted to be 100% safe.

**K:** What is safer sex to you with your female lover?

**L:** Latex gloves for any vaginal/anal penetration, and for oral sex there's always a barrier. I like gloves a lot. If you get gloves that really fit it's smoother. You don't have to worry about nails. With a lot of water-based lube it works really well. Lube is great, but it's a mess. When you take off the glove you peel off all the goo.

**K:** What enabled you to start having safer sex with a woman?

**L:** Meeting lesbians with HIV was one of the things. This put a woman's face on the epidemic. Mostly though the fact we don't know much is a reason to be safe. They don't collect statistics on lesbians, but there are three women I know who come to the clinic who say that the only way they could have gotten HIV is from another woman. Also we can't forget other STDs—herpes, HPV, and chlamydia.

It's easier to be safe with somebody who really wants to make it fun. We have made it fun, but we've only been sexual for two months. I love going down on women, and I love bodily juices. I've cried a lot about having to give that up.

Many times I'll be making out with my lover, and then start going down on her and realize that I can't do this the way I used to. I got used to gloves early on, but using a barrier for oral sex was not at all comfortable for me. Having to stop and rip a piece of plastic wrap or even remember to have it near the bed. There are all these interruptions. Sometimes I get down as far as her belly and start to cry, because of the loss. I think it's important to allow ourselves that feeling of loss and to grieve.

With safer sex you have to be creative and flexible. You have to bring your sense of humor to bed. If you've never allowed yourself to just have a good laugh over some ridiculous thing that's happening, then safer sex is probably going to be harder for you. It forces you to talk about sex. "How was that for you? Did you like the plastic wrap?" Or, "When I start breathing heavy the plastic wrap goes in my nose, and I can't breathe. I'm smothering." It forces you to talk about things that in my generation we didn't talk about. My husband and I had a very creative sexual life, but we never talked about sex. Safer sex forces everybody to talk.

One of the projects I am involved with demonstrates how to negotiate safer sex. We did this recently in a women's sex club. Two women got up in front of the whole group and talked about their history. They talked about what they didn't like sexually, and what they did like. Their attitude was so matter of fact.

I think a lot of women are raised with this very romantic scenario that somebody's supposed to whisk us off our feet, and they're supposed to know exactly how to kiss us, exactly how to touch us, and exactly when to do what, without our saying a thing. So we don't take responsibility for being satisfied in sexual relationships. That's a really dangerous mindset. We need to redefine romance in a way where we are empowered in our sexuality, and it is romantic and hot, where we get to ask for and get what we want. We have to bring power and romance together.

**K:** Who are you "out" to in your life about being bisexual?

**L:** Everybody. That's been true since I was a lesbian. I've been out on every job I've ever had so far.

**K:** How does your family deal with your bisexuality and your bisexual activism?

**L:** My father's been dead for almost 30 years. My sisters and mom all live on the San Francisco peninsula 30 miles south of here. When I divorced my husband and he raised the children, that was the worst thing I could have done in their eyes at the time. So my coming out as a lesbian was not as traumatic for them. For a long time we were emotionally distant. Now, in the last three years, I'm getting invited home again for Christmas and to other family functions. We've all grown up; we've gotten more flexible.

I told them about the book *Bi Any Other Name* when I was editing it, but they never really asked about it. It only became legitimate when I was on the Phil Donahue show. Now everybody in the family is talking about my book. I'm glad that I can bring up the issue of queer sexuality for all my nephews and nieces, because some of them are going to be queer. I'm not going to be the only one. My daughter is bisexual, though, so maybe she's the one.

My son probably has the hardest time with my being public about my bisexuality. I was not very thoughtful when I came out as a lesbian. I was so excited at the time I wasn't as considerate as I could have been about my kids' feelings. I was so proud, and coming out to everybody. He was just going into puberty—not a good time to have to deal with your mother publicly coming out as a lesbian. He keeps telling me he's afraid I'm going to get hurt. He says that there are a lot of crazy homophobic people out there, and he thinks it's stupid for me to be so public.

My daughter is in the process of coming out to the family herself now. She's brought her girlfriend to a couple of family functions. At the last wedding we went to she was sitting with her girlfriend at a table with all her cousins, with their boyfriends, husbands, or wives, and she announced that she was going to be the next one to get married. The nephews and nieces are all really cool with it, but getting married is such a heterosexual thing that it wasn't a concept they could easily grasp. They were fine, but I could tell it gave them a lot of food for thought.

**K:** How is it for you dealing with the lesbian community as a bisexual woman now?

**L:** It's fine. They've gotten over themselves! I belong here in the queer community. I've been here longer than most of them anyway. Every once in a while it's still painful, and I'm getting tired of being the token bisexual and having to remind people to say bisexual when it's appropriate along with lesbian and gay.

**K:** How is it for you dealing with the straight world as a bisexual woman?

**L:** I hardly know any straight people. I operate in a queer world. I guess there are straight women where I work, but the focus of the clinic doesn't have a whole lot to do with who we're going to bed with. I don't have a lot of heterosexual contact other then being on certain committees with some straight people.

**K:** How is it for you dealing with gay men as a bisexual woman?

**L:** I love gay men. There are all different kinds of gay men. Most of the gay men that I love are just like sisters. Mainly I take people as people, and there's a certain level of chemistry that happens between people whether it's sexual, or just the feeling that this is somebody I want to get to know. It's not so much how someone identifies themselves sexually. It's that personal chemistry.

Somebody might say, "Then why don't you have more heterosexual people in your life?" I'm just not around many heterosexual people because of the work that I do, which is focused on lesbian and bisexual women. The political organizing I do is all within the broader lesbian, gay, bisexual, and transgender community. I pull all my social contacts from the organizing and political work I do.

**K:** How is it for you being with other bisexuals?

**L:** I like it a lot. I felt like I knew every bisexual in the Bay Area in the early '80s. Now I can drop into Bifriendly or the Bisexual Women's Support Group and only know the two people who helped organize it out of the 30 people there. That's amazing. Or I can produce a dance for the bisexual community and not know most of the people who show up.

The hard thing right now for me as a bisexual with other bisexuals is that there's not very many bisexual people who are doing the work of building a political bisexual community. There are people building the bisexual community through support groups and social gatherings, but the seriousness of the right-wing rising and including us in their rhetoric is not grasped by many bisexual people. In fighting the right wing it's really important for us to become visible as bisexuals and to align ourselves with the lesbian/gay movement.

**K:** Do you feel that bisexuality has political implications?

**L:** Yes, absolutely. Bisexuality is the undoing of heterosexism. Heterosexism is the assumption that everybody is heterosexual, and that if you're not heterosexual, you're homosexual. Within any "ism" there's a dichotomy that's set up. You're either this or that. When I was first coming out as bisexual I noticed that heterosexual and homosexual people were saying the same things to me. You have to make a choice. You're on a fence. You're confused. So I realized they had something in common! Bisexuality shows that there is no fence, that sexuality is fluid.

Bisexuality also shakes up gender assumptions and roles. In our society people are defined by the gender of their partner. Bisexuality challenges everybody, because it makes people deal with people separate from these assumptions. What bisexuals give to the lesbian, gay and heterosexual community is another way to look at the world.

**K:** Do you think you have a contribution to make to the world as a bisexual woman?

**L:** Yes, I do. I already have. The book *Bi Any Other Name* that Loraine and I did was the book that we both needed when we came out.

I have so much more to give. I don't know what it will be. I do know that perimenopausal middle-aged women are supposed to be invisible. But I'm not going to keep my mouth shut. Aging women aren't supposed to be sexual, but because of the work I'm doing with HIV prevention I get people to examine issues around ageism and women and sex.

For me, sexuality is a kind of chemistry that happens between me and another person, regardless of their gender. At one point in my life there was no sexual chemistry with men for five years, but I still knew the possibility was there. I cannot say that I am a lesbian who sleeps with men. For me that's like saying, "I'm a vegetarian who eats hamburgers." Bisexuality says it all, because it's living with the possibility. It means I could be with a man or I could be with a woman or I could be with myself. It feels comfortable. It feels good.

I don't like the word bisexual, because it perpetuates the myth that I'm half heterosexual and half homosexual. It's confusing. It would be great if we could come up with a better word. Probably the most radical word would be "sexual."

**K:** What would that mean to just say that you are sexual?

**L:** I don't want to be defined by the gender of the person I'm with. Period. That's radical. The truth is we're all sexual whether we act on it or not.

**K:** Is there anything else you want to say?

**L:** I'm middle-aged now. I'm not young; I'm not old. I'm supposed to be confused and having a midlife crisis. It's like being in the middle is not okay. It is okay. I am in the middle. I cannot get away from being in the middle—I am mixed heritage, middle-aged, and bisexual.

I don't want bisexuals to make the same mistakes that have been made in other movements. I find it hopeful that bisexuals see the world and people in a non-dichotomous way. I hope that we can transfer that bisexual mindset to issues around race, class, and all the other divisions in the world, so people aren't polarized. This is my vision: that our community will include all of us.

# 9 ▼ Susan

*Susan is a 43-year-old mother and social worker who lives in Marin County, California.*

**K:** Tell me about how you grew up: your family, your class background, your ethnicity. Were you raised in a religion?

**S:** I grew up on a farm in southern Virginia. I am Southern Caucasian from a mixed-class background. My parents kept telling us how poor we were, but they put on airs and were in the Lutheran Church, which is the "society church." We weren't raised religious. We definitely were members of this church, but it was more of a social thing. We didn't have the fear of God put in us, but we were supposed to be good.

There were five of us kids. I was the fourth child and second daughter. My father was a farmer, and my mother was a homemaker, and I'm an incest survivor.

**K:** Tell me about the incest.

**S:** It actually started with my sister who is three years older than me. My father decided that he needed to examine her, because he thought she had been running around with an older boy and that maybe they had been sexual together. After that he would come and get in our bed almost every night from the time I was 10 until I left home. The last time he made an attempt to be sexual with me was when I was about 25, and was home for a visit. He came in my room, and I yelled at him, "You get out of here!" And he ran. He only had on his underwear, and he looked like a plucked chicken running. I can remember the image very well. I felt so powerful, because it was the first time that I had found my voice with him.

**K:** So when were you first aware of sexual attractions and to which gender?

**S:** I had boyfriends in the first grade. I don't remember ever being conscious of having sexual attractions toward women until I lived in a commune and ended up in bed with a woman. We were both flirting with and attracted to the same man, and neither one of us was willing to give up. So we all went to bed together, which shocked the hell out of me since I had come from the farm to this commune in DC.

**K:** Did you date boys in junior high and high school?

**S:** Yes, I dated boys all through high school.

**K:** Were you sexually active?

**S:** I was sexually active, but I wasn't going all the way. That was probably from ninth grade where I began to—what did we call it—let them feel me up. There was a big thing in my family about saving your virginity until you were married. It was constantly drilled into me by my father as he was molesting me that this was an important thing to do.

**K:** Was he having intercourse with you?

**S:** He was fondling my breasts and my genitals a lot. I don't remember having intercourse with him; I think it may have happened a few times, and I'm blocking the memories.

I didn't go all the way with anyone, although I used to do everything but for years, until right after I was out of high school. I was dating a man who was going to Vietnam. The fact that he was leaving to go to Vietnam, and also that he was very smooth, made me let fooling around with him go a little farther and a little farther, until finally I really wanted to have intercourse, so we did. I was like, oh gosh, we did go all the way, didn't we? It wasn't like I made a decision to do it. It just happened. That was probably when I was 19.

**K:** Tell me about your relationship history.

**S:** I was with this man who was going to Vietnam, and I slept with him. I was also very involved in the Lutheran Church. I was the youth representative from the diocese of Virginia to the national general convention of the Lutheran Church. I went to this youth conference where there were all these radical peace church people, and started getting into the peace movement. At the same time my boyfriend was in school learning how to speak Vietnamese. He was an officer in the military. We were definitely going in different directions. But we did park in front of the justice of the peace's house in North Carolina for about three hours one night trying to decide whether to go in and get married or not. He decided that we shouldn't.

By the next summer I had broken up with him, and I just started going wild. I went to the second Lutheran convention and slept with ten different men in seven days. At the preconvention youth weekend in New York City I actually met a bisexual couple. The guy was trying to get me to join them in their hotel room for the night, and I just didn't know what he was talking about. I just didn't understand until I lived in the commune after the second general convention and ended up sleeping with a woman.

In high school my best friend and I used to run around with our arms around each other. She and I adored each other, but there was nothing sexual about it. We just were very close to each other. My older brother thought we were lesbians, and he was upset that we were acting like that. I didn't know what he was talking about; I didn't have a clue.

**K:** So what happened with this woman in the commune, and how old were you at the time?

**S:** I was 20. She lived in the commune with me, and she and I were both up one night listening to music with this man, smoking dope. I wanted to go to bed with him, and she wanted to go to bed with him, and he wanted to go to bed with both of us. Finally she just said, "Let's go down to my room." We went down to her room, took our clothes off, and got down. After that she and I were occasional lovers.

Then I went to my sister's, and there was a friend of her husband's there named Frankie. We hung out together for the weekend, then he and I dated for a while. He invited me to come and live with him in Connecticut. I said, "Are you out of your mind?" He said, "If you change your mind let me know." He was in the military and going to be on a submarine that was going under for three months, but I could send him a familygram. He said, "Let me know, and meet me in Connecticut if you change your mind."

That spring was the May Day demonstrations in DC, and I got

arrested for leafleting on the street. I was in jail with 8,000 other people and was totally freaked out. All I was doing was handing out leaflets, and they basically swept the streets of anybody who was there. I just freaked; I was terrified. So I sent Frankie a familygram and said I was coming, because it seemed like a safe haven.

He and I lived together for six months, and then we got married. We were together about nine months and then separated, because I was doing this number where I had to find something wrong with the relationship, because I couldn't feel comfortable really experiencing pleasure. It was too hard, because of the incest. I was smoking a lot of marijuana at the time; for years I smoked marijuana to be sexual.

While I was still with Frankie, a childhood friend of mine came to visit us and slept with the two of us, mostly Frankie. I watched and felt very crushed. I used to set up situations where I would be part of a threesome, but then I would either feel like I was leaving somebody out or I was getting left out. It was never very comfortable for me, but there was always something really titillating about it. I was so out of touch with my emotions that I didn't know that these situations were hard for me.

After I separated from Frankie, I really dedicated myself to working with a drop-in learning center, which became my life. The woman who started the center was bisexual. She put out sexual vibes to me, and I didn't pick up on them. She got really angry at me, because she thought that I was putting out sexual vibes to her, but was not willing to follow up on them. So I had sex with her out of guilt, probably feeling like I had done something wrong. We had a short relationship.

Then I became a Vista volunteer, and met a lot of people from Boston. Eventually I moved to Boston. I had an affair with one of the men that I met. Occasionally he wanted to get together with me and another woman and get it on sexually. I did that a few times with him. They were one-night stands.

Probably by that time I was using the word bisexual to describe myself—not as an identity, but because it was an exotic turn-on. I would push people and situations to the limit, and that was one way of doing it. All of this, of course, is in the context of not ever having orgasms when I was sexual. My sexuality was very screwed up at this point, and I was having a lot of sexual activity with different people.

In Boston I started being even more randomly sexual. I would get stoned and call men who had ads in the paper and have phone sex with them. Sometimes if I felt good enough about them I would invite them over. I also tried to call women who had ads in the paper, but they never were into it. They weren't lesbians advertising for phone sex. They were straight women who were trying to make money.

**K:** Why do you think you did this?

**S:** I got great feedback about how hot I was. I knew how to perform well in bed. It was a place where I got lots of good attention, but I also had shame around it. I was leading two different lives. I had a set of friends who didn't know that I was doing this. Eventually I moved because I had invited somebody over who was dangerous and scary, and I was afraid of him coming back.

**K:** Do you think there's any correlation between what you were doing and the incest?

**S:** Yes. My father praised me all the time and told me how precious I was. He always talked about how wonderful sex was, and how it was the most beautiful thing that two people could share. But I had very little respect for myself after being molested by him. I just didn't value sex within the context of a relationship.

One man that I was in a relationship with used to say that I seemed to need a backup, that I always had to have somebody waiting in the wings in case it didn't work out with him. I remember one night having three different men who sort of passed each other in the hallway. One was there and left as the other one was coming. Then he left and someone else was coming. I had constant, multiple sexual relationships, but I never felt "present" during sex. The men I related to didn't know I wasn't very present, but I ended up breaking up with this man because he did know. He said that he needed to have a sexual relationship with someone who was able to be there and enjoy it.

**K:** Why do you think you were having sex with so many different men when you weren't enjoying sex with them?

**S:** I enjoyed pleasing them. I enjoyed being hot. I enjoyed being attractive to them. It was a powerful position to be in to be that seductive and free. They were amazed that I could be that hot and good, and yet so tender and tempting and adorable. I got off on it. It was a way that I knew I was good. I had jobs at that time that weren't very rewarding to me. This was a place where my ego got stroked. I was seen as being good and being attractive. Being seen as a beautiful woman was real important to me at the time. I look back now and think I should have charged money for it, because I gave it away so freely.

**K:** What happened from that point?

**S:** I moved in with a woman and her baby, and began going to school. I started having a different kind of life and doing something that was meaningful to me.

Then I started sleeping with different professors at the school I was going to. I ended up sleeping with my advisor one time on the floor in his office. I wanted to seduce him, because I was madly in love with him, and because he thought I was wonderful; but it was awful for both of us, and it really broke my heart.

It really wasn't any fun. He didn't want to come home with me and drink champagne and have decadent sex all day. He was married, had a little boy, and had another baby on the way. Having an affair was not what he wanted to do. He had just fallen into it. Now I realize there were boundaries to be kept, and it was his job to keep the boundaries.

I also had affairs with several different therapists throughout the time I was in Boston. One of them was into hypnotizing people. When he hypnotized me I felt like I was pretending to be hypnotized. Then he molested me while he thought I was in trance. I stopped seeing him.

I proposed a sexual relationship to another therapist. My rationale for this was that I needed to work on my sexual relationships, and I needed to do it with someone who could be conscious about it, since it wasn't working with the man I had been seeing. The therapist agreed and was sexual with me off and on for two years. He was married also.

**K:** How do you feel about that now?

**S:** I feel angry about it. I feel that it was the therapists' job to keep the boundaries, and they didn't do it. Being sexual with me wasn't helping me to heal. It was a continuation of the incest.

**K:** Some people will say that because you were pursuing these men that it was your responsibility. What would you say to that?

**S:** You could say that I was an adult, and therefore, that I was responsible, but I was an adult who had been abused and molested as a child. I didn't have a clue about what I now know was acting out with men in powerful positions over me. A professor gives you grades. They have an impact on your future. In therapy you surrender to the therapist whose job it is to help you heal. Instead these therapists were continuing to perpetuate the abuse by not keeping the boundaries and not teaching me about boundaries.

**K:** What happened after that?

**S:** I came out to California to visit, and I decided to move out here. Then I went back and a woman who worked at the school I went to helped me with moving. We started hanging out together. She came onto me, and we started being sexual with each other. For the last nine months that I was in Boston I had a relationship with her. It wasn't monogamous, but the time that we spent together was very intense and frequent. So it was an important relationship for me, but it was all in the context of my leaving. She's still a good friend and has come to California to visit me.

**K:** What year did you move to California?

**S:** I moved here in December of 1979. Two weeks before I left Boston someone told me about Judith Herman, who wrote the book *Father-Daughter Incest*. She was creating support groups in the Boston area for women who were incest survivors. I called her and asked her for a referral on the West Coast. She gave me Sandra Butler's name [author *Conspiracy of Silence: The Trauma of Incest*]. So I contacted Sandra when I moved out here, and she gave me the number of a woman therapist that she knew who was running a women's incest survivor group.

In that group I met a woman who was going to the West Coast Women's Music Festival. She and I started seeing each other. I was looking for a companion to go to the festival with, but she was looking for a sexual companion to go to the festival with. I didn't realize that. About two weeks before the festival she said to me, "Well, are we going to be sexual or not? Because if we're not, I'm going to find somebody else to go to the music festival with." So I started a sexual relationship with her and was in a relationship with her for about a year. It didn't work out. She left me for another woman, and I was crushed by that.

In the meantime I went to a conference in Washington, D.C., and met a man who was a professor of anthropology at Stanford and had written several books and articles that I had read as a student. I flirted with him a lot at the conference. He was very flattered, because he was 20 years older than me. He was 50, and I was 30. He called me and asked me out when I got back here. So I started seeing him for a couple of months before I went to the next year's women's music festival.

I decided at that music festival that I was going to be celibate for a while. I connected with this woman, Louise, at the music festival, and we had a celibate, intimate relationship for three months from September until December. I was also seeing this professor. Sometime around Christmas I decided to sleep with him, and then I decided since I had slept with him I should sleep with Louise as well. So I slept with her. Eventually I broke up with the professor, and started living with Louise. She and I lived together for maybe two years.

Louise and I had a very intense relationship that eventually became physically abusive. The sexual part of it was wonderful even though again I couldn't accept the pleasure that was there. I loved her body; I still love her body. I loved connecting with her, but I was not in a monogamous relationship with her. She knew I was bisexual.

Then I started seeing Jim. I had known Jim through work for a couple of years. During that time he was married and was very into his work. Then he got divorced and started pursuing me. I was very flattered.

I'm always flattered when people pursue me. I also frequently have a feeling of obligation, that if they like me I have to be sexual with them. I didn't realize for a long time that I had any choice, that I didn't have to sleep with somebody just because they liked me.

So I was in a relationship with Jim and with Louise. My hope at the time was that I could merge those two relationships and have a poly-fidelitous family. Jim was open to that, but Louise was not into it at all. She had met Jim, but she would not think about spending time with him. She saw him as a competitor. I probably dated him for about a year while I was still in a relationship with Louise.

But my relationship with Louise was not working well, and I decided to stop living with her. I wasn't trying to break up with her, but I didn't think it was working well for us to live together. She saw my decision to move out as the first step toward breaking up. It was too painful for her to stay in the relationship, and she felt very angry with me. At that point I moved in with a friend who had a spare room.

A few months later I accidentally got pregnant. Jim and I decided to get married. I've been monogamous ever since I got married.

**K:** Is that a commitment that you made as part of your relationship?

**S:** I'm not sure. I'd have to ask Jim if we have actually made that commitment. When I first met him I was stoned a lot when we were making love, and it was the hottest sex we've ever had. My daughter is six, and I stopped smoking dope when I was pregnant with her. Since I've not been getting stoned, I've not wanted to be sexual. It's a real shift in the sexual part of our relationship; I don't want to be sexual with one person, much less anybody else.

After I got pregnant I gained a lot of weight. I took real sanctuary in that. No longer was I physically attractive to men, and that was really good for me. I haven't had people coming onto me for years now, and I'm really enjoying that. It's been a real shift for me to not be dealing with sex or sexuality.

**K:** What do you enjoy about that?

**S:** Finding value in myself that doesn't have to do with sex. I like not having to deal with sexual issues.

Jim is truly supportive of me. He doesn't always do the same kinds of psychological work on himself that I do, but he supports me to do what I need to do. He's hung in with me through lots of times when I've tried really hard to negate everything that we had. We have separated, and we've talked about divorce.

**K:** If you could have your ideal situation in terms of relationships, what would that be?

**S:** I don't know enough about healthy sex yet to say what that would be. Given my commitment and my longstanding relationship with Jim, I'd like to keep working on this one to get to a place where it's healthy. From a healthy place I'd like to figure out whether or not I want to be monogamous.

I feel like there are a lot of reasons not to be monogamous, but there's a lot of depth that comes from the safety and trust of monogamy. I know that there were times when I felt very jealous when I was in a sexual triad. Especially because I was frequently in a relationship with two other people who were orgasmic, and I wasn't. I always felt left out, "not as good as," and bad about myself. I'm just not ready to try that out again until I feel healthier.

In some ways I feel like I'm just beginning to scratch the surface of being able to relate to myself. When Jim and I were about to separate it wasn't like I was going to leave him for someone else. It was like I was going to leave him so I could have some time by myself, so I could have a relationship with me. There's still a part of me that feels like I need to do that, even though I feel real connected to Jim and in love with him. I still need a lot of time and space for myself. I know how to get that when I'm mad at him, but I'm not sure yet how to get that when things are good in our relationship.

**K:** How does it feel to you having been nonmonogamous and in relationships with both men and women, to now only be with a man and be monogamous and married?

**S:** I feel left out of the women's community. There are ways that I don't get to be in that community anymore. I don't trust that I would be welcomed there as a married woman. I have a bisexual friend who lives in Oakland. She has been telling me that there's a woman there who gives her a lot of shit because she's bisexual. This woman thinks that my friend should confess ahead of time that she's bisexual to lesbians as though otherwise she's ripping them off. That just makes me furious.

I know that I had a lot of trouble being accepted as a bisexual woman in the lesbian community. I have a lot of pain around that. I wasn't accepted even in an incest survivors support group in San Francisco that I had helped found. I spent lots of time with this group and lots of energy trying to organize around the issue of incest. What happened was that a lot of attention got focused on the fact that I was bisexual, instead of people working on their incest. It was like it was too scary to look at incest directly so let's pick on this other issue.

In that situation it felt safer to say I was confused than to say I was bisexual. I was confused. I'm still confused, but that doesn't mean I'm not bisexual. I feel nurtured by relationships with women, and often by relationships with men. That's what defines me as bisexual.

**K:** How does Jim feel about your being bisexual?

**S:** His first wife left him for a woman, and I left a woman for him. We balanced the scale is the way we joke about it. It doesn't seem to bother him enough to have been an issue in our relationship. He doesn't seem to be threatened by my relationships with ex-lovers. I'm very close to two of the women I was lovers with. They come out here to visit, and I spend lots of time with them. I don't think he'd be happy if I had an affair with somebody, but he probably wouldn't mind if we had an affair together with somebody. We've talked about that, but I'm not really interested in it right now.

**K:** How are you different in relationships with men and with women, emotionally and sexually?

**S:** I think it's a lot easier to be intimate with women. There's more common ground. Sexually, when I was with women I always missed penises.

**K:** Is there anything else you missed about not being with a man when you were with a woman? Anything emotional?

**S:** It would have to be the other way around. It's more that I miss the kind of connection and intimacy that I can have with women when I'm with a man. In some ways, because men are less expressive of their emotions, things seem easier with them. They don't get as messy as with women, because women can get down into their feelings a lot more. With men you can get away with not saying how you feel. I don't know whether that's good. It's less complex.

**K:** Is there anything sexual you miss about not being involved with a woman?

**S:** Yes. There's a kind of tenderness and gentleness that I miss, and I miss touching women's bodies.

**K:** Did you ever tell your parents you were bisexual?

**S:** No.

**K:** Do any other family members know?

**S:** Yes. My middle brother, who was my closest family member, came to visit me when I was living with a woman lover and stayed with us for ten days. That was good. I felt real accepted by him.

**K:** What about people in your life now. Do people in your life know that you're bisexual?

**S:** People I'm close to know. There are some people in this town that I've come out to that are shocked by it, but mostly people are accepting. I'm much better now about not revealing things to people I don't feel safe with. I used to spill my guts and let it all hang out and feel judged and ashamed, but I don't do that so much anymore. I keep my Bisexual Pride button on the back of the front door so that when people leave they see it. It probably raises questions in some people's minds. The people that are important to me in my life know that I'm bisexual.

**K:** How is it for you being with other bisexuals?

**S:** In some ways it's real validating. In other ways it's challenging. When I went to the Bisexual Conference in San Francisco I felt like I was a prude, because I'm a monogamous married woman. That's almost like being straight. It's not adventurous.

Of course my first woman lover was there and going to the "Jack and Jill Offs" and to all these exotic S&M parties. She talks about being a sex-positive, swinging, bisexual, cross-cultural, S&M, non-monogamous woman. So she's very out there. In contrast I felt like I was ordinary and plain, like the kid from the country in the big city.

**K:** Are you a feminist?

**S:** Yes.

**K:** What does it mean to you to be a feminist?

**S:** It means to fight back. To be woman-identified. To not succumb to the patriarchy.

**K:** Give me a definition of woman-identified.

**S:** Being woman-identified means that I don't look to men to define who I am. I look to myself and to other women. I don't wait for men to take care of me or to say what I need or to define where I am. I claim that for myself.

**K:** Do you think that bisexuality has political implications?

**S:** Yes. I think about that question in two ways. One is that I think about it in terms of bisexuals as a group of people, and how it's important that we always be able to accept any group of people. I think it's very important that the entire world become inclusive of everybody's identity. The act of becoming inclusive is a political act. When all groups of people are accepted it will be a massive and wonderful change in this world.

Bisexuality also revolutionizes sexuality, and how people relate to each other in the world. I think probably in the best of all possible worlds there wouldn't be monogamy. We would all be able to love everybody. We wouldn't have the same kinds of hang-ups, frustrations, and difficulties that we now have with sexuality. And that is political.

# 10  ▼  VIDYA

*Vidya Vonne is a 45-year-old "out" bisexual woman, living and working in Santa Barbara, California. She is half-Jewish/half-WASP and was raised in working-class poverty by a single mom in Los Angeles.*

**K:** When were you first aware of sexual attractions, and to which gender?

**V:** I think that my first attractions were not sexual at all. My sexuality only really bloomed in my late 20s. I remember at 14 being attracted to my best friend, but I don't think there was a sexual component to it. She was very heterosexual, but we had this deep love. I think of that as being the first time I was in love.

Not much later than that I started getting crushes on young men in my junior high and then my high school set. I was an only child of a single mom, so I think it took longer for me to feel close to boys. It was more natural for me to feel safe around women.

**K:** Were you aware that you were attracted to both boys and girls at that point?

**V:** I can't remember whether I thought of it that way. I do remember at age 17 when I was having my first affair with a man, we had a double date with the young woman who I was in love with. I remember her sitting in the back seat with her date while I was in the front seat with mine, and thinking how much I'd rather be back there with her! I shouldn't have been having sex with this man, because I didn't have sexual feelings for him. He was much older than me and was like a father-figure to me.

After him there were some one-night stands, and I was acquaintance raped. Then I had a long period of celibacy when I got into yoga and was living in an ashram.

I was a celibate monk for many years when at age 27 I fell in love with a man whom I worked with in the ashram. He had just gotten out of a marriage and felt safe talking lovingly and seductively to me, because supposedly I had no sexual feelings, or at least wasn't acting on them. No one had ever talked to me like that. I fell completely in love with him.

**K:** Were you actively sexual with him?

**V:** No. I would have been if he would have gone for it, but the mores of that group were you're either celibate, or you're married. He probably would have married me. I could have left the order and married him, but I felt more like a 13 year old, like, "I want to kiss you. I want to find out what this is about." I wasn't ready to marry him or anyone.

**K:** When did you become sexually active again?

**V:** It was part of the decision to leave the monkhood. It took me about a year and a half to make the decision to actually leave, because it was a lifetime commitment that I'd made. During that time I got involved with another man there at the ashram. I was attracted to women there also. I've always been aware of being attracted to both men and women, although I don't think I knew about bisexuality at the time, or at least I didn't connect it with myself.

**K:** Was it an issue for you that you were attracted to both men and women?

**V:** No, not at all. Because I wanted to transcend sexuality at that time, I would have felt bad that I had sexual feelings at all—but not specifically about my feelings toward women.

When I left the ashram in 1978 I moved to the nearest big city. I was sexual with various men at that point. They were mostly men that I had known through the ashram, so it felt safe. These were men who were yogis even though they weren't as full-time as I had been. So my first real sexual experiences were with men who were more like brothers to me.

**K:** When did you first get involved with women?

**V:** I knew that I was attracted to women all along, but I didn't know how to get involved with them. So in the early '80s I took myself to a women's night at a bar. It turned out that a good friend of mine from my yoga days was also there looking for a woman partner.

I started dancing with women. It seemed like there was a lot of costuming involved at women's events. I remember just being thrilled about wearing my boots. Instead of "frilling up" to go out, I was "butching out" to go out. That was really fun.

There was a woman who was studying to be a therapist who was the first woman I felt a real strong attraction to. We never became lovers, because she didn't want to be. I would have. We did sleep together and cuddle. Her body was voluptuous. That was my first sensual experience with a woman.

The first actual sexual experience was with a woman I met on a yoga retreat. She was obviously dykey. We got to be friends, and I invited her home. I don't think I invited her to my home to have sex with her, but just to spend the night as a place to stay. We ended up having sex, but it wasn't very good. In fact I haven't had a lot of really good sexual experiences with women yet.

The next thing that happened was I got involved with the Rape Crisis Center. That was a big move. I did it mainly to get involved with other women. Now that I think about it, it was a big political step, too. That's when I discovered feminism, because I'd been in the ashram during the '70s so I missed the '70s women's movement.

I got involved with a man who I met at the Rape Crisis Center and fell very much in love with him, but if we were, say standing in front of the Rape Crisis Center, I remember feeling embarrassed that I was with a man. It felt politically correct to be with women and be dykey. So the heterosexual part of my bisexuality seemed shameful.

K: How did you evolve to where you are now openly being bisexual?

V: I went to a women's music festival and met Lani Ka'ahumanu there at a support group for bisexual women. I must have been already thinking of myself as bisexual, but it was like a private label. Lani talked about how important it was to come out as bisexual, because it makes us visible, and it creates a safe space for us to be who we are. I just felt, "Yes!"

I bought one of the Bi Pride T-shirts that she was selling. It was hard to wear it at the festival, but a number of women came up to me when I wore it and said, "Nice T-shirt" or, "Me too" or, "I've been thinking about it." I was blown away.

**K:** Did you come out in the lesbian community as bisexual?

**V:** I was selective at first about who I came out to.

**K:** How were those experiences?

**V:** One on one they were good, but now I notice that lesbians don't ask me out. Even on the rare times that I go to the gay bar, if they know who I am they don't ask me to dance. I don't get invited to the impromptu "Let's go see the lesbian movie that just came out" kinds of things, where a couple of lesbians will call their network of lesbian friends. Maybe I'm not seeking them out either. I'm tending to go towards the bi community, because I want to develop it, and I feel more comfortable there.

**K:** Can you tell me about your current situation?

**V:** I've been celibate for the last six months. I was involved with a man, and now we have a platonic, committed relationship. We're building an intentional community together. So far there's three of us, and one child. None of us are sexually involved with each other. They're my committed partners.

We're trying to create a family situation that's not based on the traditional nuclear family of two people who are sexually involved with each other. We're intentionally creating a family unit of people who have similar goals and want to love and support and be committed to each other. We will probably all move into a big rental house together to start with.

**K:** What do you want in terms of being sexually involved with somebody within this arrangement?

**V:** My fantasy has always been that I'd be involved with a man and a woman at the same time, but my best experiences have been being sexual with two men. This happened for me at a conference on polyfidelity. It was beautiful and touching to see two men be tender with each other. Men really need to hear that, because they've been taught that their bodies are ugly, and that sex or even affection between them is ugly.

**K:** Do you practice safe sex?

**V:** Yes, my version of it. We have to call it "safer" sex, because I don't really think any sex these days is safe. I always have a major talk. I find out where the person has been sexually, and where they are now, and what they've done, and how safe their sexual practices are. We talk about AIDS tests, and what they've done since their last test, and what they were doing the six months before it. If their answers don't satisfy me, but I still want to be sexual with them, I just stick to our touching each other and things that don't involve bodily fluids.

**K:** What do you do if their answers satisfy you?

**V:** If it's somebody whose been monogamous with somebody else whose been monogamous with them for the last nine years, I might feel fine about using no protection at all. The kind of people that I'd be attracted to I would have gotten to know, and most people are really careful now even though they weren't long ago. I do use condoms a lot. I can't get pregnant so I don't have to worry about birth control.

**K:** So you're not fertile?

**V:** Right. I had a tubal ligation done so I don't need birth control.

**K:** What are your safer sex practices with women?

**V:** Lesbians' sexual histories are usually just incredibly clean. They have long, monogamous relationships. It hasn't been much of a problem.

**K:** How are you different when relating to a woman and to a man?

**V:** I don't think that I am. I try to have equalitarian relationships. There are remnants of sexist patterning that I see happen, but I wouldn't say there's a big difference in how I am with men and with women.

**K:** When you're involved in a relationship with a man what do you miss most sexually or emotionally about not being with a woman?

**V:** It's not real clear cut to me that men are one way and women are another way, so I don't miss much about one when I'm with the other. If I'm with a man I miss that they're aren't breasts around, and when I'm with a woman I miss penises, but it's not a big deal.

**K:** Do your parents know that you're bisexual?

**V:** Yes.

**K:** How are they about it?

**V:** It's not a real big deal. I came out to my mother when I started dating women in the early '80s. She told me how she wished that she had been sexual with one woman friend whom she would have wanted to have that experience with. There're no real issues; they're "California people."

**K:** How is it for you dealing with the straight world as a bisexual woman?

**V:** I don't see the world that way. There are all these communities of people who feel that they're not a part of the mainstream. Everyone thinks that there's a mainstream out there, but I'm not really sure that there is, because everybody seems to feel left out of it.

**K:** Do you think there are political implications to bisexuality?

**V:** Yes. For me being bisexual has been very political. Bisexuals are oppressed, because of our connection with being homosexual.

We're also oppressed because we're not monosexual. It's easier for straight people to accept gay people, because it's the same scene: they just do it the other way around. But bisexuals have another minority factor: we're not monosexual, which is scary to the straight community. We appear to be more of a threat to the straight world than the gay community, because we challenge the stereotype that polarity is what sexuality is about, and that it takes a butch and a femme or a man and a woman to create a sexual bond.

**Postscript:** Vidya has recently seen the break-up of the intentional family she mentions in this interview. It's been a painful process—she hopes she has learned valuable lessons for the next try, especially the lesson of humility. She recently completed a Bachelor's Degree in Sociology and Communications and awaits the call for her next step in life, both in terms of relationships and of career.

# 11 ▼ RACHEL

*Rachel is a 28-year-old white student from a wealthy background who lives in San Francisco.*

**K:** When were you first aware of sexual attractions, and to which gender?

**R:** In junior high I was attracted to boys. I considered myself straight until about halfway through college when I was 19 or 20.

**K:** What happened that changed the way you viewed yourself?

**R:** I realized that I was attracted to a woman, but didn't do anything about it. Later I started thinking of myself as bisexual when I was attracted to a woman who was attracted to me. That happened when I was 21.

The actual situation with this woman was a bisexual nightmare. She was interested in me first. I was falling hard for a man who was a friend of hers and met her through him. She let me know that she was interested in me. I was also interested in her. I didn't know what to do, because here were two people that I was interested in, one of each gender, who were friends. It was messy. I had been interested in the man for several months, and that was finally starting to turn into something. With her it was all very quick and exciting. It had a glamorous, dangerous, heady feeling to it.

I feel like I didn't handle it very well. I decided that it would be better to pursue a relationship with the woman. There were ways that we seemed more compatible. Also, a relationship with her would be new and different for me. So I told the woman that I wanted to be in a relationship with her, and ended up spending the night with her.

The next day I had to tell this man that I was going to stop our relationship. He and I had had sex a couple of times by then. I started telling him this. Then all of the things that I liked about him became very apparent; I thought, I can't leave this man. I'm totally crazy about him. So I ended up spending the next night with him.

So I had spent one night with each of these people in a row. Then I had to figure out what was going on. What I realized was that I was getting swept up into something with the woman that might have been really nice and fun, but that I had stronger feelings for the man than for her.

I had another relationship with a woman a year and a half later that was fun and easy. I wasn't deeply involved emotionally. We were only together for about a month and a half, because she was moving out of the state after that. What was really nice was that she was completely happy and comfortable with her bisexual identity.

After that I had another relationship with a woman that didn't quite get off the ground. It ended painfully when I got involved with another woman, who I was then with for two years. That relationship was so absorbing that I didn't ever think about being with anyone else during the time that I was with her.

**K:** Did you ever go through an identity crisis about being bisexual?

**R:** Yes, I did, because it seemed that being bisexual was a very hard label to have. I felt like no one really got it. Lesbians didn't trust me, and straight people didn't really either; they seemed weirded out talking about it. So I didn't use the label. I would just tell people that I had relationships with men and with women. There have been times when it's been easier for me to call myself bisexual, but it's never been a label that's sat comfortably with me. During my last relationship I had a more lesbian identity, because I was with a woman who was very strongly identified as a lesbian.

**K:** Was it hard for you to label yourself as a bisexual when you were with her?

**R:** Yes, it was, although I was also around people for whom it was a positive thing for me to identify as bisexual. I was often in groups of women where a real attempt was made, often successfully, to create a safe bisexual space.

I think my partner had some issues about the possibility of my going off with a man. She had the impression that my being bisexual meant that before I was with her I was jumping from bed to bed and gender to gender. Her relationship history is very different from that. It seemed to me that she felt that I had slept with a few too many people, and the fact that they were of different genders made it all the more suspicious. I really felt like I was being judged.

Also she wanted me to choose to just be with women. There's so much stuff in my family about trying to please everyone and do the "right" thing. Eventually she realized that her putting pressure on me to choose to be lesbian felt just like my family, who had expectations of the way that I should be in the world, and she stopped.

**K:** Tell me about your current situation.

**R:** Part of what caused that last relationship to end was the level of intensity that was always there. So now I'm seeking out relationships that are not going to be so intense. I'm finding myself more drawn to men than women these days, just in terms of who's attracting my attention.

**K:** Are you dating now?

**R:** No, because I can't be bothered going on a date with someone I don't know very well. When I picture myself with someone at this time I can only picture myself with someone I already know. I don't want to go out with somebody to see if I'm attracted to them. I don't want to be spending time with people starting from ground zero, trying to figure out whether I like them or not. I would like to already have gotten to know someone and know that there's a certain level of attraction and compatibility already there before I spend time with them.

I feel pushed in some ways to choose someone and settle down. My parents are dying to see me married, and there are a whole lot of prizes that come with that. There's silver place settings, and a wedding dress, and jewelry, and an enormous amount of approval. Also, a lot of my peers are settling down either with the same sex or opposite sex partners. Part of that is an age thing. I'm finding myself part of a dwindling number of single people in my age group. People I know are starting to have children. But because of this last relationship, I feel I need some space around me.

**K:** It sounds like right now you're not particularly into looking for a monogamous relationship. Is that correct?

**R:** Yes.

**K:** Do you want to be in a monogamous relationship in the future, or do you always want to be in relationships that are nonmonogamous?

**R:** I have found myself caring about that differently depending on how the relationship with my partner was. If I feel very secure with my partner then I have no problem having them be involved with other people. If I don't, then it's a big issue.

When I am very much involved with someone I don't tend to think about being with someone else. So for me there are times when being interested in being with other people is a sign that the relationship is on it's way out. During one relationship I went out with somebody else just because I felt so bad about the relationship I was in. I needed to feel attractive and to not give my primary relationship so much of my attention.

**K:** Do you practice safe sex?

**R:** Yes. Definitely. I always use condoms with men for intercourse and for oral sex. The safe sex I've had with women has either involved dental dams or no oral sex, except for the last relationship I was in. We didn't do safe sex because I had been tested, and she went over her history with a fine tooth comb.

I like using condoms for sex with men. I like not having a big wet spot on the bed. So I don't have a problem using condoms with a man until we are really comfortably, safely, thoroughly committed to monogamy. I give blood a lot. So I have updates on my HIV status regularly and would want the same kind of ongoing assurance from my partner.

**K:** How do your parents deal with your bisexuality?

**R:** They think of me as a lesbian although we have talked about my being bisexual. The bulk of the time since I have come out to them I was involved with a woman.

**K:** How do they feel about you—in their eyes—being a lesbian?

**R:** Awful. They remind me frequently how hard it has been for them. My father actually doesn't talk about it. He went out of his way to make sure he never met the woman I was involved with. My mother has met her, and was sort of okay with it, although I could tell that she was trying really hard to be okay with it more than that she actually was. She's written off the idea of my ever having children, because she thinks of me as a lesbian. Lots of lesbians have children though. I've just never wanted to have children.

One interesting thing that did happen was that my grandparents figured it out and they didn't care. I think they think that I'm a lesbian also. I don't know if someone's being bisexual would occur to my grandparents. My father had taken this stand about what a horrible thing I was doing and made a big deal about me not telling them. I didn't tell them but, as I said, they figured it out, and they don't care.

**K:** Do you relate differently to women and to men in the context of a relationship?

**R:** Yes. With men I buy more into conventional ideas of how I look or how I act. I have a lot more experience being with men than women, so I don't have to think about what I'm doing as much. In a way some of it's just a well rehearsed dance. There are certain things about being with men, especially in the early stages where you're getting to know each other, that's so spelled out that it's easy to just follow along with it. I'm very shy about ever asking people out, and with men I don't have to.

With women everything is more conscious. I have more of a sense of having to figure out all kinds of things. I feel that way sexually, too. I think that there's this idea that because another woman's body is so much like my body that it's easy to know what to do. I haven't felt that way. Having sex with men requires less thought.

**K:** What do you miss sexually and emotionally when you are involved with a man and not with a woman?

**R:** There's some ways that I feel emotionally safer with men, because they're not going to try to get as close as women will, but I also miss that closeness. With men either it's very hard to get that real emotional closeness, because they don't know what it is and how to elicit it and handle it, or they don't want to bother with it, because the feelings are so messy and so boring.

I don't show very much of myself to anyone. The people who have gotten to really know me have all been women. I think that is because women will go after my core issues—what I'm really afraid of, what I really think about things, and how strong I really am.

Sexually it's harder to say if I miss anything, because I've had some very good male lovers and some not-so-great female lovers. But I really hate having to deal with birth control. That whole thing is a big drag. What I really appreciate about using condoms for safe sex as opposed to just contraception is that I can demand a much greater level of responsibility from men, because now there's a truly compelling reason for them to wear condoms. I find that a real relief.

**K:** When you're involved with a woman, what do you miss sexually and emotionally that you get from a man?

**R:** There's a way that men are really easy in the world, and sometimes that's fun to be around. I think that they have a sense of entitlement that is often infuriating, but there are times when it's fun to be around people who are so confident of who they are in the world. There are some things about men's bodies that I like. I like men's arms and shoulders.

**K:** How is it for you as a bisexual woman dealing with straight people?

**R:** It's hard, because I don't feel that very many straight people think of bisexuality as a real identity or a real kind of life. I think that the gay and lesbian community is much more aware, especially recently. Straight people tend to think that if you're not straight you're lesbian. So it's a weird thing.

Just recently I was with an old friend that I wasn't really out to, and I was just matter-of-factly talking about my last couple of relationships. I thought I'm going to let her figure this out on her own. I'm not gonna walk her through it.

Most people assume that I am straight, because I don't look like the stereotypical lesbian. But if I mention a girlfriend to them they assume I'm a lesbian. If I mention a boyfriend they assume that I'm straight. That gets tiresome.

**K:** How is it for you as a bisexual woman to deal with lesbians?

**R:** Lesbians aren't quite so overt anymore about making anti-bisexual remarks, but I've heard a lot of them. That's a hard thing to deal with, because I already feel that I don't fit in with them. So I don't generally feel safe enough to take a stand and say, "I'm one of those people that you're saying these things about." I feel bad about that. Lesbians that I haven't known well have assumed that I was a lesbian, because I was involved with a woman, and I haven't done anything to correct that. I always feel like that's a cop-out; I feel bad about not being more out as a bisexual in the lesbian community.

**K:** Why weren't you out as a bisexual in the lesbian community?

**R:** When I was in the middle of the last relationship I had with a woman it didn't really matter to me. I was with her, and that was all anyone needed to know about my relationships and private life. People that I'm closer to know the full story. Also I wanted to be accepted and to be thought of as trustworthy by lesbians.

**K:** And you would not be thought of as trustworthy by lesbians if you were a bisexual?

**R:** That's my sense. When I don't feel safe with lesbians that's usually what it is about.

**K:** Do you have close lesbian friends?

**R:** Yes.

**K:** How are they around the issue of bisexuality?

**R:** They're really okay about it. Part of the reason that I can be close friends with them is that they can handle my being bisexual.

**K:** Do you consider yourself a feminist?

**R:** Yes. I started calling myself a feminist when I was 12, and I haven't really looked back from that. I don't know how it would be to be another way.

Something must have sparked my thinking about it at that age. I don't remember what that was. It just started making sense to me that women had a worse deal than men did in the world. Then I started noticing all the ways that that was true.

Defining myself as a feminist started out by my being really aware of and upset by the inequality between men and women and actively looking for ways to change that. Now I feel like that experience has been useful for me in appreciating other kinds of oppression as well. So now I feel like being a feminist was the beginning of doing other kinds of anti-oppression work, like anti-racism or anti-classism work. How I think is much more integrated now. The ways the world is unfair doesn't seem to me to be just about men and women. There are a lot of other ways that people are oppressed.

**K:** Do you think that bisexuality has political implications?

**R:** I think that anything that's about making a group of people visible who are not the standard traditional American nuclear family has political implications. I also feel that any time you start talking about a different way of living your life it gets exciting. There are a lot of lesbian and gay male couples who have lives that look like a regular old nuclear family except that the two partners are the same sex. It's really great that people can do that, but I think that it's also really great to have relationships that have the possibility of not being a regular monogamous couple.

**K:** Do you think you have a contribution to make to the world as a bisexual woman?

**R:** One always likes to think that by being who we are and being clear and out about it that it's going to do good. I think about people I know who know only straight people, or who have only been friends with other gay people. As a bisexual, I give people a chance to have a relationship with someone who is different, someone who thinks about the world differently, and who lives their life differently.

I'm in school with a group of young men of color who, as far as I can tell, have absolutely no experience that they know about with bisexual people, and almost none with lesbians or gay men. It's been quite an issue for them to deal with my bisexuality. They like me, and they're curious. They don't really get it, but they're trying, and they understand a lot more than they did before.

**K:** What do they get from knowing you?

**R:** I would like to think that they get a heightened appreciation of differences among people, and how you can be close to people who are not like you or don't fit your ideas of how women should be or how men should be. There's quite a lot of homophobia at my school. I have been trying to educate these young men about that by using one kind of oppression to illuminate another.

Some of these guys will talk about not liking gay men calling them "honey," and I say women don't like to be called "honey" by men that they're not interested in either. I compare how they as people of color feel when somebody says something that's racist, with how I feel when someone says something that's homophobic or sexist. So I think that they're getting something from me.

# 12 ▼ JUDY

*Judy Freespirit is a 57-year-old disabled writer who lives in Oakland, California.*

**K:** Tell me a little bit about how you grew up; your class background, your ethnic background. Were you raised in a religion?

**J:** I grew up in the Midwest. My parents were both first-generation American Jews of East European descent. My father's family was not religious. My mother's family was extremely orthodox, but when my mother married my father she dropped it. So I was not raised religiously. I was always raised to know that I was Jewish and to identify as a Jew from a cultural perspective, but I never had any religious training or education. Anything I know about the religion I get second hand from other people.

I identify my class background as self-employed working class. I was born right at the end of the Depression. Where we lived at that time you couldn't get a job if you were a Jew; the only way to make a living was to have your own business. My parents started a used furniture store when they got married with some pieces of furniture that my grandfather took out of his used furniture store to give them so that they could get started. We lived behind the store. We always had food, but money was tight. My parents worked very hard, because their business was very labor intensive. They worked six days a week, and many times 12 hours a day.

My first eight years were spent in a very poor neighborhood where we were practically the only Jews. During the Second World War, my parents sold the business. My father went to work in a defense plant, and we moved to a Jewish neighborhood which was lower middle class. We were on the lower end economically in that neighborhood. While I didn't consciously see class, I always felt class oppression. In high school, my clothes were not always up to snuff. So I've always been conscious of not quite making it classwise.

**K:** When were you first aware of sexual attractions, and to which gender?

**J:** It gets a little complicated because of incest. I was molested by my father probably from the time I was a small infant. So I don't have a memory of not being sexual. My father was not brutal or vicious or mean. He was just seductive and secretive. For years I had a really hard time dealing with the fact that there was a part of it that I liked. At age five I was a sexual being who was acting on her sexuality and enjoying it despite the negative parts of it. These did not have to do with being injured physically, but more with the secrecy of it, and feeling dirty and bad.

I was attracted to boys as a young child. I always recognized that boys had more power than girls, and I liked being in the presence of that power. I also liked being able to compete with that power.

I played with whoever was in my neighborhood until I was eight. We lived on a main street that had stores so there weren't many other kids around. I remember having a boyfriend before I was eight. He was a neighbor, and I liked him, but I also had girlfriends.

I also remember being really in love with my second grade teacher. There is nothing I wouldn't have done for Mrs. Gardner. I did the best in school I ever did in my life when I was in Mrs. Gardner's second grade class. I can almost tell you what she looked like. She used to wear these beads that had rainbows in them.

I started going to an all-girl summer camp when I was seven and went for nine summers until I was 16. I can remember having crushes on women counselors there. I also had one girlfriend when we moved to the Jewish neighborhood when I was eight. She lived a block away and was a really close friend. I can remember being attracted to her.

**K:** Were you aware of this as an attraction?

**J:** It was more like she was my really good friend, but we used to practice kissing, and I can remember being turned on and her getting scared. Not that we did that much. We were mostly French kissing. I instigated that, because I knew about it from my father.

The first boy that I can remember being attracted to was a boy that lived across the street when I was probably 10 years old. I was real attracted to him.

**K:** When did the sexual molestation from your father stop?

**J:** When I was 15, I stopped it. I told my father that I was feeling resentful, like he was using me. I said, "If you didn't have me you would have to go to a prostitute and pay her. So you're going to have to pay me." He said, "How much do you want?" I said, "Ten dollars." So he gave me the money. The next time I asked for more. I kept upping the price until he didn't want to pay any more, and that was the end of it.

**K:** Was he having intercourse with you at that time?

**J:** It's hard for me to remember. There's a lot I blocked out, but yes. I remember he would withdraw before he ejaculated.

**K:** When did you start dating?

**J:** I started going to parties with boys when I was about 11 and playing kissing games. They would turn out all of the lights, and you would pair up. I started dating when I was 14. I always dated older boys. When I was 15, I started going out with a guy who was a freshman in college. When I was 16, I started going out with a guy who was 27. I dated him for a couple years.

**K:** Give me an overview of your relationship history between then and now.

**J:** I never had what I considered a sexual relationship with a woman until I was in my 30s.

**K:** What happened up until that point?

**J:** I dated men. I started being sexual with the 27-year-old man, although we didn't have actual intercourse. We did heavy petting and mutual masturbation. I broke up with him when I was a freshman in college. He wanted to marry me, and I didn't want to marry him. One of the reasons I didn't want to marry him was because he was in the furniture business. I didn't want to get stuck in the furniture business like my parents. Also he just wasn't what I wanted.

When I got to college, I dated a few guys in my freshman year.

Nothing real serious. Then in the middle of my sophomore year I met the guy that I ended up marrying. He was a graduate student. From the time I started dating him I never dated anybody else. We got engaged after about six months, and then before a year was out we were married. I can remember being attracted to other men once or twice while I was married. One was a man I was working with, and one was a friend of my husband's, but I never really considered acting on either of these attractions.

I don't recall being sexually attracted to women during my marriage, although I had very close women friends—women that I was intimate with on an emotional basis, but it wouldn't have occurred to me to act on my feelings sexually. In fact my husband worked as a juvenile probation officer and would occasionally have to work with lesbian couples because he did a lot of custody investigations. He would talk about having to interview these lesbians. I didn't know any lesbians, and I couldn't understand why anybody would want to be a lesbian. I always used to say that I really liked men better than I liked women. I think what I liked about men was their power; and I didn't like myself, so it was easier to like men than to like other women.

I was very unhappy from the minute I got married. It wasn't a good marriage. I stayed in it, because I made a promise that I would. I stayed in it, because my husband didn't say he wanted out. I stayed in it, because I had a child. After the first year I never considered leaving.

That first year my husband was very abusive to me. He had a violent temper; he was like a little two year old. So if he didn't get his way he would just lash out, one hit. It wasn't like he beat me. It was more like poor impulse control. He would just flail out. He was accustomed to having his own way all the time and getting everything he wanted and being totally taken care of; he just expected it. That wasn't my idea of what I wanted to do. So we had some real problems.

He got drafted into the military and was sent away. I wrote him a letter and said, "If you ever hit me again, that's it. You don't get any more chances." And he never did until after the women's movement began, and I left. That was 14 years later.

There were a lot of things wrong with our marriage, but there were some things that were okay about it. For instance, he was a very good father. He was very much into child rearing, and he was very open to my doing whatever I wanted. So when I decided to go back to college and get my degree, he was supportive. He encouraged me to work if I wanted to. So I started working and getting more independent.

I worked as a social worker in a psychiatric hospital, and I was making fairly decent money for the first time in my life. Every time I'd get my paycheck I would think I could just cash this and get in my car and leave. Then I would have this fantasy of getting in my car and going out on Route 66 heading east. The fantasy would take me to where I ran out of money in some little town where there wasn't anybody that I knew, and where there was nothing to do but get a job as a waitress and sling hash in a greasy spoon and sleep on the floor in the back room. At that point I would cash the paycheck and stay.

**K:** Were there other things that were good about the marriage?

**J:** Being married gave me community approval. Once I had a child I couldn't conceive of being a single parent. I didn't want to spoil the child's life. I stayed for him. But emotionally my husband just wasn't there for me. He was very secretive, and he lied a lot for no apparent reason.

**K:** What about sex?

**J:** Sex was always okay, but my husband hardly ever wanted to have sex. I found early on that if I tried to instigate it for sure I didn't get it. The only way I was ever going to have sex was if I waited until he instigated it. So we would have sex maybe once a month. I probably wanted it more like once a week. Eleven years into our marriage my husband told me that he had intentionally withheld sex, because he thought I had tricked him into marrying me, and he was punishing me.

We had had sex once while we were engaged, and I didn't get my period. I went to a doctor and was told that I was pregnant. So I called my future husband and told him this. He said, "We were going to get married anyway. Let's just get married sooner." His mother didn't want us to get married, and she did everything she could to stop it.

About a month after we got married I woke up one day with blood on the sheet. We thought I was having a miscarriage. So I spent three days in the hospital with them trying to save a baby that wasn't there. It was grotesque. Then his mother said to him, "She tricked you." As if he was such a prize. He had this tucked away and never expressed it. He just punished me for the next 11 years before he finally told me.

**K:** What happened after he told you this?

**J:** I think things got a little bit better sexually, but by then I was on my way out. It was the '60s. It was the period of the human potential movement and weekend marathon therapy sessions. I started going to those things, because I was meeting people at work at the psychiatric hospital who were doing them. I started getting in touch with how angry I was at my husband, and how upset I was, and how unhappy I was. I used to have this feeling of silently screaming inside my head all the time. I felt miserable and unhappy. He just didn't communicate. He would come home from work and turn on the TV, or turn on the stereo, and read a magazine like there was nothing between us.

**K:** You did enjoy sex with him. Is that true?

**J:** I did enjoy sex. I always enjoyed sex. I enjoyed sex with my father. This is very hard to acknowledge, but I did. It's very linked with power for me. I enjoyed the power that I had when I had sex with my husband. It gave me some power over him that at some point he would need me, and I had the power to give or not give sexually. I had the power to please him or not please him.

   I had orgasms fairly easily. I'm the only person I know of who has faked not having orgasms. I didn't want to give him the satisfaction of knowing that he had given me an orgasm. So I would not let him know, and he wouldn't know. I was so powerless in so many ways in that relationship that this is how I had some power.

**K:** Some people would read this part of your story in which you say you enjoyed sex with your father and say maybe it was all right for her father to have sex with her. Maybe it was a positive thing in her life. What would your response be to those people?

**J:** It was not a positive thing. It was an abuse of power on his part and has in fact negatively impacted my life. He took advantage of me. He used me in a way that made me feel that it was my job to be used. That's why I stayed in that marriage for 14 years. He hurt me by telling me that I couldn't tell my mother. Therefore, I spent my entire life estranged from my mother, because I had this major secret that I couldn't tell her. He hurt me, because my self image was one of being a dirty, bad person for many years. It hurt me, because it made me feel that I was different from everybody else in the whole world. Until I was 17 I didn't know that anybody else ever did this, and I thought I was this freak, this monster. I honestly believe, although I have no proof, that the fact that I'm disabled and very ill is linked to the fact that I was under this incredible stress my whole life, because of the sexual relationship with my father.

**K:** If your mother had known about it, and if there was not a society that made you feel that it was dirty that you were doing this with your father, do you think that it would still have been abusive?

**J:** I think that when one person has power to give and take livelihood for somebody else, that using that person sexually is an abuse of power. I was not in a position to take care of myself, to feed myself, to clothe myself, to emotionally support myself. I needed my father, and he used me. What it does to one's psyche is devastating. I will suffer from the consequences of this all my life.

I've denied that for years, saying I've worked this out in therapy. It's not a problem any more. Now I recognize that it's always going to have an impact on my life. How I see the world, how I relate to people, how I feel about myself, my physical condition, my emotional state, everything is impacted by having grown up under that kind of power abuse.

A lot of the problems I've had in relationships had to do with being an incest survivor. If I'm feeling sexual and my lover isn't, it's very hard for me not to take it personally. This is because so much of my feeling of being loved has to do with whether someone will have sex with me. My Daddy loved me. He wanted to have sex with me. So I have a very hard time when somebody says they love me but doesn't want to have sex with me. I've never been able to work through that yet.

I had a relationship for five years with somebody who never wanted to have sex, and it was awful. I love this woman to this day. We haven't been together for 15 years, and I still madly adore her. We're very close friends, but we couldn't be lovers.

**K:** What finally ended your marriage?

**J:** A couple of things happened which foretold the end of my marriage. When I went back to college, I got involved in the civil rights movement. I joined CORE, Congress on Racial Equality. We decided to picket the administration at my school, because they were giving students referrals for housing in the community that were discriminating based on race.

I came home one day very excited, and said to my husband, "We're gonna picket." He said, "I forbid it." Up until that time I had been very compliant. I had been unhappy. I had been miserable. I had occasionlly complained, but I had always ended up doing what he wanted me to do . But this time I just said, "Sorry. I'm doing it." He was incredulous.

The next thing was that after I graduated from college and got my job at the hospital, my ring finger started itching. I just couldn't stand that ring on my finger any more. This is before I knew about the women's movement. I started thinking this ring shouldn't be on my finger—it should be through my nose. I just wanted to take that damned ring off.

So one day I came home, and I said to my husband, "I don't want to wear my wedding ring any more." His response was, "If you're not going to wear yours, I'm not going to wear mine." So we both took our wedding rings off. It was a big relief. It didn't mean to me that now I could be sexual with somebody else. It was just stating my independence; I am not this person's property.

A couple years later I discovered the women's movement. I started getting really involved in it, and started talking about rape and men oppressing women. Whenever I opened my mouth on that topic at home my husband would get really agitated. He started old behaviors that he had done when we were first married. He didn't hit me, but he would get enraged and red and clench his fists and scream. A couple times he threw plates across the room. He was obviously very unhappy with this movement and these concepts.

I was feeling very powerful. I had all these women supporting me. Within six months, I started going to women's consciousness-raising groups. I started a hotline at the Women's Center. I started a drop-in rap group once a week at the Women's Center. I started teaching radical therapy from a book, keeping a chapter or two ahead of the class.

Things were happening really fast. My life was real busy with all this. My husband was getting more and more upset. One day he hit our son who was 11 at the time, because he drank the last of the milk. I realized that he was hitting him because he was angry at me.

Meanwhile in my consciousness-raising group I was talking about the fact that I had lived in my parents' house, and then I had lived in a college dormitory, and I had gone right from that into marriage. I had never had any time in my life when I lived on my own, and I was really longing for that. The women in the group encouraged me to take a vacation from my husband. They said, "Why don't you make a deal with your husband that you'll get your own place for three months? Why not do it?" People were doing all sorts of things in those days. It never had occurred to me before that I could leave him for just three months. Before this I thought that if I left him I had to leave forever.

So I went to my husband and said this was what I wanted to do. He didn't give me any trouble at all about it, which shocked me. I think he was feeling threatened and thinking that he wanted out. He said, "I've never been happy with this marriage anyway. Maybe it will be good."

We talked with our son about what was happening. At 11, he was more connected with his father than with me. They did sports together. They did hobbies together. Plus my husband was really into parenting, and I needed to be alone. So it was everybody's feeling that it would be best if Joe stayed with his father, and I move out. So I moved out into a little furnished apartment.

After I left, all of a sudden my husband got real interested in me sexually. So for a while we were having sex a lot more regularly than when we were married. He would come to my place, or we would go out together. It was fun. I could be with him or not be with him. It didn't have the same feeling as when we were living together as a married couple.

After a couple of months it became clear that neither of us wanted to save the marriage, and that our separation was going to be a permanent thing. We didn't get divorced for a long time, because he had me covered on his medical insurance, and there was no reason to get divorced. He's had a lot of girlfriends over the years, but he's never gotten remarried.

At this time, as I was going through all this change, I went to something called a gay/straight dialogue at the Women's Center. At this event different women got up and talked about their sexuality. There was one straight woman, one lesbian woman, one bisexual woman, and one asexual woman.

The asexual woman talked about freeing up your time and energy by not giving any energy to sexuality. She wanted to have all of her energy to put into making historical changes that would make the world better for women. I was very idealistic about feminism at that time, so I decided to be asexual for a while.

At that point I made a commitment that I have never wavered from, and that is, that the rest of my life would be spent with women and devoted to the betterment of women in some way. I wasn't going to put any more energy into making the world better for men. I felt that women had been shafted for too long, so some of us had to make this commitment.

Nobody before this had ever told me that I could change anything in the world. No one had ever said to me, "You're somebody who can make history." It was monumental in terms of my self-image to think that I could be somebody who could change the world in some positive kind of way. It was worth making a decision that said, "I will never give my energy to men again, because men have so much power that no matter what I do I will lose more than I gain with them."

Up until that time any time I had spent with a man in any way I had ended up somehow taking care of him: educating him, getting him what he needed, bending so that he would be pleased, putting him before me. I didn't do that with women, and they didn't expect it. So I decided that I wasn't going to give any more energy to a system that supported men having that kind of power. It felt like it would take something away from me. Even to explain feminism to men was taking energy I didn't want to give them. I wanted to focus my energy on women instead of getting it syphoned off by men.

**K:** So after you stopped being sexual with your husband, were you ever sexual with a man again?

**J:** No. I never have been sexual with a man since I made this commitment. I have never wanted to be sexual with a man since then. There's never been a moment that I've questioned this commitment.

But by this time I was getting to know a lot of lesbians. Going to the Women's Center the first few months was just shocking for me. Seeing women kissing each other. Seeing real butchy women. Being around women who were saying out front, "I'm a lesbian." My mouth was hanging open, but I didn't feel critical. I was just amazed. Then I started thinking, "Why not? They seem happy. Maybe it's okay."

Around that time there was this purge of lesbians from the National Organization for Women (NOW), because the straight women were afraid that they were all going to be accused of being lesbians if there were lesbians in NOW. Rita Mae Brown, a lesbian who had been involved in NOW, was going around the country making speeches saying that if every woman were to stand up and say, "I am a lesbian" they couldn't divide us this way. I thought, "That makes sense. Okay, I'm going to say I'm a lesbian." So I took on the identity before I was open enough to have sexual feelings for a woman. I identified as a lesbian and became a lesbian-feminist activist.

About two and a half years after I started calling myself a lesbian I got interested in getting into a relationship with a woman, but I didn't know how to do it. I just didn't know what to do. At that time I had a little flirtation with one woman. She wanted to get into the radical therapy collective I was in, and she knew I wanted to come out, so she slept with me. That was my first sexual experience with a woman. It was nice. I liked it. It was like sleeping with somebody who was my kind.

The next woman I slept with shortly thereafter became my first relationship. This woman took a class I was teaching at the Women's Liberation Center. She was a working class, baby butch, bar dyke who had just ended a long-term relationship and decided that she next wanted to be with me. She just charmed the shit out of me. She was a wonderful first lover for me.

It was her goal in life to bring every woman in the United States out. She was really into it. She was very sexual and very much into teaching. She used to say that she saw sex as a performing art, and that she was an art teacher. So she taught me a lot about being a lesbian both sexually and culturally. The sex was hot. I used to keep track by making X's on my calender. We had sex every day of the first 36 days of our relationship. Sometimes there were several X's on a date! It was a really good sexual relationship.

But power issues were a problem between us. She did not have as much privilege as I did. She was more butch looking than me so she was less acceptable even in the women's movement. And there were things that she wanted from me which I wasn't willing to give. I did not want to be married. I was just coming out. I wanted to have other relationships. Nonmonogamy was the "in" issue of the day. I liked the idea of nonmonogamy. I wanted to be open. The point that we really started having a lot of problems was when other women showed up, and I got involved with them. She got really jealous and angry, and we broke up. Shortly after this I had two other overlapping relationships which lasted for a long time.

I've always been nonmonogamous. I've had three and four lovers at the same time. None of my relationships were one-nighters. They were all from three months up to several years, but overlapping with other relationships.

At this point in my life, I haven't had a partner for six years. Right now being 57 years old and, not having a lot of energy, I am open to being in a monogamous relationship, just because it takes a lot of energy to be nonmonogamous. When I was younger and had the energy I didn't want to close my options. I had been closed for the first 34 years of my life. I didn't feel that I wanted to spend the rest of my life being connected with just one person.

Monogamy also has some political implications for me. If you are in a partnership with just one other person then you make a power block of two, so that when you're with any single people you have more power together than they have. Plus people tend not to take their friends as seriously as their lover when they're in a monogamous relationship. Their lover always comes first. If there's time left over they spend it with friends.

**K:** Do you think that your disability has something to do with your being single for so long at this time?

**J:** It has a lot to do with it. My particular disability limits my ability to be out in the world and meet people, because I can't walk very much. I can't stand very much. I can't sit in many seats so I can't go to a theater. There are places I can't go, because I have Environmental Illness (EI). I can't go to anybody's house who has a cat or a dog. I can't go where there's incense, or people wearing perfume. So it's very hard for me to get out and meet people.

Also I haven't really been very open to relationships. At first I was having relationships while being disabled. In fact I was much sicker than I am now, but then I decided that my health had to be my very first priority. Relationships take energy. What I'm doing with my life right now is healing. It takes everything I've got.

My relationships in the past have been extremely exhausting. Trying to do them and getting out of them. It made me worse. On several occasions I have ended up being terribly ill during a breakup. So much so that one of them ended up with a four-year asthma attack. That was horrendous and made me sicker than I've ever been in my life. I'm real clear that I'm never going to do that again.

**K:** If you could have your ideal situation in terms of relationships, what would it be?

**J:** Most of my lovers have been significantly younger than me, because feminists tend to be a lot younger than I am. My ideal relationship would be to be with somebody within my age range, like five years one way or the other. It would be with someone who has done a tremendous amount of work on her own emotional issues, worked out whatever was dysfunctional in her past and is real centered within herself. She would be somebody who wants to connect in a meaningful way, but not be tremendously needy, someone who could allow me the space I need to do what I need to do, but who wants to share and play with me. So she would have to be somebody who was well adjusted and didn't need a whole lot.

Ideally she would be somebody who wasn't real athletic, because people who are athletic want to do things. When they have a lover who can't do a lot they feel deprived. In that situation I feel guilty, and then jealous, because my lover's out doing something that I can't do.

Also, ideally she would be somebody who either has tremendous consciousness around EI or is also environmentally ill, because very few people who aren't environmentally ill have a real understanding of what that means. It's just too hard to have to always be telling someone don't do this and don't do that. This limits me a lot.

**K:** Would you want to be monogamous or nonmonogamous?

**J:** I think I would be open to either. If the other woman wanted to be nonmonogamous then we would have to have some really clear guidelines for what that meant, but I would be open to being non-monogamous, because I have successfully done nonmonogamy. I'm one of the few people I know who has actually had very little problem with nonmonogamy, because there were really clear guidelines that all my lovers agreed to.

**K:** And what were those guidelines?

**J:** That you don't prioritize your relationships. That you tell everything to everybody. You don't keep any secrets so that nobody's feeling paranoid. As long as I'm getting what I want from my lover, and she's getting what she wants from me, I don't have any jealousy about the fact that she's also with another person. I think uncompromising honesty is absolutely necessary in nonmonogamous relationships.

**K:** What are your feelings about safer sex if and when you next get into a relationship?

**J:** I have a lot of concern about it. I have not started a new relationship since there have been lesbians who have gotten AIDS. During my last relationship, the AIDS epidemic was happening, but that lover had been a separatist in a monogamous relationship with another lesbian separatist for ten years. Even if either one of them did ever sleep with anybody else it would have been with another lesbian separatist. They didn't even relate to nonseparatists. So it was about as safe as you can get in terms of AIDS. I didn't even think about it; we just fell into bed one night.

Now things have changed. I know that it's still safer if you relate to separatists, but there are no guarantees. I have some fears that I'm never going to have another relationship. That would be very sad. I've decided though that if I ever do find somebody, I won't care what she says. I won't care how much I like her. I would want us both to be tested for AIDS and retested in six months, because sometimes the AIDS antibodies don't show up for six months after you contracted the disease.

I think about all these things that I hear about and I've never even seen, like dental dams and finger cuffs or rubber gloves. They sound grotesque. Tasting latex is not my idea of a good time. I think it would take some of the fun out of it. But it makes it a little easier not to rush out looking for somebody. I hear about how people get into using all the safer sex stuff, but I'm not real anxious to experience it. It doesn't feel like a fun experiment.

On the other hand, it wouldn't stop me from being sexual if I found somebody I really wanted to be with who also wanted to be with me. It would make it more complicated though, because I wouldn't assume anymore that just because somebody was a lesbian that I was safe. Chances are I'm safe, but who knows if they were with somebody who had been an IV drug user in their past and didn't tell, or who had slept with somebody who slept with somebody who used IV drugs. It's too much of a crap shoot. I don't take a lot of risks. My life is scary enough.

**K:** Is there anything that you miss emotionally or sexually that you got from relating to a man?

**J:** Sexually there's nothing I miss from men. There was nothing that I did sexually with men that felt any better than what I do with women.

What I miss emotionally about not relating to men is that it's so much easier; they're so much more disconnected from their bodies and from their emotional selves. So it's not as intense, and I can be more distant. It's countered by other shit so I wouldn't exchange places with what I'm doing now, but I do miss that.

Because most men are so non-understanding emotionally there's no point in even trying to explain to them what you're feeling, so you don't. Whereas with women, we are so close that even when we have differences we feel like we have to nit-pick every little item to understand everything. It takes a lot of work; it's tiring.

**K:** Why are you calling yourself bisexual since you are only open to being in relationships with women?

**J:** Because I recognize that by nature I am bisexual. By choice I'm a lesbian, which to me means I only to relate to women sexually and for the most part, emotionally. How I define a bisexual is somebody who is able to sexually relate to both sexes. I can do that. I have done that. Sex was fine for me with men. I'm not one of these lesbians who always hated sex with men, or who never had sex with men, and I also find it very easy to love women and to be sexual with women. I don't like to have to call myself bisexual. It's not something I embrace, but it is something that I have to acknowledge.

For many years I was a lesbian separatist. I don't call myself that anymore, but actually my life is essentially lesbian separate. I don't identify now as a lesbian separatist, because some purist separatists would want to argue with me, and it's not worth arguing over. I have a son that I care about and am close to, and I'm not willing to throw him away; also I want to leave open the possibility that there might be a few men in the world that I could have some kind of friendship with. I have a male co-counselor who is a wonderful co-counselor for me. We've been working together for two years now. I value that relationship and really care about him. He's the closest man in my life—he and my son.

**K:** How has your relationship with your son been?

**J:** For a long time he was axed. When he was growing up I don't even know if he knew he was axed, because I occasionally saw him. He didn't want to see me that often; teenaged boys don't hang out with their moms a lot. So I had two separate lives. I was living the life of a lesbian separatist, and my friends never met my son. I have friends that I've had for 20-some years who've never met my son, although they know I have a son. My son and I have a very caring relationship, but we don't seem to need each other a lot.

**K:** Give me your definition of lesbian separatism.

**J:** Lesbian separatists put lesbians first before anybody else and want to live their lives as much as possible with lesbians only. This does not mean women only—this means lesbians only. They're hostile towards bisexuals as a group, because they consider bisexuals to be straight women with homosexual options. They feel, and I have felt this at times, that bisexual women put lesbians at a disadvantage since bisexual women have the possibility of taking the energy of the lesbian community and giving it to men. So it feels like a ripoff. Lesbian separatists don't want to give energy to men in any way, including through straight or bisexual women. Some would take it so far as to want to live on women-only land and never see a male and not ever even have a male child around. Others are more moderate, but all lesbian separatists want to have some lesbian-only space—someplace where they don't have to have any males around them, including boy babies.

I still want to have those spaces. I don't feel I have to be in them all the time, but I like sometimes to have the option to be in lesbian-only space. It feels really good to me to be in lesbian-only space.

**K:** Who are you "out" to in your life in terms of being bisexual?

**J:** I don't go around saying I'm bisexual, because it's not really my identity. It's my nature rather than my identity. It's very hard for me to tell some of my friends who are separatist that I am bisexual, but I think I've told them all in one way or another, at one time or another.

I've been very careful to not say to lesbians that I am a bisexual, because I don't want them to think that I identify as a bisexual. I don't. Many of my lesbian friends have known they were lesbians their whole lives. They know I've been married. They know that I'm not the kind of lesbian who has never been with a man.

I feel it's important now when I talk to people about my sexuality that I say if the world were perfect, and there wasn't all this oppression of women, I probably would be bisexual. But since things are so screwed up between men and women I've made the choice not to give any energy to men. In all honesty though I have to say that my sexual nature is bisexual; I'm just choosing not to act as a bisexual. I feel very much a lesbian. That's my identity, and that's my commitment.

I feel it's necessary for me to say I am a lesbian, because of lesbian invisibility, because of the hatred towards lesbians, because of wanting to stand up with lesbians and be counted. I feel that if lesbians are ever going to get any acceptance or power or parity in this society people have to know that we exist. One of the ways we have been kept down in the past is by denying that we exist. As long as lesbians stay in the closet and people think that they don't know any lesbians, that they don't have any lesbian daughters or relatives or friends or coworkers, then people can delude themselves into thinking that everybody's straight, and that lesbians are these strangers out there that it is all right to abuse.

**K:** How do you feel about people possibly knowing that you are in some sense, anyway, bisexual?

**J:** I'm having a lot of feelings about whether I want to use my name for this interview instead of a pseudonym. It's interesting to me that it's bothering me, because I have told the people that need to know— meaning anybody I'm at all close to. But I have a public name of sorts as a writer. I'm not sure that I want to open up that can of worms, because it's not important to me and it will upset a lot of lesbians. There are women who would no longer approve of me if they knew I was bisexual. I would hate to lose my good name in the lesbian community.

I used to feel a lot of hostility towards bisexuals myself, or at least a lot of suspicion. I'm not sure that I don't still feel some wariness. I've mellowed out a lot over the years. I have straight friends that I trust implicitly, but when somebody I've just met tells me they're bisexual I'm cautious. I'm certainly not open sexually to a bisexual woman, because I don't want to give my energy to somebody whose going to take it and give it to men. This is probably going to be something that women who are identified as bisexual in a different way than I am will find offensive, but I don't think I'm the only one who feels this way. I would feel horrible if anybody I was lovers with was involved with a man after me. It would make me feel like shit. It would be like being devalued.

I think that what's really going on with me is that I think lesbians are better than bisexuals. So if somebody is my lover, and then they are involved with a man, they're lowering themselves and what we had. I don't even know why. Certain buzz phrases come up, like consorting with the enemy. There's a way in which men as a class are the enemy. Here's an analogy: You're a dyed-in-the-wool progressive, and you're with somebody who says they're progressive. You think that you're on the same wavelength and that you agree with each other on some basic bottom line things. Then they join the John Birch Society. It's like they fooled you into thinking they were somebody they weren't, and it feels like a ripoff.

I know of a lot of women who were lesbians for a while, then got married, and now call themselves bisexual. To me they opted for the easy, socially acceptable way out. It's fine with me that they do that unless I have a personal investment in them, like having been lovers, in which case I feel ripped off. They're now able to give to a man who already has more privilege than women, additional knowledge of the values of the lesbian community.

I think every marginal group develops certain strengths. People were always ripping off the Black community. We ripped off their music, and we rip off a lot of their culture and style. It feels like when a woman identifies as a lesbian and then goes back to relating to men that is what is happening.

Married bisexual women get to have it all. They get to have the societal approval of being in a heterosexual marriage. They get to have the option to sometimes have relationships with women, possibly even lesbians who are part of the lesbian community. So they get to be part of the lesbian world, and they get to be approved as a heterosexual.

Lesbians who are born lesbian don't have that. That's one of the reasons why I don't want to call myself a bisexual, because I don't want to separate myself from lesbian-born lesbians. I don't want to make them think that in any way I put them down or don't want to identify with them.

It's hardest to be a lesbian. It's hardest I think to say, "I am a lesbian." I know that some bisexuals think that's not true, but for me it is. When I get up and say, "I'm a lesbian," I'm a target. That's much more socially disapproved of than being bisexual. I don't want to desert lesbians by identifying as bisexual in public even though it would be so much easier to say "I'm bisexual" than to say "I am a lesbian."

**K:** Why do you think lesbians are more a target?

**J:** I think that lesbianism threatens patriarchy, because in order for patriarchy to work men have to have power over women. Men don't have power over lesbians to the same degree they have power over straight and bisexual women. If I don't want anything from you, you have less power over me. If I choose not to give you my energy, you have less control over me. Hatred for lesbians comes from the fear that they can't be controlled.

Lesbians tend to be more independent. We tend not to buy in so much to societal norms. I don't know any lesbian who buys high-heeled shoes or girdles or makeup. Some do, but not many. We don't diet as much. I know these are gross generalizations I'm saying about lesbians, but I think it's part of how we threaten patriarchy.

Plus a lot of men are terrified that when women get together they like each other better than they like them, and many men think they need women to survive. I don't think women need men as much to survive as men need women, because men have been programmed not to be able to take care of themselves. So they think they need women or they'll die. If all women became lesbians, how would they survive? They'd have to darn their own damned socks and do their laundry and cook. And they wouldn't have somebody to feel superior to. So it's terrifying to them.

**K:** You've talked about being feminist. What does that mean to you?

**J:** My feelings about being a feminist are similar to my feelings about being a lesbian. I am not going to desert feminism—and a lot of people have—because it's gotten unpopular.

A lot of women are feminist and don't even know they're feminist. To me a feminist is a woman who recognizes that patriarchy has set her up to be one-down, and who doesn't like the position and feels that it's important to do something about it on a political level. I'm not talking here about partisan politics. I'm talking about women taking some kind of political stance, at least to help make the world better for themselves by making it better for all women. It means naming oppression and refusing to participate in it wherever possible. It means not putting men first, which is the opposite of what we're all raised to do. It means seeing ourselves as whole rather than half of a person who needs a man to complete herself.

My pre-feminist self thought women weren't so hot. Men were better than women. I liked being around men better than I liked being around women. I know why now. I got a lot approval for being a good hostess and cook and servant to men. But women didn't need me to do those things for them; therefore, it was harder to get approval from women.

Now everything I do is political. When men say and do things that are oppressive and sexist I point it out. When women demonstrate internalized oppression around me, I support them to figure out what's going on. I write and publish and speak about being a feminist. At speaking engagements I might be talking about fat liberation or aging, but I always do it as a feminist.

My primary focus is on making the world better for lesbians first, then women in general. I see issues in an historical context, not as people's individual or personal problems. I look at how money and power and class and race impact people's lives, and then use that information to do what I can to make women's lives better.

I'm also a fat activist, which evolved from my being a feminist. Traditionally, women have had to live up to certain standards around physical appearance to be considered sexually attractive or socially acceptable. The fashion industry has created a standard that keeps getting thinner and thinner so that nobody fits into it anymore. There are very few women who feel okay about their weight. Usually they feel too fat. Occasionally they feel too thin. Millions of women are starving themselves daily, and many are literally killing themselves trying to make their bodies fit this standard.

There is a liberal fat movement called the Fat Acceptance Movement which is mostly straight people talking about trying to change social attitudes towards fat people, and dealing with job discrimination, housing discrimination, the lack of clothing that fits, and the social stigma fat people have to deal with in our society. They get together socially and help fat people build up their self-esteem.

I've been a part of the Fat Activist Movement since the '70s. Fat Activism teaches people about the facts as opposed to the mythology about size. How being fat often has to do with heredity. Sometimes it has to do with a malfunctioning system of the body, but more often it has to do with starving yourself. When you starve a body by dieting it becomes more efficient at storing fat, so that all this dieting that people are doing is causing them to become fatter.

**K:** Judy, do you feel that bisexuality has political implications?

**J:** It certainly has some political impact on the lesbian community and the gay community in that it blurs the definitions a lot. It's easier when you're an outcast to have clear definitions and boundaries. So it feels unsafe that bisexuals want to be seen as part of the same movement. I would have no problem with the political implications of bisexuality for lesbians and gays if there was an independent bisexual movement.

It's not that I think bisexuality is not an okay way to be. It's more that I have a problem with what feels to me like a usurpation of something specific and making it something more general by lumping bisexuals with lesbians and gays. I don't think being a bisexual is the same as being a lesbian anymore than I think being a gay man is the same as being a lesbian.

Not that I wouldn't be an ally, but, see, I'm a lesbian. I sometimes do coalition work with gay men, and I sometimes do coalition work with straight feminists, but lesbianism is my politics. It's like the difference between a melting pot and a stew. I like the stew concept where the pieces retain their separate identities and work together rather than everything blending together in a puree so that you can't identify anything anymore.

Then there are lesbians who say, "I'm a lesbian, but I sleep with men." To me that's a bisexual. If you sleep with women and you occasionally sleep with men, you're a bisexual who prefers women. I'm a bisexual who doesn't sleep with men; therefore, I can call myself a lesbian. But if I decided to sleep with men again I would have to stop identifying as a lesbian.

I think that bisexuality has a lot of political implications for the straight community, because it's a threat to the status quo. It's one way that people are saying that religious fanatics don't get to tell them how to live their lives. I think it's a tremendous threat to established religion, and therefore it's very political.

I think that any time people are able to break out of the constraints of the established order it changes the body politic. Openly being bisexual can't help but have an impact. Just like the sexual revolution had an impact. It used to be that if people lived together you didn't mention it, now it's, "so what?" So bisexuality will become eventually, "so what?" It's changing how it is okay to be. There're more choices now. Although it's not accepted everywhere by everyone, still it's more accepted.

Bisexuals are being actively political. They're writing about bisexuality. They're speaking about it. They're demanding to be part of the Gay Rights Movement. It's clearly a political movement. There's always been bisexuality, but it hasn't always been political. I think it's probably good overall.

K: Do you think you have a contribution to make to the world as a bisexual woman?

J: Any contribution I make, I make. The question is do I have any contribution to make to the bisexual community? Possibly, but it may not be something that the bisexual community wants. It's this: acknowledging that people can choose not to be bisexual, and that lesbians have concerns about getting ripped off because of bisexuality, and that it's okay to voice those concerns.

I'm not assuming that every bisexual's going to rip me off, but I'm concerned about it. I think that that needs to be said. I want this interview to be in this book, because I want other women like me to know they're not alone. So for those kind of bisexuals who are like me, this is a contribution. It's also a contribution to people who never thought about this who can expand their perception of what bisexuality means.

K: Is there anything else you want to say?

J: There is something else. I don't know if I want to say it, but it's the truth. Sometimes I think that I've cut off my nose to spite my face. I sometimes think about what if I met this perfect man. I don't really believe there is one, but let's say this perfect knight in shining armor showed up who was absolutely in love with me, offered me the world, would take nothing away from me. All he wanted was for me to be his wife. In other words I could still have all my friends, those who would have me, which would probably be almost none, but that it wouldn't be anything he was doing. That would be hard to turn down given how ill I am and how difficult it is for me to function in the world.

So what I have decided is if that perfect man shows up, and he truly is that perfect, I would then consider it. Not do it, but consider it. Until then, forget it. I'll be lucky if a woman who's half that good shows up, and I'll grab her. It's a total pipe dream, but just on a what-if basis, I do sometimes have that thought. The old sleeping beauty syndrome. After all these years of feminism, there's still a part of me that would just love to have some man come and make it all better.

That's the kind of thing you don't admit with your separatist friends unless everybody's telling their deepest, darkest secrets, and then only maybe. It would be hard, because I think there are lesbians who would hold it against me. When you get in an oppressed community the rules are very tough. People who are very put upon feel self-protective, and often don't want to be with people who aren't exactly like them.

If I was with a man, I'd lose all my friends. It would be like starting all over again. I would be at his mercy, because I would have only him and his friends and his family. Everybody who I have now would be out of my life. It wouldn't be my choice, but I know that's a given. There might be one or two people who would still be my friends. And I like being a lesbian; it would be a big thing to give up.

Lesbians are my people. There are some things that we understand that nobody else really gets. There are some things that we've lived through that nobody else has lived through. There's a connectedness in oppression that happens to people that creates bonds. I don't want to lose that. If I were to identify as a bisexual, or if I were to relate to a man, I would lose that. I even lost some lesbian friends by having as close a relationship as I have to my son.

**Postscript:** Judy Freespirit is currently the Coordinator of the Feminist Caucus of NAAFA (National Association to Advance Fat Acceptance) and editor of *New Attitude*, the Caucus's publication. For information, contact her at P.O. Box 29614, Oakland, CA 94604-9614, or by e-mail at 0005348398@mcimail.com For more information on the Fat Liberation movement (sometimes referred to as the Size Acceptance movement) contact NAAFA at P.O. Box 188620, Sacramento, CA 95818, phone (916) 558-6830, or e-mail fatmaven@aol.com. NAAFA has a catalog of pamphlets and books available by mail.

# 13 ▼ CAROL

*Carol is a 36-year-old Caucasian woman who lives in Berkeley, California. She is an editorial assistant for a magazine and also works in an art center.*

**K:** Tell me about your family, ethnic and class background.

**C:** My father is English, German and Dutch, and my mother is all Italian. In fact she was first generation.

I always claim that I am middle class, although my background certainly is blue collar. I suspect I have middle class values, but sometimes I just think that what we strived for when we were working class was to get middle class values. So I never know exactly how to answer that question.

My father was in construction originally. Then he bought his own business, a gas station, in which he basically worked alone. So even though he owned it, he was just scraping by. My mother didn't work after I was born, because he wouldn't let her; she had done office work before that.

I'm the youngest of three children. It's a blended family. My father had a daughter, my mother had a daughter, and then they got together and had me. One sister is 17 years older than I am and the other is 7 years older. So it's almost like being an only child; leaves room for lots of spoiling.

**K:** Were you raised in a religion?

**C:** I was raised Catholic. My father didn't have much of a religion, or if he did I didn't know about it; so he just let us be Catholic, which is what my mother is. I went to public schools, though, so I am not a product of Catholic schools. I consider myself a recovering Catholic now.

**K:** When were you first aware of sexual attractions and to which gender?

**C:** I just always knew it was there.

**K:** What did you know was there?

**C:** Feelings that are at such a deep level that it's hard to find the words to describe them. I can remember from a fairly young age being interested in girls. Not in what girls did. I mostly played with boys. I can remember being eight and nine and being interested in girls. We used to play nurse and doctor, and I always had to be the doctor. Feminism must have been coming out in me before I knew what it was; I would never let them make me the nurse.

I remember practicing kissing with a girlfriend of mine. We had known each other since kindergarten. We must have been 12 or 13. I'm pretty sure for her it was like this is kind of stupid, but let's figure it out. But for me I knew it was something more. I always felt that way about boys though too.

**K:** How did it feel to you to know that you were attracted to both boys and girls?

**C:** I didn't feel confused for some reason; it felt okay. I remember assuming that I would end up with a man, because that's just the way it was. I wasn't aware there was a woman's community and lesbians out there. I wasn't aware of bisexuality. I just assumed that all my girlfriends felt the same way. I'm not sure I ever knew it was different until I started hearing people talk about other people at school.

I remember very distinctly in the eighth grade there was this girl who wrote a love letter to Barbara Eden of "I Dream of Jeannie." It was truly a love letter. It wasn't just, "I admire your outfits, and I would love to look like you." It was, "I love you, Barbara." People made such fun of her. You get messages that it's not okay to talk about your feelings for girls. Whereas all of my friends talked about boys.

**K:** When did you start dating?

**C:** I didn't date a great deal. As a fat woman I had to really put myself out there, and I often didn't do that.

The first person I dated was somebody I'd known since I was three years old, named Billy. We started officially dating, that is going places where it was definitely boyfriend/girlfriend, at about 15 or 16.

Nothing sexual happened until I had a car, or nothing much happened, because you have to have a car. I think those are the rules. We were 17 when I had my Dad's car.

Billy actually wrote me a letter once in which he proposed to me, which I thought was so funny. I think we were 16 when he did that. Then his parents got divorced, and he moved out of the area. All through junior college, I used to see him for three months in the summer, and then we used to write and call a lot during the rest of the year.

**K:** When were you first sexually active?

**C:** That would have been with Billy—heavy petting at 15 or 16. Some mutual masturbation somewhere in there.

**K:** When did you first have intercourse?

**C:** I was on the birth control pill for a couple of months before I actually did that. I was so proud of myself, because I was very clear that I knew how you got pregnant, and I wasn't going to do that. I went away to college when I was 19, and my second week in college I went to the women's clinic and got birth control pills. A couple of months later I had intercourse with a friend of a friend that I'd met at a party. So many people talk about having sex the first time without protection, but I was on the birth control pill for two months before I would even consider getting that close to a penis.

**K:** So you were involved with various men through college?

**C:** I dated a few men here and there, but there was nothing serious. I dated a woman, too, for a while.

**K:** How did that come about? What happened?

**C:** It was the first semester in college. I woke up one morning, and it was foggy. I looked out the dorm window and saw this person jogging across the courtyard. It turned out that this woman lived down the hallway. We became friends.

I remember when she told me she was a lesbian, because we were at the Blue Flame Lounge having a drink. Having a drink in a bar was very important then. I guess I was maybe 20 at that point.

I don't remember exactly when she said, "I'm a lesbian." I suspect that at some level I already knew. I looked at her and said, "Does your Mom know?" I don't know why that was important to me. It just was. I had to know whether her mother knew. Of course as soon as that came out of my mouth I thought this is probably the dumbest question in the world. No, I suspect the dumber question is, "So are you the man or the woman in the relationship?"

**K:** Did you go through an identity crisis around realizing you were attracted to this woman?

**C:** No, I always knew; my bisexuality was always in the back of my mind.

This woman and I were friends for awhile. It was the first time I had a chance to sit down with someone who was a lesbian and talk and find out about this group of people that I hadn't known anything about. Then we drifted apart as she went off in one direction, and I went off in another.

**K:** Tell me about your relationship history since then.

**C:** After I got out of college, I moved back home and wasn't involved with anyone. I had a year's supply of birth control pills, and I kept taking them thinking, "You never can tell." Then when the year was up I stopped, thinking, "I'll deal with it if it comes up."

By the time I left college I knew that I was in love with my current partner whom I had met at a science fiction club in college, but I didn't know how to approach him. He had moved out to California. I had a chance to go to California to visit an uncle. So I made arrangements to do that, and then my uncle died. I had a week planned in California and no place to stay. So I ended up staying with my current partner for a week instead of just seeing him for one day. That's when the relationship started. That was 13 years ago. We've been living together for 11 years.

That takes care of a great deal of my relationship history, but not all of it. We have had an open relationship. I know that sounds like you have this revolving door, in this culture that has to have everything be black or white. You're either monogamous or you're this other terrible thing.

I've never liked the word, nonmonogamy. Polyfidelity is a word I've liked, because it implies that you're in another relationship. During these 11 years we've been together there have been two other people that I've been involved with. One was a man, and one was a woman.

The man was someone I had known for several years. I had actually met him in college. That relationship lasted about four years. We're still friends, and we still talk. He lives in another city.

The relationship with the woman was the first and only time, I hope, I ever break the rule of being involved with someone I work with. Unfortunately she was a woman with a lot of problems that I wasn't aware of at first. The relationship lasted about a year and a half total. She lived with my partner and me for a while. I had to do a lot of rescuing and a lot of things didn't work out, but sexually it was wonderful. One of the things I found out was that if you are going to have more than one relationship, the primary person and the other person have to be able to get along. These two were pretty opposite.

This woman had had a hard childhood. That's something I had never dealt with before. Now I have more friends than I would care to count that have had hard childhoods, because of being abused. This was the first person I ever knew that closely who had had a hard childhood. Later on I could understand some of what went on between us.

I found myself rescuing her a lot, which I was very good at. When she was kicked out of her former lover's house, she moved in with us. She needed a bank account, so we helped get her a bank account. She'd been in the state for eight months and hadn't gotten a California driver's license. I found myself organizing her life.

She was the first woman that I felt an emotional and sexual attraction for on a long-term basis. It taught me a lot about myself, on the relationship level and the sexual level.

K: Tell me about your current situation.

C: At the moment there's nobody else in my life except for my partner.

K: Are you married?

C: No. There are a couple of different reasons why we don't get married. I'd rather the state not be in my business, and as long as the state makes rules that say that only men and women can marry, neither one of us are interested in being married.

**K:** Do you and your partner always tell each other about relationships?

**C:** My partner has always been the first person to know when I was interested in someone. It is very important that that level of openness be between us.

**K:** Has your partner also had other partners?

**C:** No, he hasn't. He's a disabled man. He claims, probably rightfully so, that it's harder for men to find other partners than for women, and it's probably harder for disabled people than for nondisabled people.

We've spent an awful lot of time processing and talking about this issue. In 11 years we've had plenty of time to deal with it. Both of us recognize that ours is a primary relationship. Whatever is going to happen, we're probably going to be together for the rest of our lives. With the caveat that I know that a lot of people say that, and a lot of people break up. I truly think that on some deep level there is a real connection between us that I don't see being broken easily.

**K:** If you could have your ideal situation in terms of relationships, what would it be?

**C:** More time for relationships. That's certainly an issue with having more than one relationship.

Besides the physical differences between men and women I don't feel a real difference in sex with either one. I don't feel unfulfilled if I don't have a woman in my life, and I wouldn't if I didn't have a man in my life. It's truly a whole lot more important who the person is.

**K:** Would your ideal situation be to be involved with other people besides your partner, or does that not matter?

**C:** It truly doesn't matter. If someone comes along, that's great and wonderful, and we'll see where it leads. But I'm not out looking.

It's been about five years since I had another relationship, and I haven't felt they were five frustrating, unfulfilled years. They have actually been wonderful, incredible years in a lot of ways—good and bad. Since I don't think we can have too much love in our life, if there's anybody else out there that I end up getting involved with, a woman or a man, that'll be wonderful. I'm just not out searching.

**K:** What do you get out of being in an open relationship? Why do you have an open relationship?

**C:** What I get out of it is not so much that the relationship is open, but that it's not closed. The not-closed part means that if someone else comes into my life I don't have to deny my feelings or hide them.

I saw one of my sisters go through four husbands, a couple live-in boyfriends, and lots of intrigue. When I was younger, she would call me on the phone and say, "Call me back." Then when I called her back she would pretend I was a sick girlfriend so she could get out of the house and go see someone else. That level of dishonesty and lack of integrity bothered me. I was maybe nine years old. I didn't understand exactly what was happening until I was older. She also used to take me to ceramics class and drop me off. She was supposed to be there with me, but she'd go off and see someone.

What I get out of nonmonogamy is not closing the door. Not saying this is what it must be forever after; it can never be anything else. My current partner may be my only partner for the rest of my life. I don't know, but what I do know is that if someone else comes into my life I don't have to go into major denial about it, and I don't have to cheat on him. That's what I get out of an open relationship.

**K:** Do you practice safer sex with your partner, and do you have agreements about practicing it with people outside your relationship?

**C:** The man that I had a relationship with many years ago is HIV-positive now. He was diagnosed about three years ago. We had not been together for about a year at that time.

I thought there was a level of honesty between us—that I knew absolutely everything about him, and he about me. I was certainly always very up front about being bisexual. I thought that we were clear that he had been practicing safer sex with anybody else that he was involved with.

What I found out was that he had been having some relationships with men, but was in very heavy denial around that. He would not claim the word bisexual. It was like, I'm straight, and this sometimes happens.

At that time my partner and I got tested for HIV, and practiced safer sex while we were waiting for the results. We've been tested twice since then and haven't been with anybody else so now we don't practice safer sex with each other, but we certainly went through a heavy emotional period. I was probably as close as I ever got to being nonfunctional.

It was a couple of days before Christmas that we got this news. So I went through the holiday season and into the new year waiting for our test results. It was scary. If nothing else that has certainly put the fear of unsafe sex into me. I have no doubt that if either one of us would be involved with anybody else that we would only do safer sex with them.

**K:** What is your definition of safer sex with a man and with a woman?

**C:** Condoms for oral and anal and vaginal sex. Dental dams for cunnilingus. I think kissing is okay.

**K:** What about genital touching?

**C:** I know that gloves should be used. I understand the concept. I suspect that would have to become part of the erotic play. It hasn't been a part of my life yet, but there's nothing like having an HIV scare in your life to make you go out and get the information. Considering that I was on the birth control pill for two months before I even had straight sex, I have a feeling that as soon as I go beyond kissing with somebody I'll be reaching for the latex.

**K:** What do you do for birth control now?

**C:** I don't use any sort of birth control currently, mostly because penis-vagina sex isn't a big deal in our life. Luckily we're very compatible. We're both orally oriented.

**K:** So you don't have intercourse?

**C:** Very rarely, like once a year, and then we do it with a condom.

**K:** How does your partner feel about you being bisexual?

**C:** I don't think he has any trouble understanding why someone would be attracted to women, since he's a straight male. Our philosophy about life is similar—there's too little pleasure in this life and certainly too little love to try to limit other people's options. Mostly his political work is done in the disability community, but he works at the gay freedom day parade every year. So he supports the gay/lesbian/bi/transgender community.

We have had conversations like, "If I left you for a man, how would you feel? If I left you for a woman, how would you feel?" I think we both agreed that it would be painful, no matter what. As far as I can tell he doesn't feel any more threatened by men than by women or vice versa. Maybe because he doesn't feel threatened. Maybe in the final analysis that's it; he trusts our relationship, so he's not threatened.

**K:** Do you relate differently to men and to women?

**C:** Yes. It's easier to be physical in public with a man. Of course everybody assumes you're heterosexual until you prove otherwise, and then the other choice is you're gay, so I often find myself not wanting to be physical with men in public, except with my partner. Because he's disabled there's a way that he's not viewed as a man in this culture. So when I'm physical with him in public it's almost a political statement all by itself that disabled people are sexual, and I'm not his sister or his mother or his attendant.

If I'm physical with an able-bodied man in public, it sets up this dynamic that I cringe at. It says that I'm his woman. I know it's getting better in general, but still the man's deferred to. Being physical with a woman in public you run into the danger of being stoned on the street, but I don't feel the same kind of cultural bullshit that says she owns me, or that she should be deferred to. On a one-to-one basis I don't think I act differently with men and with women.

**K:** Being only involved with a man now, is there anything you miss emotionally or sexually about not being involved with a woman?

**C:** I don't think sexually I miss anything, because as I said earlier, sex is sex. Emotionally there are some differences, but I think I get some of those emotional needs met from close women friends. There's certainly a way in which women know other women that men don't.

There is a kind of connection between women on a level that is different; you share the shit of being a woman in this culture.

**K:** In terms of how you feel about your body and how attractive you feel, is it different with men and with women?

**C:** Body issues are something that have changed a lot over the years with me. Seven years ago I wouldn't have been able to say I'm a fat woman. I would have said I'm a thin woman just waiting to get there. I'm chronically dieting, and I will be thin one of these days.

But I've changed since I became aware of the size-acceptance movement and became a fat activist. Now I don't believe that dieting works. So that means I'm going to be a fat woman the rest of my life.

My experience with my disabled partner is that we both have issues about our bodies that we're dealing with all the time. With other women, competitive issues can come up around our bodies.

**K:** Do your parents know that you're bisexual?

**C:** We don't talk about it. I think my father was always worried that I was a lesbian, because I rarely had dates. By the time I got involved with my current partner I think my Dad was just glad that it was a boy and not a girl.

My Mom knows that I have a lot of women in my life that are lesbian and bisexual, because I talk about them, and I talk about their relationships. My oldest sister knows.

**K:** Do any other family members know?

**C:** If my older sister knows I suspect other people know.

**K:** What is her attitude about your being bisexual?

**C:** She asked me the standard question, "Who takes the part of the man." I think I just laughed.

Then she didn't believe that my partner knew that I had been involved with other people. I was home in Illinois, and my partner was out here in California when this came up. So I actually had to call him on the phone and hand the phone to her so she could hear him say that he indeed did know about my other relationships. The fact that

I had been involved with a woman probably blew her away less than the fact that my partner knew about it.

**K:** Do your friends and coworkers know that you are bisexual?

**C:** I just told one of my coworkers recently. She's a straight woman in her early 20s. She was taking a Human Sexuality class, and she was telling me that these bisexual people came to the class. She was talking about it in such amazement that I couldn't help myself. I just had to let her know that indeed she even knew a bisexual woman, and I was right in front of her. She was surprised. I think taking the class helped her though. She seems fine. The other two people I work with know. One of them is a lesbian.

Almost all my friends know—even my straight friends from high school and junior college.

**K:** How is it for you as a bisexual woman dealing with lesbians?

**C:** Sometimes it's difficult with lesbian women, because I'm involved with a man. There are certainly issues for some lesbians around bisexual women. I try to be very aware of that. When I'm at women's events and someone starts to flirt with me, I make sure that somewhere within the next ten minutes I use the male pronoun for my partner. I certainly won't let it go on without letting them know that there's this man in my life. For obvious reasons I don't have many lesbian separatist friends.

I had someone who I met at a women's dance get in my face, because I am involved with a man. The fact that it was a fat women's dance implied for many women that it was lesbians only. But I looked around the room and saw plenty of other straight and bi women— some of them not out about being bi.

There are not a lot of opportunities for fat women to dance unless you have a partner. You don't just go to a place and know that somebody's going to ask you to dance. So these dances are very freeing for us.

This person asked me to dance. We danced, and then we separated. I ran into her later in a laundromat. We were talking, and shortly into the conversation I said something about my partner, and I used the male pronoun. She got right in my face, and said, "You're with a man!" She was just inches away from my face. I said, "Yes." She said, "You're straight?" I said, "No." I think the conversation had about two more sentences to it, and then she went to the other side of the laundry room.

That's one of the things that made me aware that I didn't want to be under any pretense when I'm in the women's community that I'm a lesbian. I suspect it can be very painful for some lesbians and even scary to be involved with a bisexual woman. I've certainly heard lesbian friends talk about not wanting to be involved with bisexual women, especially a bisexual woman who's involved with a man. That's a major no-no for many of them.

**K:** Because?

**C:** If I'm in a primary relationship with a man, any relationship I have with a woman is not going to be primary. That automatically puts them at the back of the bus. In this culture you get kudos for being involved with a man. You don't get it for being involved with a woman. So for a lesbian not to be put first in a relationship like this is really difficult.

Also, it's so much safer to be involved with a man in this culture. If you're a bisexual woman, you're always seen as having the option of having the "protection" of a man in your life. If you're a lesbian, that's not an option.

Oftentimes if you call yourself bisexual, but are involved in a homosexual relationship, lesbians see it as a bridge before you become homosexual. Other lesbians see it as just testing the waters and playing around. Some lesbians see it as fence-sitting. In this culture everything's got to be yes/no, right/wrong, left/right, black/white. Nothing can be in the middle. To be bisexual means that you're not lesbian. You're not straight. You're somewhere where people have trouble dealing.

I find this is true for me when I deal with very androgynous people. I have this need to know whether they're a man or a woman. If I'm truly having a hard time figuring that out, I don't have a gender base from which to relate to the person or to understand their life experiences. So when people are having trouble dealing with a bisexual person, maybe that's what's going on.

**K:** How is it for you dealing with straight people as a bisexual woman?

**C:** Unless I'm even a little bit close to these straight people it's not an issue, because they assume I'm straight. Of course, what happens is just like what happens in a roomful of white people where a racist will feel totally comfortable saying something racist. If people suspect that everybody they know in that room is straight, they're not expecting any feedback on a homophobic remark.

For me if someone three steps above my boss makes a homophobic joke, I won't laugh. If I feel safe enough I say something. In some social situations where I'm not worrying about people having power over me, I may say something to make the person suspect that it wasn't copacetic to say that in front of me. Obviously I'm not a black person, but if someone says something racist to me, and I react negatively to what they said, then hopefully they'll think about it.

**K:** How does it feel to you when you're in a situation with straight people, and somebody says something homophobic?

**C:** It bothers me just like when a friend says something negative about fat people. I'm their friend, so *I'm* not "fat." If people make negative comments to me about somebody else's body size it's like I'm invisible.

As a bisexual, I'm certainly invisible to them, too. It can make me feel anywhere from angry to uncomfortable to righteous. If I get righteous, they're in trouble, because I'm probably going to lecture them. I've only lost it a few times and just yelled.

Living here in the Bay Area there is a certain consciousness level that doesn't exist most other places. My partner and I were in Houston, Texas recently for a conference. The conference was held in a very fancy hotel, above our economic level, but somehow we were able to do it.

I never felt class issues as strongly as I did there. I'm not used to seeing so many white people in one place and seeing so many people of color in lower service positions. It really hit me.

And the heterosexism hit me stronger than it's ever hit me before, too. Everybody was paired male and female, male and female. We were at a conference around disability issues, and the people at the conference were diverse, but many other people were at the hotel.

We were there for a week. Because I didn't have anything else to do, I did a lot of walking around and observing in the hotel. I felt very outclassed. It was such a white bread, straight world there, and I wasn't fitting in. My body wasn't right. My politics weren't right. My sexuality wasn't right. My economic status wasn't right. I never felt so out of place in my life. It was a very new experience. I am aware that as a white woman involved with a man there are ways in which I walk through the world that are fairly comfortable. But there I wasn't so privileged.

When we came back, as soon as we got to the airport here it was different. There were people of color doing all kinds of jobs. And it wasn't like everybody is on Noah's ark, sexually speaking.

That hotel was just like Noah's ark. In all the social situations you never saw a man without a woman. You never saw two women together, or two men, unless they were part of a group of business-men; you never saw a group of businesswomen.

**K:** How is it for you being with other bisexuals as a bisexual woman?

**C:** Usually comfortable. I don't know very many bisexual men. I have some very close straight men friends. Most of my friends are bi or lesbian women and a few straight women. Just like when I'm with a group of fat women I feel more comfortable, there's a level of comfort with other bisexuals. It's like you're home. Even though we may have a lot of differences among us, we acknowledge the fact that we're attracted to both sexes.

**K:** Are you a feminist?

**C:** Yes, with a capital "F".

**K:** What does that mean?

**C:** The funny answer is that I'm not going to take shit from the patriarchy. Except I also realize, that just like there are layers of Catholic teaching inside of me, there are patriarchal values inside me around women's roles in this culture. To be a feminist means constantly being aware and questioning every time any kind of assumption is put on me or women in general, and doing what I can to make a difference with what energy I have. Letting people know that something is sexist. Why does the woman have to do that, or why can't the man do this? I am constantly questioning the roles, and questioning any assumptions made along gender lines.

**K:** Do you feel that bisexuality has political implications?

**C:** I think anytime you take sexuality out of the bedroom it has political implications. It's a political statement being bisexual. It's a form of questioning, and when you question something it starts a whole thought process that ends in your being able to articulate to someone why something should be changed.

**K:** Do you think you have a contribution to make to the world as a bisexual woman?

**C:** Yes, because it's a part of me and I hope that I have something to contribute. I don't know if I'll ever do anything specifically around being bisexual, because of lack of energy and time. Right now my time mostly goes to fat activist issues and Democratic politics. I don't know if there's any direct correlation between these activities and being a bisexual woman. I like to think that had I been straight or lesbian I would still be making some kind of contribution that would not necessarily be directly linked to my sexuality.

**K:** Is there anything else you want to say?

**C:** We were talking about self-acceptance. Sometimes I have trouble with the word, acceptance. In the size-acceptance movement, there's a bit of a kowtowing to the powers that be when you're asking for acceptance. I'm working to get to beyond mere acceptance and beyond the demanding anger of some movements. There's certainly anger in me too, and I want more acceptance, but I want to go beyond all that to this is who I am, and this is what I need. This is not something that you can fix or change about me. I'm not asking for your permission to be myself. I simply am.

**Note:** For more information on the Fat Liberation Movement see Judy Freespirit's postscript on page 164.

# 14 ▼ MICHELLE

*Michelle is a 42-year-old nurse-midwife who lives in the Northwest. She is in a polyfidelitous relationship of ten years duration with Casey (whose interview follows this) and Casey's husband, Doug, and has one child.*

**K:** Tell me a little bit about your background; how you grew up, your family, your class background.

**M:** I grew up in an upper middle class Jewish family in Southern California of two parents and two kids in the 1950s. My father was college educated. My mother was a "Mom at home." My father died at age 52, unfortunately. My mother still lives in Southern California.

I was raised in a very reformed Jewish household. In fact my grandmother was an avid Christmas celebrater, because she liked the holiday.

I went to college right after high school not really knowing what I wanted to do. I spent nine years working on a bachelor's degree, and got it in nursing in 1980 after I married my college sweetheart. He turned out to be gay and we separated. That was quite a growth-producing experience. At the time I was unfamiliar with homosexuality. It wasn't that I was opposed to it; it was just something I didn't know a whole lot about.

**K:** When were you first aware of sexual attractions and to which sex?

**M:** I don't know that I've ever had a strong sexual attraction to either sex. I've always felt intimate and loving with both sexes, but I'm not a highly sexual person. I went with guys throughout high school that I was physically intimate with, but not sexual with. Until I met Casey, I had never even thought about the fact that I could be sexual with a woman.

**K:** Give me a brief sexual relationship history.

**M:** My first actual sexual experience was with the man I eventually married who turned out to be gay. Then I had quite a few male sexual relationships after that time that were never terribly satisfying. It always seemed to satisfy them rather than me. I had a real wild sexual relationship with a Panamanian black man who was a broadcaster in Boston. That was probably the best male sexual relationship I ever had.

Then I met Casey and Doug in 1986. Casey and I had known each other very briefly professionally. On a trip to a conference, Casey and I started talking about the continuum of sexuality that we both felt people were somewhere on. Some people were much more hetero-sexual than homosexual, some people were the other way around, and some people were in the middle. We both felt like we were somewhere in the middle. We realized then that we were attracted to each other.

Doug and Casey at the time had been married for 13 years, and they had spoken about adding another woman to their family. Casey knew she was attracted to other women. This was the first time I had realized it about myself. We started an intimate relationship about two weeks after this trip. Doug was very supportive of it. He admits that in the back of his head he hoped that maybe there was something in this for him, but he was also very excited that Casey finally was involved with a woman and could develop the other part of her sexuality.

**K:** How was that for you? Did you go through an identity crisis?

**M:** No. It seemed like the most natural, normal thing in the whole world. Like it was part of me, and I just never knew it was there. I think because it isn't okay in this society to be attracted to someone of the same sex, it was something that I had never even looked at. It just took Casey to wake it up. We went through that new relationship high. I don't think either one of us ate anything for two-and-a-half weeks. I don't think we slept for two-and-a-half weeks.

It felt really good except it was very clear to me that she was never going to leave Doug for me. But I don't remember that consciously crossing my mind. I don't know that there was ever a thought of how we were going to work this out when she had a male partner, and I wasn't part of that relationship. There didn't seem to be a whole lot of barriers to us getting together except that we were wondering where we fit into society. We took it day by day. The first three weeks were just a haze.

Then we started to look at the logistics of the whole thing. I was living with a man at the time who also happened to be bisexual. He was very supportive, but wanted me to continue the relationship with him. Also I wanted children, and he did not. We ended up separating. I moved into an apartment by myself where I lived for all of two months.

In the meantime Casey and I were teasing each other in the bedroom one day, and Doug happened to come in. He started tickling me. I fell on the floor in the bathroom, and that was the beginning of our sexual relationship. It was that silly. Our relationship has always been somewhat silly. We've done that I guess to cope with the rest of the world, because we don't fit in real well.

**K:** What is your relationship with these two people now.

**M:** These two people are my soul mates. They are my confidants. They are the people that know me better than anybody else in the whole wide world. I would be lost without either one of them. I enjoy the sexual aspect of our relationship, but for some reason I don't make much time for it. So that's been a problem in our relationship, particularly since my child, Meade, was born. Having a baby, especially a premie which he was, takes a lot of time.

Most of the time Casey and I are cuddly. We're intimate. We're close, but we're not usually sexual. Yet that is more comfortable and more necessary to me than the sexual relationship with Doug. So I think I'm a little more on the lesbian side than Casey is. She would like to have more men in her life. I don't have a need for that at all.

**K:** Are you saying that the sexual relationship with Casey is not a real strong one?

**M:** My relationship with Casey is very intimate and loving and tender and touching, but it's not strongly sexual.

We had another male that we had added to our family, Jarrett, Meade's biological father. It didn't work out. He didn't have the psychological and emotional makeup to be part of a multiple adult family.

Right now we're still in the process of rebuilding from that. So sexual issues have been difficult, but as far as intimacy is concerned I would be more lost without Casey than I would be without Doug.

**K:** Would you use the term polyfidelity or group marriage for your relationship?

**M:** Absolutely.

**K:** Give me a definition of that.

**M:** Like a monogamous dyad the three of us are primary to each of the others just as if we were married to each of the others. We are lifelong committed partners. We do not have outside sexual relationships. We choose to keep our sexual relationships within our triad. As far as the connection among the three of us, it's just as strong for all of us to each of the other two.

**K:** What do you get out of being in the family you are in? Why did you go into this? Why do you stay in it?

**M:** I can live with my best friend and still have a man in my life as well. I found when I was in relationship with just a man that there was never enough time for the women in my life. Now I live with my best friend, the dearest female person in my life, and also have a deep connection with a male partner. How much better can you get?

**K:** Do you want to add somebody to your family?

**M:** We think about it. Doug and I are not as open to it as Casey is. Casey feels a need to have more male energy in this household, and she would like Doug to have a male sexual partner. Doug feels a very strong interest in exploring his bisexuality, which he has never done. Casey also feels that she'd like to have other male sexual relationships.

We see other dyads and triads looking for people to add to their families, and it's a hard thing to do. When you're a single adding a single that's hard enough, but when you're adding another single person to three other connected people it's almost impossible. I feel that someday it may happen. It may be a situation where I'm not sexually involved with that person, and that feels okay to me.

I just think that right now, for me, there are too many other things going on in my life. I'm in the process of getting back into my profession. I have a child who is almost three years old. Although he is parented by all of us and has two almost-adult teenage sisters who are wonderful at helping out, it's still very energy and time consuming for me. So as far as the energy needed to add another person, at this point I don't have that.

**K:** Did you deal with safer sex when you three got together, and will you deal with that if you bring other people into your family?

**M:** Absolutely. We're health care providers. How could we not? When we got together I had an HIV test. Casey and Doug had never had other partners, so they couldn't have been HIV-positive, whereas the partner that I had been with was bisexual. Jarrett, the person we tried to add to our family, had had an HIV test when I was using him as a donor to try to get pregnant. He had not been with another partner for over six months before being tested, so we knew he was HIV negative and did not use condoms.

We would screen anybody before adding them to our relationship. Because of the mistakes that we made with Jarrett I can't imagine that we would court anybody less than six months before we'd have a sexual relationship with them anyway. If the potential seemed to be there I know we would all insist on HIV screening.

**K:** If you could have your ideal situation, what would it be?

**M:** I'm a realistic person, so talking to me about idealistic situations is difficult. I've pretty much got what I want. There are pieces of our relationship that are difficult and that I would change, but as far as how much difficulty I've had dealing with the world, I've had very little. Sometimes I wish I could have more energy to go out and search for more people to be part of our family to meet some of Casey's needs, but as far as my ideal situation, I really think I have it. There's not much I would change.

**K:** Tell me how the situation is for the children in this family.

**M:** Casey and Doug's girls are 14 and 17. They're very well adjusted teenagers. They have their rebellions, but they're not rebellious teenagers by definition. They have said to us that they love us, but they think we're weird. I don't know how much they talk to their friends about our lifestyle. Friends come over and spend the night all the time. Nobody says anything about it. We have never had either one of them come home and say, "So and so can't come over, because their parents are worried about your lifestyle." I can't imagine that there are any better adjusted teenagers out there who live in traditional families.

We talk about our lifestyle when it's brought up, but we don't insist that they discuss it with us. You don't do that with teenagers. That's just not where they're coming from. They don't want to spend time sitting and philosophizing about their parent's relationship. They are both mature in their thinking and very insightful, but neither one of them are at a point in their sexual development where they're asking questions. When they're ready they know that we're open to any kind of discussion, because we've had discussions about everything else under the sun.

**K:** How is it for Meade?

**M:** He knows that he has Daddy, Mommy and CC. I would say he's more connected to me, because I do more of his care, but as far as his emotional connection I think he's connected to all of us equally.

**K:** How is it for you dealing with other people about being in a polyfidelitous family?

**M:** I talk to people about my life when I get to a certain level with them. I'm not sure I can describe to you what that level is, but, for example, the people I work with are very close, and they all know about my lifestyle. Some have asked me questions about it, because they know me well enough to know it's okay to discuss it with me. Others say, "That's interesting," when I have told them and never bring it up again. I'm in an OB/GYN practice, and we deal with all different kinds of women. I deal with lesbian women, bisexual women, and straight women, as do the rest of the office staff. So my lifestyle is not an issue for them.

**K:** Do family members know that you're bisexual? Do family members know that you are in a polyfidelitous relationship?

**M:** We have five living parents between us, and they all know about our relationship. Doug's mother says, "Well, if it works for you I guess it's okay." Casey's folks really haven't said much of anything, but they both treat me like I'm another daughter. My Mom is fine with it.

Because of the generation that they're in, none of them understand it or even attempt to, but they see that we're happy, and that it works for us. As far as our bisexuality is concerned, it's never been discussed. I think there's an assumption that Casey and I are involved with each other, but in their generation that is something you just don't discuss.

**K:** What about siblings?

**M:** I have a brother who is a middle-of-the-road conservative. He thinks his sister is weird. We have a close relationship, but our lives are very different. He has a sarcastic facetious way of talking about his sister; he's always thought I was a leftover hippie. I think inside he really is a very liberal, open-minded person, but he's been in the automotive trade for years and hangs around people who don't think openly. One of his dearest friends is gay so he's very accepting, but as far as having actually discussed it, we never have.

**K:** What about friends?

**M:** For years, we had some friends that we saw frequently until they moved out of the state. We never discussed our relationship with them, because they never brought it up. We still have some friends that have never said anything to us about our lifestyle, but they like us, and we like them, and we spend time with them. I guess we don't have a lot of really close friends that we spend time with. Part of the reason for that is that the relationships with some of the people we used to spend time with were so superficial that we weren't interested in putting out the energy to continue them.

We do spend a lot of time with another triad. We would like to develop more friendships with people who are like minded and accepting of our lifestyle. We hoped that the Group Marriage Alliance that we recently started would produce people to spend time with, but it hasn't really.

I don't think we've ever had any friends that have stopped seeing us, because of our lifestyle. People get to their level of comfort, and then they don't discuss it any further.

One of the other triads that we spend time with has an interesting story illustrating this. The woman used to work in a very large law firm, and she decided she was ready to share her lifestyle with other people in the law firm. She'd been there long enough, and she felt comfortable. So she took the office gossip out to lunch, and though she told her all about her lifestyle, nobody else in the office ever heard a thing about it. Because many people aren't comfortable with the lifestyle itself, they don't know what to say. When I tell people that aren't comfortable with it, they don't ask me any more questions.

**K:** How is it for you dealing with lesbians and with the lesbian community as a bisexual woman, and as a woman in a group marriage?

**M:** Being in the health professions I do see quite a few lesbian women. I have a feeling that my comfort level with lesbian clients is much greater than most of my heterosexual colleagues, because I'm bisexual.

**K:** Because you're sexual with a woman so it's not a weird thing?

**M:** Right, exactly. Also, I feel that I can hone in on their particular needs without having to go through a thinking process. I just know, because I can identify with their way of functioning. Although I find that one of my areas of expertise is that wherever somebody is coming from I can connect with them.

**K:** Do you have other situations when you are around lesbians? Do you have lesbian friends?

**M:** It's more lesbian colleagues.

**K:** How is it for you with lesbian colleagues? Do they know you're bisexual?

**M:** Some do. Some don't. We did tell a couple of our colleagues six years ago, and they were overjoyed that we had shared it with them, but I don't think it went any further then that. We had wanted to get to know these people better, and we wanted a connection with them other than just being nurse-midwives; but after that things started to happen in our lives—like getting involved with Jarrett, and building our house. So there were other priorities, and we just really haven't connected with them again. Like I said, friendships with people that are like minded and can connect with who we are, are becoming more important to us.

**K:** How is it for you dealing with the straight world and straight people as a bisexual woman, and as part of a polyfidelitous relationship?

**M:** For me it's nothing I ever hide from people. I'm just as likely to tell people about my family as I am about my sexuality. Those who I feel close enough to tell, I tell the whole story. Those who I don't feel close enough to tell I don't tell any of it. It isn't like I'm hiding from the straight world. I don't feel any difficulty in connecting with anybody. As long as they're open to who I am as a person, they're going to be open to who I am as somebody in a group marriage. Connecting with anybody in the straight world or the gay world has never been an issue for me.

**K:** I would ask about how it is for you with gay men and with other bisexuals, but it doesn't seem relevant for you.

**M:** There are people who don't see color. I don't see sexual orientation. I just don't.

**K:** Is your comfort level different in terms of how you feel about your body with a man and with a woman?

**M:** I would say it is. I have always had the feeling that men have a meat market attitude about women's bodies. So nudity for me is not as comfortable with Doug as it is with Casey.

Doug is very touchy-feely, and the minute I have my clothes off he's got his hands all over me. Sometimes that's not what I want, and it's difficult to say, "I don't feel like that now," because he feels rejected. It has taken me a long time to get to a comfort level with Doug that's close to how I feel with Casey.

With Casey I feel very comfortable. I can't remember ever feeling uncomfortable at all with her. She's like my other self.

**K:** Do you consider yourself a feminist?

**M:** Absolutely. Without a doubt.

**K:** What does being a feminist mean to you?

**M:** The battles I choose to fight usually have to do with getting me and my sisters an equal place in the world. The issues most important for me have generally been professional ones—getting hospital privileges, and being accepted by the medical community as a nurse-midwife. Usually that's a male/female issue. I happen to be in a women's practice at this time, so that hasn't been true where I work now.

As far as other women's rights issues go, I've been very involved in the abortion issue in the past. I am pro-choice. I feel that it is a woman's right to choose. I was involved with the National Abortion Rights Action League and was vocal and visual in that group.

Once I got involved in private practice I didn't feel safe being so outspoken on that issue, because we had a lot of fundamentalist Christian clients. I felt very strongly that first of all it could have ruined the business, and second of all the abortion issue was heating up around people being violent to pro-choice professionals, and I didn't feel safe.

Right now I don't feel safe marching for any cause, because I've got a young child. It hasn't changed how I feel about feminist issues. It has changed how I will support them. But my major energy has been toward my professional feminism in that I am a nurse-midwife competing within the medical community, and that has been a male/female issue, at least until recently.

**K:** Do you think you have a contribution to make to the world as a bisexual woman in a polyfidelitous relationship?

**M:** I think my contribution to the world is in my offspring and in my profession. I've chosen my issues, and where I put my energy; bisexuality and polyfidelity aren't where I chose to put my energy.

**K:** Do you feel that bisexuality or your lifestyle has political implications?

**M:** I know it does. Legalizing our relationship, and being able to file tax returns together are things that could become real big political issues for us, but I just don't have the energy to work on them. It isn't that important to me that the rest of the world recognize my relationship.

**Note:** For more information on relationship options see the "Other Resources" appendix on page 252.

# 15 ▼ CASEY

*Casey is a 42-year-old nurse-midwife with two children who lives in the Northwest. She is involved in a triad with her husband, Doug, and with Michelle, whose interview precedes this. Michelle makes some comments during the course of this interview.*

**K:** Tell me about your background. How you grew up, your class and race. Were you raised in a religion?

**C:** I had a standard "white bread" background with an intact family. My parents have been married for 47 years now. I was raised Presbyterian. My mother went back to school when I was in junior high, went through college and got a master's degree, and ended up teaching. My father worked for the railroad for 37 years. I have one sister who is five years younger than me.

**K:** When were you first aware of sexual attractions and to which sex?

**C:** There was a group of us that hung around together in eighth grade. So I would say I was first attracted to males in eighth grade. I'd been sexual with some of my girlfriends in the sixth grade.

**K:** What did you say to yourself at the time that you were being sexual with these girls? Was it something that you even thought about?

**C:** I don't know if I thought about it in terms of a label. I really resist labels strongly. It just felt good to be with my girlfriends. Talking and sharing and physical closeness and having sleep-overs was enjoyable. There was an excitement about being together and there being a secret part of us that was the sexuality thing. Yet with the boys it was also exciting and sexual. Being attracted to someone didn't seem to depend on the person's sex so much as it depended on who that person was and their receptivity toward me. I don't think I put a label on it then or even later, really. I had "working relationships" with both sexes by the time I was 19.

**K:** Did you have relationships with women in high school, too?

**C:** Yes, but not sexual ones. It was mainly grade school sexual relationships with girls just because we were all going through this period of time where we were uncertain, and other girls were comfortable. There was bonding that happened just because we were young, and we were female, and we understood each other. Boys represented this unexplainable mystery. So it was like the attraction of the alien, and the attraction of the self, and I didn't feel like I wanted to give up either one of those.

**K:** What happened that you started getting involved with women after high school?

**C:** College was really great fun, because there was more freedom. There was less concern about parental values. My parents are very traditional. They hugged and kissed, but we never saw them being sexual with each other, and we knew that they frowned upon masturbation and such things. So there was a sense that you needed to keep this exciting sexual part of yourself hidden from them.

So college was a time to explore. I fell in love with a woman who was in one of my classes. She was very tiny, and I felt protective toward her. I couldn't quite figure out why. She and I had a lot of long talks late into the night trying to figure out whether I was really attracted to her, or whether this was just my maternal instinct. It was wonderful. At the end of my freshman year I went off to nursing school, and she went off to Alaska where her family had moved. So I didn't see her after that.

**K:** Were you sexual with her?

**C:** Not in the traditional sense of being sexual. We were close. I certainly felt intimate with her mind. I think she felt close to me, too, but she wasn't ready to explore it any further than that.

While I was in nursing school I decided that it was time to get out in the world and do something a little bit on the wild side. So I volunteered to work at a free clinic downtown in the city I was in. There was a crash crew which worked at night and went out on calls to people needing help. People called us when they were having bad trips, or when they took too many tranquilizers with too much booze, or if they were prostitutes on the street and tired of the life, or whatever. That was really an eye opener. I met some real characters.

**K:** What did you do for birth control with men?

**C:** Did we have birth control then? There wasn't birth control then, was there? (laughing)

**K:** Yes, there was.

**C:** We didn't use it, though.

**K:** When did you meet your husband?

**C:** I met my husband, Doug, in March of '72, and we became engaged the following November. We got married September of '73, my senior year in college.

**K:** Tell me about your current situation.

**C:** Doug and I had lots of talks over the years about what we wanted in a family. We read some interesting books on multiple adult relationships, and we thought that would be fun. We were corrupted by reading [Robert] Heinlein and other science fiction writers and just had the desire to be more inclusive than exclusive.

I'd known Michelle, the woman who became our partner, professionally. When my first birthing center business partner left the practice, I needed assistance in attending some of the more difficult births. Michelle was in a start-up private practice herself and thought we could combine forces and help each other out.

We were both concerned that our practices thrive so we went to a marketing workshop in another city together. One of my pet theories is about the continuum of sexual expression from complete homosexuality on one end to complete heterosexuality on the other. I explained this theory to her on the way to the workshop. She didn't seem to object to it.

When we got back to my house she kissed me goodbye. It was like now, was that just a thank you kiss goodbye, or was that a "I want there to be something more" kiss goodbye? Maybe she's just a kissy person. I talked to Doug about it. I said I have to know what it is, because otherwise I'm going to go off on this flight of fancy about it. So I said, "I'll call her."

I had it all worked out in my mind exactly what I was going to say to her when I called her, but her boyfriend, Jim, picked up the phone. I almost asked him what the hell he was doing picking up his phone, because he wasn't the one I wanted to talk to. But I thought I can still do this same scenario. I've just got to talk to Michelle. So I asked if I could talk to her. He said, "She's not here right now. If you want to leave a message I'll be happy to tell her why you called." It was hilarious.

K: So what happened? How did you get together?

C: To this day it's a red haze.

*(Michelle enters the interview.)*

M: We talked about did we want to do this? Didn't we? Where was our comfort level?

C: What would Jim say? What would Doug say? What would we say? What would our patients say?

M: Basically at that point we decided we didn't really care what other people would say, but we didn't know what we were going to do about it.

C: Or where.

M: Then it turned out that Jim, my boyfriend, was going out of town, and Casey came and spent the night with me.

C: That's right. The night we didn't sleep! It was one of those 13-hour nights!

M: Casey and Doug had come over to my house while Jim was away. They insisted on both going home, because Casey's folks were there taking care of the kids. But then Casey drove all the way back, and we spent the night together and had all sorts of experiences neither one of us had ever had. It was lovely.

**K:** So you had not been in a sexual relationship with a woman before?

**C:** Not really. It was fun.

**M:** I had never been intimate with or kissed another woman.

**C:** In the following two-and-a-half weeks, I lost 15 pounds. The typical-—not eating, not sleeping.

**K:** It was just the two of you at that point? Doug was not involved?

**C:** At that point Doug and Michelle were not sexually involved, although the three of us talked a lot that summer about Michelle's relationship with her boyfriend. About my relationship with Doug. About her relationship with me. We had very long involved discussions. Michelle's goal at that point was to have a child, and Jim was not willing to agree to that. She was willing to wait until he was ready to agree. Except she and I complicated things by falling in love with each other. So I told her that she should leave Jim.

We had a big fight over this. She was trying to convince me that there was no good reason why she should leave Jim. I said, "Let me get this straight. You want to have a child. Jim will not commit to having a child. You still want to stay with him. Doesn't this seem like number one counters number two." She didn't want to hear that, and she didn't want to hear it from me. So I said, "I really think you should think about this a lot. Besides there's always another option—that you could come live with Doug and me."

She wasn't sure she wanted to do that. She didn't want to have to think about leaving Jim. She thought it would be interesting to live with Doug and me, but she wasn't sure she wanted to go from one relationship to the other. That didn't seem like a good idea to her. She really wanted her independence, but she really wanted to have a baby.

She thought about it. She decided I was right, but then she had to go through the separation from Jim. And there was also a concern about telling family and friends. How do we explain this? Whether we would explain it.

**K:** What happened at that point after Michelle separated from Jim?

**M:** I rented an apartment for two months.

**C:** You must have stayed there at least three nights. But it was important for her to do that. That was the break between her old life and her new life. After Michelle moved in with us, her relationship with Doug started.

**K:** Did you call yourselves polyfidelitous at that time?

**C:** I don't think we called ourselves anything then. We didn't even know the words. We didn't know about Kerista.[1] We didn't know about the concept of polyfidelity. We didn't know about PEP.[2]

**K:** What did you say about it all? What were you saying to each other?

**C:** "We're happy."

**M:** Yes. "We're happy." I'd say it took us a couple of months to start talking about how do you tell people about this?

**C:** We were just too wrapped up in each other to really notice much else. There wasn't a time when we said, "Stop. Let's wait for a label before we proceed." We proceeded. We said, "This is what feels right, we're all in agreement, and we're all adults." We talked about what each person's bottom lines were. What we would and wouldn't do.

**K:** What were your bottom lines?

**C:** Mine were that I would never leave my children, and that I believed very strongly they should have a father in the house, and that if having a relationship with Michelle meant I had to leave my children, I wouldn't, and that was that. I wanted us to share equally, which I felt

---

1. Kerista was a communal living experiment which pioneered the concept of polyfidelity.

2. PEP (Polyfidelitous Educational Productions) is now Loving More. See Other Resources on Page 252.

we could do from the beginning, because I don't have a real sense of possessiveness.

**K:** Do you mean in terms of the relationship and relating to each other?

**C:** And the household. The house and everything. That was hard for Michelle, because she felt that Doug and I had been together for 13 years, and had kids, and had built up assets, while she was coming with nothing. I didn't see it that way. It took us a while to understand each other's point of view. We moved from that to the intention to create a family—to create a household together. Until she was comfortable in belonging as an equal partner, we would not share income. We would each make our individual contributions to the family.

**K:** What is the situation now?

**C:** We've come through so many stages and phases since then. Right now we share income 100%. Everybody puts their money into the pot, and we pay everything out of the pot. We own the property and the house in three people's names, all with right of survivorship. We have everybody on everybody else's wills.

**K:** Describe what your relationship is like.

**C:** I think each of us has a different perspective on that. I would say that Doug feels like he has two life partners, two wives. I think for him that's very ego gratifying. Not that that was his prime reason for participating, but I think that has really strengthened his ego.

I would say for myself, it's having my cake and eating it too. It's having all my best friends at home, which is fun. There's always somebody to talk to. Some of the things I don't like doing I don't have to do. Other things I like doing I can do more of. For Michelle, I think she has a family that shares her values.

My kids have two Moms. We have different schedules so there's usually someone here for the kids. They have three adult perspectives. I guess the kids would also say it's rotten, because they have three parents to mind instead of two, but they seem to weather that fairly well. I don't know if Meade, Michelle's baby, has an opinion yet other than he knows who everybody is.

**K:** At one point you added another male partner to your relationship that didn't work out. Why did you do that, and why do you think it did not work with him?

**C:** At that time I was still interested in expanding the family, and that was a genuinely felt need on my part. Secondly, though Doug had a vasectomy reversal, it didn't work in terms of getting Michelle pregnant, so we needed a fertile male partner to be able to add a child to the family.

Jarrett, the man we tried adding to our family, was the husband of a friend of ours. Michelle had used him as a sperm donor, but hadn't gotten pregnant. At the time, he and his wife had recently gone through a divorce. We felt he was supportive and of good character. Plus we liked him, and he was funny.

**M:** We'd known him three or four years. He's in construction, and he was helping us with remodeling our house, and needed a place to live.

**C:** So we decided that in exchange for room and board he could help us finish the house. Then we all talked about bringing him into the family as another partner and decided to do that.

In retrospect I think that at the time we were each trying to be supportive of what we thought were our other partners' needs, but we weren't stating to each other what our own needs were. Doug was being generous to me since he knew I wanted another partner, and he knew Jarrett, although he didn't have an attraction to him. Michelle felt that she would have an opportunity to have a fertile partner as well as enjoying Jarrett, and that it would help me meet my need for another male partner in the family. I felt that it would meet Doug's need to have a close male friend. Even if they weren't sexual, they would at least be close. So we did it for everybody else instead of for ourselves.

Michelle figured she wouldn't need to use birth control right away with Jarrett, because she hadn't gotten pregnant before using him as a donor, and of course she got pregnant the first month. I'm very fertile so I used a cervical cap. The period of time that Michelle became pregnant until the baby was nine months old was an incredible strain on everybody.

Jarrett had not been parented well. He grew up in a very abusive family. I think that contributed to his inability to bond. He, I think, would say that he was doing everything he could to be a good role model for his son in that he was going to school and working as hard as he knew how to work. When he wasn't studying, he was at work, and when he wasn't at work he was studying; and that was the best he could do.

But unfortunately it's hard to make a relationship work if someone's never there, and it was hard for him to have a relationship with his son since he never was there for him. It wasn't something that Jarrett could understand. He has a one-point focus, and while he could do one thing he couldn't do the other. He just didn't have the capacity to have a relationship with each of us and to Meade in addition to working. So things didn't work out with Jarrett as part of our family.

**K:** How has it been for you to have one of your partners have a baby?

**C:** Having a baby is something I'm familiar with professionally as well as personally, but having Michelle have a baby, there was no clear role for me. I know what to do when you're the mother. I'm not so good about knowing what to do when you're the father. So if you're not the mother, and you're not the father, what are you? There's no rule book written about how to be a second wife. Primarily I got a chance to experience what being a father must feel like.

Michelle went into premature labor when I was on the other side of the country. At that point, I needed some time away to clarify issues in my mind about the baby and my business, so I decided to visit some friends who had a boat off of Delaware Bay on the East Coast. About fifteen minutes after I arrived at their place, I got a message to call home, because there was a problem.

I got the first flight home that was available and arrived the next morning. Doug picked me up at the airport and drove me to the hospital where Michelle was. They had her on all sorts of medications. That was Monday, and things were calm.

On Tuesday she stood up to go to the bathroom, and water poured down her legs. Her water had broken, which meant that we were going to have this kid soon. Despite a whole raft of things that intervened, we finally had Meade. He was 2 lbs. and 6 oz. He didn't even look like he weighed that much when he was born.

**M:** We brought him home from the hospital when he was three-and-a-half-weeks old. We told them, "all you're doing is keeping him warm and feeding him my breast milk." So we brought him home, and he started to grow. Casey and I took three-hour shifts night after night with him, because we had to constantly tube feed him. We did that for a month. There's no way I could have done this without Casey.

**C:** And somebody had to make a living, so that's what Doug did.

**K:** So both of you were just taking care of this premie?

**C:** And the house and the kids.

**K:** I know many lesbian couples with children who consider that they are both mothers. The child has two mothers.

**M:** I can understand that, but Casey was already a mother to two wonderful children, and it's different. When you start out parenting together, and it's both your first parenting experience, I can understand how you could establish your roles.

The other piece is there's a biological connection between Meade and I, especially with his prematurity. In spite of the fact that Casey did spend time at the hospital with me and Meade, she still had to continue the rest of our lives, which freed me up to stay at the hospital with Meade day after day. So there was a delay in her even being able to establish a bond with him.

**K:** How has it been for your two older children in terms of your relationship?

**C:** I think the kids have dealt with it better than most adults. They've had a chance to experience different kinds of families. They consider Meade their brother. They don't say, "He's my adopted brother, or he's my stepbrother." He's a brother.

**M:** They're talking to a friend on the phone, and he's bothering them, "Oh, that's my little brother." There's no question in their mind who he is.

**C:** As far as our relationship goes, they're 17 and 14 now, and we've been together ten years. So they were little kids when we got together. There were issues about how much mothering Michelle would do of my kids. From the beginning Doug and I tried to encourage her to participate and to uphold a united front with us in terms of how we wanted to deal with the girls. We still have discussions about that. I think we're all better parents because of it.

The girls are at a point in their lives where they're beginning to reach out to other people. They're both very interested in boys. As far as I know they've not had relationships with girls other than best friends, but I'm not sure a mother knows that necessarily. They tend to think we're weird. Fortunately another polyfidelitous family that we spend time with has a son, and he thinks we're just as weird.

This other polyfidelitous family shared with us their experiences attempting to enlarge their family. I have come to believe that it takes a confirmed and committed dyad relationship experience before you can really think about moving to three or more partners. Whenever you add a member to your family you risk everything. You risk the original relationship, and you risk coming out of it not in the same space you were when you started.

**M:** Adding partners to your family is going to change the relationships you have with the people already in your family. No matter who you add, the relationships are going to be different.

**C:** We're quite content in our society to say that if you add a child to your family it changes your relationship. What's different in adding another partner? When you add a child to a family you risk the whole family. Families that have babies with birth defects often fall apart due to the seriously ill child. We've had a premature child, we've lost big bucks, and the three of us have weathered it.

I think for the kids that's beneficial, because they see how you weather crises. I think the experience of seeing how people work things out is invaluable to them, because they're going to need to do this in their lives. If they don't learn it at home it's going to be real hard to learn it in the outside world. I think they've done well with it. They think we're weird. I think that's fine. We certainly are not staid middle of the road kind of people, but by the same token I don't think we're that different from so-called "traditional families."

**K:** How are you like a traditional family?

**C:** We're in a committed, long-term relationship that values raising children and having a comfortable lifestyle and wants the best for each of the members. I think that's what all healthy families want. By the same token, there are unique things about having three adults in the family.

**M:** We're going to Doug's high school reunion in September, and he had to add lines to the form, and figure out how when they charge this much for a single, and this much for a couple how much they would charge for three. That's how it's different than a traditional dyad relationship.

**C:** But it's not different in terms of having disagreements. It's not different in terms of being committed. It's not different in terms of your relationship growing over time. So it's not as odd as some people think.

**K:** If you could have your ideal situation in terms of relationships for yourself, what would it be?

**C:** I'd have exactly what I have now, except I'd work three days a week instead of four. So there'd be more time, and I think we'd have another partner or partners. I can't see our family growing much beyond five adults. I just don't think there's enough psychic energy for more than five adults.

**K:** Would you want to have more men? More women? Does it matter?

**C:** I'd like another male partner. I used to say all I wanted was four adults in my family, two women and two men, and that would be ideal. I think it would still be ideal in some ways, because it's balanced, and I think a gender balance is nice if you have the right folks involved. But over the years I've learned that we're intimidating. We've been together so long that one person coming into our family may feel that it's impossible to achieve equality with the three of us. So it might be easier to have a couple join the family, because they would have their history together and their connectedness. I'm open to either of those possibilities.

**K:** Do your parents know that you're bisexual or that you are in this group marriage?

**C:** Yes, they do. We were selling our house before we moved here. My mom's a realtor so she was walking through the house, and she noticed we have a huge bed. She said, "This is a big bed. Does Michelle sleep here, too?" "Yes." "This isn't a platonic relationship you have with her, is it?" "No." "Okay." And essentially never said another word about it.

**K:** Does that mean your father also knows, and have they been basically accepting?

**C:** Yes.

**K:** Do you have siblings or other relatives who know?

**C:** I have a sister. My sister is five years younger and has never been married and would very much like to be married and have a family. We have a big family, and I think she feels that I have everything, and she has nothing. If I were single and had two kids she probably would be quite happy to be more involved, but it's obvious that we have three children, and we have two partners each, and she doesn't have one, and where's the justice in that? I don't think she has malice towards us; I just think she's so wrapped up in her own feelings about what she doesn't have that it makes it hard for her to relate to us.

When Michelle was pregnant it was real hard for my sister. She had a friend who lost a baby and had been trying for many years to get pregnant. So my sister asked if Michelle would mind not coming to a Thanksgiving dinner, because her friend would be there, and it would be like throwing it in her face. While I really think she believes she asked for the sake of her friend, I know she's uncomfortable with our group marriage. But I wouldn't say that her feelings are directed at Doug or at me or at Michelle; I think it's more her regrets at this point, and maybe over time they'll become less. She's getting ready to turn 40, her biological clock is ticking loudly, and there's nothing I can do to help, unfortunately. That's hard.

**K:** What about friends and coworkers? Do people generally know that you're bisexual and that you are in a polyfidelitous relationship?

**C:** In the beginning I felt like it was important to stand up and be counted for the lifestyle—to be out there. I've mellowed over the years. I'm living my life, and my life is my example. If people want to know, they'll ask. Occasionally I get uncomfortable wondering about how a particular person will react if I tell them. At some level I don't want to even worry about it. I want to live my life.

**M:** Preface that by saying you've only been at your current job for two years. She's in a supervisory position in a public agency.

**C:** And that makes it a little difficult. I have co-workers who are gay, and we can have good discussions when we're not working, but it's difficult to make friends, because of my supervisory. So that's a barrier that doesn't really need to be there from my perspective, but is there in terms of the other folks. There're several that know about my family, but I'm selective about who I tell.

**K:** Is that true with friends? Do you have friends who don't know about your family?

**M:** We have friends who we've never specifically told. For example, we're close to some of the neighbors that don't know specifically. None of them have ever asked, and we've never told them, but we're very close to some of them. We have conversations about life and children all the time.

**C:** They know we live in the same house, but they don't ask about it.

**M:** One of them has come over and used our shower when their water went out. So he's obviously aware of what size bed we have in the bedroom.

**C:** But then again we may pay more attention to that than other people do. We have a king-size bed plus a twin bed pushed together. We think that people would look at that and automatically know, but I don't think in general people do.

I used to be more out there, but I'm not anymore. It will be interesting to see how time changes that.

I tend to be more reticent when it comes to the kids, and their friends. We try and make it real clear that there are three adults in the household so that when they have friends over for an overnight that's known to the parents in advance.

**M:** None of their friend's parents have ever said they couldn't come over. Each of the girls has a fundamentalist Christian friend, and their parents know that there are three adults living in this household. The parents have talked to all of us and been in the house. Nobody ever said anything.

**K:** How is it for you as a bisexual woman in a polyfidelitous relationship dealing with lesbians and the lesbian community?

**C:** For the most part it's comfortable, although occasionally there's a sense that I'm neither fish nor fowl. For some lesbians it's like, "You can't make up your mind? What's wrong with you? You're really gay, so forget men." It doesn't work that way. Our colleagues who are gay were thrilled when we told them that we were in a relationship, but they automatically assumed that meant that Doug wasn't a part of the relationship. They just don't address that. To them it's like we're gay.

**K:** How is it for you as a bisexual woman in a polyfidelitous relationship dealing with straight people and the straight world?

**C:** I think people are people. I tend not to put labels on people. I guess if I had to label myself I'd say "bisexual," but I tend to think that I like loving people. So whether they're male or female, why should that make a difference? If you have a son and a daughter you love the son and you love the daughter regardless of which sex they are. So why is it so odd to love both men and women?

Dealing with different people is like speaking different languages. If I'm speaking to a Christian fundamentalist woman in a monogamous relationship whose been married for 20 years and has three kids, I know how to talk to her. There are parallels from my existence that mesh with hers quite nicely. We can talk about teenagers. We can talk about driving permits. We have common ground.

If I'm talking to a gay couple we can talk about how the relationship's going, and how difficult it is to be in a nontraditional relationship, existing in this legal climate, and do they have power of attorney for each other? Do they have advance directives? We see heterosexual, bisexual, gay, and celibate all as viable choices. People need to be accepted for who they are. I find it easy to relate to most anyone.

**K:** Are you different in how you relate to a man and to a woman?

**C:** The thing that flew into my mind when you asked that is that men are easy, and women are hard. Turning on men is easy. It's straight-forward. It's plumbing. It works. Turning on women you have to know more about what they like, and what they don't like. It takes longer. It's fun both ways.

I'm different in how I relate to Michelle and to Doug, but I think that has more to do with their personalities, because I relate to Michelle differently than I relate to other women, and I relate differently to Doug than I relate to other men.

**K:** In terms of how comfortable you feel about your body, is it different with men and with women?

**C:** I think so. I think with men I try to present my most svelte self. I feel like I have to hold my stomach in. With women I'm not sure that the body image isn't equally important, but there's more reality there. A typical male perception of a female body is comparing it to the model of the week. With a woman it's not a model that you're compared to. It's more like this is my body, and this is your body. It's the bodies of the real women themselves that your body is compared to, not a fantasy that you'll never measure up to.

**K:** Are you a feminist?

**C:** Yes.

**K:** What does it mean to you to be a feminist?

**C:** That brains are equal. That if I can add two plus two I should get paid the same as someone else who can add two plus two. I think that raising children should be equal opportunity employment for males and females. I think it should be more highly valued than it currently is. I think women should have the right to do with their bodies whatever they want just as men have the right to do whatever they want with their bodies. I don't think women should be subservient to men or the other way around. Respect doesn't see sex as a barrier.

**K:** Do you feel that bisexuality and your situation being in a group marriage has political implications?

**C:** I think that it has political implications and that it has economic implications. People living in larger groups within single households only have need for one refrigerator. If we were living separate lives we would have two of everything. Anytime you get into economics you're making a political statement. The pooling of incomes, the sharing of resources, the sharing of assets is threatening to those folks that believe in an ever-expanding economy.

Group families tend to think more about stewardship of the land and resources. We do. I feel that in group marriages a higher value is placed on relationship than on things. You realize that there are important needs of the family that can be better met if there are more than one or two adults in the family.

**K:** Do you feel that you have a contribution to make to the world as a bisexual woman in a polyfidelitous relationship?

**C:** My main contribution is how I live my life; my example. I try to live the best way I can. What I will leave in terms of a legacy is how I live my life.

I don't really feel much pressure to go out and proselytize for the polyfidelitous lifestyle at this point, but at the same time it takes speaking up about it to have other people know that this is happening. People tend to think that relationships like this went out in the '60s. That it's part of the hippie movement, or it's part of New Age ideas. It's really just part of life, and it probably has always been a part of life. It's been called a lot of different things. There have been lots of extended and expanded families of various sorts throughout history.

# 16 ▼ PAMELA

*Pamela Willard is a 33-year-old massage therapist and libertarian activist who lives in San Francisco.*

**K:** Tell me about your ethnic background, and where you grew up.

**P:** My ethnic origins are English-German-Irish. I grew up in a lower middle-class, mainly white, predominantly Mormon (excluding ourselves) small city in Arizona with both parents working two jobs to make ends meet.

**K:** When were you first aware of sexual attractions, and to which gender?

**P:** My first sexual attractions were probably at around 10 or 11, and they were to girls. That went on all the way through high school, but I just didn't know how to deal with them. So I squashed them. Also, it was obvious that my younger brother was gay from a very early age, and that was always a problem in my family. So I didn't feel like I had a choice at that point.

**K:** Did you act on the attractions?

**P:** I did. Mostly when I was a teenager, with my girlfriends. There was a little group of us that hung out together. It just seemed right at the time. After a couple of times I think it freaked everybody out, and we stopped. It didn't stop my attractions.

**K:** What did you do with your girlfriends?

**P:** We were kissing and feeling and touching. I don't remember orgasms or anything like that, but we were exploring. It was passionate for teenagers.

There were a lot of situations during those teenage and young adult years where I'd run into women that I was attracted to or maybe they were attracted to me, and I would just freak out about it. I would go with my brother to gay bars and have fun. I really wanted to be there, but then I wouldn't let myself actually be attracted to or find a lovemate. To this day I have not sexually acted out with any women since my teenage years.

**K:** When did you start being sexually active with men?

**P:** When I was 19. I feel like now I only did it because it was the thing to do. I was at a place in my life where my sexual feelings almost had to be acted on. There was a lot of it I really never enjoyed. It was the only way I knew how to relate to people, and so I began relating to men mostly through sex.

I felt at that point that my worth was only in what I could give to other people. When I began relating to men my self-worth was mostly wrapped up in how I could please them, or how much they enjoyed being with me. I was fairly successful at it. I did go out with a lot of men, because it made me feel like I was a good person.

I would probably change that today. A tremendous amount of what I did then was abusive to myself. If I had been able to feel comfortable with myself I probably would have been more particular, and would not have dated as many men as I did. And I would have sought out women too instead of just seeking men.

**K:** What is your current situation?

**P:** I'm been married to my husband for almost five years. It has been a monogamous relationship, although he's very supportive of my coming out about being bisexual. We've talked at great length about it and what it means. He understands that at some point I might feel it's necessary to validate that part of myself and explore a relationship with another woman. In our marriage I feel we're strong enough and we love each other enough that it would be possible to have a relationship with a woman as long as I'm honest about it, and he's aware of it, and the other person's aware of my marriage.

At this point I'm not ready to say to my husband, "I've got this new side to me, so I'm just going to dump you." That's part of what makes it difficult. It would be different if I discovered this before I made a commitment like this. But I do have a commitment and I want to honor that, though I also want to honor this new part of myself.

**K:** What do you think would be different if you had known you were bisexual before you got married?

**P:** I may not have gotten married. I might be with a woman now, instead. I don't know. It's something I can't know. Until I've been in a relationship with another woman there's a part of me that feels like it's missing. If I had dated both men and women before I got married, perhaps I would have chosen to be with a woman and would not have gotten into a traditional marriage.

**K:** How did you come to acknowledge your bisexuality?

**P:** Through my relationship with my husband. It's the healthiest relationship I've ever been in in my life. He is a very open-minded individual, has lived in San Francisco for many years, and has no judgments against anyone. Looking back I think that he knew maybe even when he first met me. We have lots of friends who are lesbian couples. I realized that it was safe to talk to him about how I was feeling. Gradually it became part of our conversation.

Once I knew he was okay about it, I had to get okay about it. Is this just something I'm talking about or is this really going on? That process took a couple of years in which I had all these conversations with myself. All these years feeling attractions and then suddenly realizing that maybe this is real. Maybe this is not that you're crazy or you're sick or you're perverted. Maybe this is who you are.

Finally one day I just said to my husband, "I think I'm bisexual. How do you feel about that?" And he said, "Yes, of course you are." Ever since then it has been a lot easier for me to be able to say, "I'm bisexual and that's okay."

The last year and a half or so has been spent integrating my bisexuality into my body, my therapy, and everything else I'm doing. To me it's important to do something about being bisexual. It may be just talking to other people about it. Now that it is part of who I am, I don't want to keep that part in the closet all the time. I'm not sure where I'll end up going with this politically. It still feels very unacceptable.

**K:** And how is that for you?

**P:** It's really difficult for me. I feel the only person I can safely talk about my bisexuality with is my husband. I finally have been telling people, but for me it's been a challenge of who to tell, when to tell, whether to tell.

There are certain people that I do want to feel free to say, "I went to this bi women's group. Or I read this book about bisexuals." I want to be able to talk about what is really going on with me. Those people I'm telling. So far I've been surprised by the positive reception I've gotten.

Right now I feel really nervous about talking about being bisexual to lesbians. I don't like to be judged. This is a particularly vulnerable area for me to be judged on. It makes it difficult, because I have this need to relate to women right now. You go to some lesbian event, and it seems safe and there's lots of women there all together. There's this part of me that wants to go, "I'm like you!" But I don't feel that they think I'm like them.

Also, with most men I don't feel safe talking about it. I have some gay male friends who have been the most supportive. Straight men just seem to have this big lesbian fantasy thing going on.

I haven't been really good about talking to my mother. My father is dead. Maybe if I was actually in a relationship with another woman then I'd want to break it to her, so she could learn to live with it. At this point it's one more thing she's going to freak out about. I've got my gay brother that she still really hasn't dealt with. Why bring more havoc into my life?

**K:** Have you come out to your brother?

**P:** Yes, I have talked to him. There's a strain of male homosexuals who think that female homosexuals are the most disgusting thing on the planet, and he was one of them. Many years ago I put out feelers about where I was at to see how he would accept it. He made some comment like, "Pamela, don't even talk like that. I can't believe you'd want to be with another woman. That's so gross."

I was real nervous about talking to him again, but he and I have always been close. We are the only siblings in our family. So about a year and a half ago I told him, and he was completely different about it. He was totally supportive. He's been really great about it. I'm shocked about it, but pleasantly. As far as the rest of my family goes, my cousins and my grandparents are from the hills of Pennsylvania, and are just starting to figure out that my brother's gay. I'm not close enough to them that it's ever going to come up.

**K:** Did you go through an identity crisis in coming to a place of being comfortable with being bisexual?

**P:** Yes. I went through phases of thinking maybe I'm not bisexual, maybe I'm lesbian. Maybe I'm just a heterosexual with a lot of fantasies. What the hell am I? I didn't know how to identify myself. I thought, "Do I really want to be a bisexual? Do I have a choice?" I don't really have a choice. It's just a matter of how much of it I can accept, and how out I want to be about it.

**K:** What helped you become comfortable with your bisexual identity?

**P:** I think what helped me most was when I actually told people. I had felt like there wasn't anybody I could really talk to about it, or that would understand it. I felt like the only one out there, and I knew that wasn't true.

I found this bi women's group. That really helped. To be around other women and to be accepted, even though none of us knew each other. So even though I'm not actively trying to meet other women for relationships, ever since I joined that group it feels okay. It was a really scary thing for me to go to that first meeting.

**K:** How did you get up the courage?

**P:** It became imperative to the point of this is who you are, and what are you going to do? Stay in your living room and wonder about this the rest of your life? It took me about a month before I actually called the phone number and talked to the woman who leads the group. After the first meeting I felt confident that it was a really healthy thing for me to do.

**K:** If you could have your ideal situation in terms of relationships, what would it be?

**P:** My ideal situation would be to have two relationships. I don't know if that's possible. I'm truly in love with my husband. I don't feel like I should have to give up a love relationship like this with a male just so that I could explore a relationship with a female.

My hope is that at some point I will meet a woman who is willing to have a relationship with me, but would be accepting of the fact that I still have a love relationship with my husband. My fantasy is to be able to maintain two relationships where we all know each other, but not all having sex with each other. They would be separate relationships.

**K:** I assume you've worked out something with your husband around the potential for nonmonogamy in your relationship. Is that correct?

**P:** Yes, we've talked about it and he understands that this is a desire that I have, and he's cool about that. The criteria being that I be honest. He says, "As long as you tell me." It's not like I'm out having one night stands all over town. I wouldn't want that, and I wouldn't want that from him either. It's mutual respect; if I meet someone I'm interested in exploring a relationship with I'll tell him.

I have to also be prepared for the fact that it may not actually work the way I want it to when it comes down to it. At this point I can't worry about that yet. It's in the future still. It took me a while to just get that somebody could care about me enough to let me be who I am. That's really amazing. I'd like to see it work out so that all three parties would be mutually respectful of each other and that we all get what we need out of it.

**K:** Do you have any agreements or have you talked with your husband about safe sex? Are you worried about sexually transmitted diseases?

**P:** That's something we haven't really talked about, but in my mind it wouldn't be appropriate to have a sexual relationship with anybody else without making it as safe as possible. The last thing I'd want to do is bring home a sexually transmitted disease to my husband. That would be awful.

**K:** How do you relate to the straight community as a bisexual woman?

**P:** At this point I'm not relating to the straight world as a bisexual woman. With most of the jobs that I've had, I just think it would create more problems than it solved to be open. There are so many misconceptions and negative connotations about what it means to be bisexual that the average corporate American couldn't deal with it.

I have problems deciding in massage what to do with being open about my sexuality. It's one thing in corporate America, but massage is a very intimate thing. I go on my intuition whether it is important for someone to know or not. In some cases it would make people feel more comfortable with me, and in some cases it might make people feel less comfortable. I make it very clear that this is nonsexual massage.

**K:** Do you have anything more to say about how you as a bisexual woman relate to the lesbian community and to lesbians?

**P:** I really love women. It was repression that made me avoid women most of my life. I felt like I could only express myself with men. Now I want to be around women.

I've always had many gay friends since I lived in San Francisco. It's the most comfortable place I've ever lived as far as acceptance of gay people goes. When I first got here, I would walk down the street and cry. I would go into a restaurant and I would get tears in my eyes, because I thought it was so great. Two women could kiss over here, or two men could hold hands over there. It was so liberating, so wonderful. It's always been a big part of my San Francisco experience to be around that.

I never really got into the lesbian community, because I knew there was a part of me that always felt like I'd be rejected for some reason. So I've been treading lightly into it here and there, and I just love it.

I feel really drawn to the lesbian community, but then once I'm there I feel like a fraud. I feel like I can't let them know where I'm really at. It creates a lot of discomfort for me, and I don't know how to deal with that. I love being part of groups of women. Women together tend to be a lot more loving than men together. I'm drawn to the lesbian community, and then once I'm there I feel like I better just keep my mouth shut.

**K:** And why had you better keep your mouth shut?

**P:** A lesbian that I talked to put all these ideas in my head, like that lesbians hate bisexuals, and they don't want you in their space. You want to be with women, but you also want to be with those patriarchal men, and try to have the best of both worlds, including traditional marriage and acceptance in this society.

So I've been to a couple of events where I'm in this group of lesbian couples, and I'm terrified that if they knew that I was bisexual they'd all turn on me. I've also heard bisexual women say that they've had totally accepting, wonderful experiences in the lesbian community, but for me right now that's hard to imagine.

**K:** How have your experiences with gay men been for you as a bisexual woman?

**P:** So far I've had total acceptance from the gay males that I have told. I have not had any of them be against me or make any negative comments.

**K:** Do you think you have a contribution to make to the world as a bisexual woman?

**P:** I'd like to think so. There's a part of me that really wants to keep raising consciousness about sexuality. I've been fortunate in my life to have been involved with fringe movements where people tend to accept me as a person. I've always loved that.

Except people would always talk to me about what they were into, and then they'd make some derogatory remark about gays. So I'd say, "You know my brother is gay." I like that aspect of being different, and people not being able to tell.

I think it's almost required for me if I'm going to be bisexual that I don't hide about it, and that I eventually do something to further the consciousness of the world to accept it. It was really crucial for me to hear other bisexual women. That's really what did it for me. Just one meeting with bisexual women and I knew that I was in the right place. If there's anybody else out there whose suffering through the same tortures I went through, then my experience can help them.

**Postscript:** Pamela now identifies as a lesbian and is very happily involved in a long-term lesbian relationship. She feels this interview accurately describes the process through which she got there.

# 17 ▼ Revi

*Revi is a 21-year-old white student and women's health worker active in the queer women's community, who lives in San Francisco. Her mother is a lesbian.*

**K:** When were you first aware of sexual attractions and to which gender?

**R:** I cannot remember not being aware of sexuality. I can remember when I was about eight being totally crushed out on a girl who was maybe 14 or 15. As a teenager I only slept with boys, but I always called myself bi, and I always knew that I had crushes on women. I had a romantic friendship with a woman all through high school; we wrote each other love letters.

**K:** What was it like identifying as bisexual in high school?

**R:** I lived in this little hippie-dippie, theater town in Oregon. I hung out with a distinctive group of people in high school. We were called the drama fags. We were all the weirdos, and all the kids of the weirdos in town; the kids of the theater people, artists, craftspeople and the hippies. Two of my best friends were two women who were together for six years all through high school, and everybody knew. None of us cared. So even though most of the people I hung out with would have identified as heterosexual, had they been asked, it was fine for me to say that I was bi. Nobody cared.

**K:** Tell me about your family situation. Were you open to your family about being bisexual?

**R:** Yes and no. I lived with both of my parents until I was nine, when my mother left my father and got a woman lover. I lived with my father until I was 12. Then I lived with my mother and her woman lover in Tucson for a year. Then my mother and I moved to Oregon, where she met another woman, who lived with us most of the time that I was in high school. I was very close with this lover. I've been close with most of my mother's women lovers.

When I was in high school and calling myself bi, I was living with my mother and her lover and often going with them to women's land in Oregon, and to women's gatherings. But I had a very difficult relationship with my mother, despite all of this great lesbian energy.

**K:** How did she feel about your being involved with boys?

**R:** She was not happy about it. She was a lesbian separatist at that point. I think she might still identify that way. She was a pretty heavy duty separatist, at least as much as she could be living in town and working a straight job. She never told me not to go out with boys. She was always very nice to my boyfriends, but I couldn't talk to her about any problems I was having with them, because she would just say, "It's because he's a boy. Try girls."

**K:** What about with your father? How did he feel about your bisexuality?

**R:** He was out of the picture for that period of time, because he was out of the country. He came back when I was 18. I don't know if I ever officially came out to him. I don't like to do a big coming-out thing to anybody. I usually just talk about my man lover and my woman lover. But when he came back, I was coming out as a lesbian. So I think that I probably did come out to him, because there was a period when I said to a lot of people, "I am a lesbian. I'm letting you know, because you're important to me."

**K:** Why did you identify as a lesbian at that time?

**R:** I would talk about being bi with people in high school, but it wasn't a real thing for me. I had crushes on women, but I didn't really do anything about it or want to do anything about it. So when I came out as a lesbian, it was much more like I was coming out from being straight.

From the time that I started being sexual with men when I was 15 until I came out as a lesbian when I was 18, I had been on a downward spiral. Each man I would sleep with would be more disgusting and treat me worse and be more of an alcoholic or drug addict. The last one was the final straw. It was a really bad scene. It brought me to my senses. I decided then that I wasn't going to be with anybody, male or female, until I could take care of myself. So I was celibate for a year, and that was the year I came out. I came out as a lesbian in reaction to how badly I had been treated by men, and how badly I'd self-abused myself in relationships with men.

I also came out because I was getting active in the women's community as a feminist; I wanted to belong, and that was the way to belong. I was in Boston then. When I was there, if you were a lesbian you had very short hair, and you wore certain clothes. I used to go out with my girlfriend who had really long hair, and I had really long hair, and we both wore hippie-chick dresses. We used to go to girls' bars in Boston and make out passionately on the dance floor, and we would be ignored by lesbians. We were straight to them. It was 1989 and '90. We both had a lot of anger about that.

When I got into sexuality discussions with people, I would always say, "I identify as a lesbian, because my allegiance is with women. I love women. I want to be with women. I'm part of the lesbian community, but that doesn't mean that I don't feel a sexual attraction to men. What it means is that I'm choosing not to act on the attraction to men, because it doesn't seem to me to be worth it; the men that I've been with have not been worth my time."

**K:** And did you get involved with a woman?

**R:** Yes. We were best friends. She and I were both just coming out. We had a very intense relationship, and it got sexual. But she was in a phase of not being able to be sexual with people who she loved and felt intense about. She was fucking everybody in sight, but couldn't deal with being sexual with me, because she loved me. So we would make out in corners and on the dance floor, and pretend it wasn't happening. As far as actually getting down to sex, I wasn't getting that much. But we were identified as a couple.

**K:** What happened then that caused you to identify again as bisexual?

**R:** I started sleeping with a man. That's the easiest way to put it. I met this man, Jordan, at work. He was one of those few men where I've felt, "I'm really attracted to this person, and that's fine, but I'm not going to do anything about it."

He ended up spending the night with me one night when he needed a place to crash, and we ended up being sexual. I was very passive about the whole thing. I gave him his choice of where he wanted to sleep. He wanted to sleep in my bed. I was thinking, "We'll see if anything happens. Just take it step by step and moment by moment, and if anything doesn't feel okay, I'll be able to say that."

But what actually happened was that I freaked out about it, and I was thinking and saying, "Do you know that I'm a lesbian? What are you doing in my lesbian bed with all your clothes off?" I had a minor stress episode. But in the end we had really nice sex, with a nice connection and a very nice talk. I started liking him lots.

The next couple of weeks after this I was saying to myself, "Okay, I fucked a man. I don't think I'm going to do it again. I can do it once and still be a lesbian. It's not such a big deal, right? I don't have to do it again."

So that's what I told him the next time he asked to spend the night with me; but it wasn't over between us. We have ended up sleeping together regularly and being lovers. I love him.

It was very intense for me at that time, because I couldn't do a denial thing about it where I was still calling myself a lesbian but having a male lover. So I came out as bi, which was terrifying.

K: Tell me about that. Who did you come out to?

R: Everybody in the whole world.  Most of the people who work at the job where I met him were dykes; I got hired as a dyke. It was a lesbian environment. It was the hardest place to have to come out as bi. I did it in a round-about way. When I was in a situation with one co-worker, I'd casually ask her how long it'd been since she'd slept with a man and see what she said. Then I'd say, "Well, I've been sleeping with a man lately."

K: What were the reactions?

R: The individual reactions that I get from lesbians when I come out to them as bi are mostly positive. It's the overall community reaction that's generally very negative.

One friend of mine didn't have a problem with my sleeping with a man, or my coming out as bi, but she did not like it that I still wanted to be accepted in the lesbian community. She said, "Nonmonogamy is fine with me; that's what I'm used to. But I wouldn't sleep with a woman who had a male lover."

**K:** What was it like to come out to your mother?

**R:** The last person that I came out to was my mother. She was the most scary one for me to come out to. I did it by letter, and I had no idea how she was going to react. I wrote in this letter, "I'm very scared to come out to you, because the people that I get the worst reactions from are lesbians, particularly older lesbians who identify as separatists. I just want you to know that I'm freaked out about this, and I don't want you to give me any bullshit about bisexuality."

She wrote me back and basically said, "I'm glad that you are who you are." She said that she felt that being bi was a very liberated thing to be, and that it made her feel great, because it made her feel like she'd done a good job raising me. She also was defensive about my feelings about lesbian reactions. She said, "Yes, it's wrong for lesbians to jump on bisexual women, but this is why they do it"—of course listing all the reasons that I'd heard a million times.

**K:** What are those reasons?

**R:** That lesbians feel like bisexual women are really dykes who are just afraid to fully embrace their sexuality and be out, or who are hiding behind a man, or who are untrustworthy and are going to leave them for a man. Being untrustworthy is a big one. The separatist line about bisexual women is, "We want the lesbian community to be a community that only supports lesbians, because we don't want to give any energy to men; and we feel like giving energy to women who sleep with men is giving energy to men."

**K:** Tell me about your current situation.

**R:** My current situation is very complicated. First of all I am totally and completely in love, which is so great. The only problem is that she lives 5,000 miles away in London. I met Naomi two months ago when she was here. Although she's far away we have lots of plans, and hopefully some of them will happen. We're committed to each other in a nonmonogamous way.

**K:** Is she bisexual or lesbian?

**R:** She is a lesbian, but has slept with lots of men and is very "out" about having slept with lots of men. She feels there's a potential for her to do it again. I think that if she lived in San Francisco she might identify as bi. As biphobic as I still feel the lesbian community in San Francisco is, it's more acceptable to be bi here than in other queer women's communities. When I was in Boston it was not okay. When I was in the women's community up in Oregon it was not okay, and nobody came out as bi. Here women that I know and hang out with identify as bi.

**K:** How does Naomi feel about you being bisexual?

**R:** She has no problem with it at all. She thinks it's great. One of the best things about the connection that we made was that it was incredibly open. We talked about everything. She slept with five women while she was here. She told me about all of those experiences in graphic detail. I helped her scheme how she was going to get one woman into bed, and I talked to her about my relationships and my relationship with Jordan. That's how we were with each other, and that's very much how I hope that we will continue to be.

I was with Jordan only until this summer, though not by my design. I recently discovered that he was under the impression that we were having a monogamous relationship. I can't imagine why he was thinking that, since I have always said that I was nonmonogamous; he knew that I was looking for a woman lover.

**K:** Did he mean that you wouldn't sleep with any other men?

**R:** I don't think so. I think that he meant that we were committed to each other and to not being lovers with other people. But I was only with him exclusively for this past year because I didn't have much time or energy for other relationships, and also because I didn't find anybody that I wanted to sleep with.

**K:** Is this new, major relationship of yours with a woman hard for him?

**R:** I met Naomi while he was away for five weeks. He left me this witty little goodbye note before he left, and one of the things that he said was that I was required to have at least one affair while he was gone. I quite took him at his word, and had three—one of which isn't an affair, but something much more serious than that.

He came back a week before Naomi was leaving. I didn't know what to do, because I love him and treasure him, and I knew that I wanted to keep being with him. I wasn't sure that I wanted to still be lovers with him, because on the sexual level it's been much more intense and passionate for me with Naomi. I was on this total high. I didn't know if I could be involved with somebody else at that time, because she was going back to London in a week, and I knew that I wasn't going to see her for about six months.

He'd been traveling, and we hadn't been in touch very much. I would have written him had I been able to, but I wasn't. He called me the instant he got back into town, which I knew he would, and I had to say, "I can't see you right now, because I'm with this other person who is leaving in a week, and I want to be with her all the time."

I did see him, of course. I saw him for one evening the day after he got back, and then I didn't see him again until after Naomi left. He flipped; it was a big shock. He'd been with another woman lover of his, and it had been a bad scene in a lot of ways. So he'd been doing lots of fantasizing about me, and then he came home to me saying, "I'm in love with somebody else, and I can't see you for a week." So it was heavy.

That was two months ago, and we're dealing with the transition. He backed out of my life for a while, because he was hurt and processing all of it. I really missed him a lot. His backing away from me made me realize how much I love him. It's been great to have him back in my life. We've been back hanging out with each other for a couple of weeks.

Then there's another woman who I also had an affair with while Jordan was gone. I don't know what we're doing. She's having a hard time in her life, and a lot of it has to do with sex. She's very much a butch dyke, and very much a lesbian, and she always sleeps with bi girls, because she likes really femme women, and a lot of really femme women turn out to be bi. I completely have the hots for her, and I'm just dying to go to bed with her every time I see her.

But what she's saying to me right now is, "I like you so much. You're so great. I love hanging out with you. I think you're so sexy. I really want to sleep with you, but I can't be sexual with anybody right now." So I'm hanging out with her and seeing what's going to happen.

**K:** If you could have your ideal situation in terms of relationships, what would it be?

**R:** I would like to have a committed relationship with one woman, because what I have with women so far has been much more intense and passionate and deep and moving than what I've had with men. I would be really interested in having a committed primary relationship with more than one person. I don't feel that I would be able to have two entirely separate, committed primary relationships with two different people who lived in different places. We would all need to live together, and everybody love each other, though they wouldn't necessarily need to be lovers. I would like us to be nonmonogamous, and be able to have hot affairs. I would like to have kids in a situation like that.

Then there's this other part of me that feels that being with Naomi was so incredible that I almost feel I could be monogamous with her, which is a foreign concept to me. I haven't understood monogamy at all until this point, other than in a very negative sense of an ownership thing, or that love is finite. If we live together that might happen, simply because we have such an intense thing going that I'm not sure either one of us would have the time or energy to be with other people.

And I love men, which is really scary, because I don't like men. As a group, as a whole, as a stereotype, I cannot stand men. I find them offensive and unattractive and, because of their genitalia and all that goes with it, unable to have a similar focus in life to mine.

I'm a woman's health major in school. What I want to do in my life is work as a healer on the level of connecting spirit with body. I'm very much focused on women's bodies and women's sexuality. I could talk to Jordan for hours about what I want to do around women's bodies and spirituality, and he would listen, and be very aware and give me great feedback, but fundamentally he couldn't understand it, because he's not a woman.

**K:** And what do you love about men?

**R:** I meet certain individual men whom I love, and I love hanging out with them. Most of them are queer. I love to see men being gentle. I love to see men being with kids. It really moves me. I have certain men in my life who are some of the dearest people in the whole world to me, and I treasure them. That's what I mean when I say that I love men.

**K:** Do you identify as either butch or femme?

**R:** I identify as femme. The more I let myself be a femme and know that I'm a feminist, and that it's okay to be a femme and a feminist, the happier and more femmy I get.

It's infinitely more acceptable here in San Francisco for me to be who I am and look the way that I do, and also be a very "out" dyke, than in other queer communities I have been in. At least among the groups of women that I hang out with here, it's fine. It's still different. It's still not necessarily the norm, but it's okay. I don't walk into a girls' bar here and feel that people look at me like I'm a straight woman, and what am I doing there? I feel that women respond to me as a femme dyke. That's good.

Feminism is just about women reclaiming who we really are, isn't it? That's what it's about for me. We can argue until kingdom come about whether society has socialized me to be as femmy as I am. Fundamentally, this is how I'm happy. The more femmy I get, the happier I get, and the more I feel like I'm being me. For me that's what feminism is about—everybody having the freedom to be who they are.

**K:** Do you practice safe sex?

**R:** That is constantly under negotiation. I work in health care. One of the things that I do is HIV counseling. I consider myself fairly well informed. I am ambivalent about safe sex between women; that's a hard one.

**K:** Do you practice safe sex with men?

**R:** Yes, I don't do penises without condoms for vaginal intercourse, and I think I'm getting to the point now that it'll be for oral sex, also.

The fact is that safe sex is an anomaly; it doesn't exist. Safer sex exists, but it's all on a continuum, and it's where you and your partner or partners decide you feel comfortable being on that continuum of risk. In my past I have been very unsafe and have been tested a lot. So far, always negative. It was a self- destructive thing for me to be having unsafe sex at the level that I was having it.

One of the things that Naomi did with me was to say to me, "This is not okay. You're not treating yourself right. You're putting yourself at a danger level that is not okay with me, because I love you."

She felt that if I continued to have sex at the risk level that I was having it at that time, I would become HIV positive. So we negotiated on what we decided was an acceptable level of risk. Then we made a mutual vow. I vowed that I was not going to put myself beyond that level of risk, and she's going to quit smoking.

**K:** What did you decide would be your safer sex practices?

**R:** Condoms on penises. If hands go into vaginas, check for cuts. If there are any visible cuts, use gloves. If there is any menstrual blood, use gloves.

**K:** What about oral sex?

**R:** If there are any cuts in the mouth, or if she's bleeding at all or close to bleeding, then use some kind of barrier. But neither Naomi nor I can stand dental dams. I have not eaten a woman with latex between me and her; the idea makes me very sad. Saran wrap is better for oral sex, but I want to be able to taste her. I feel like if I don't get to taste her, then I don't want to do it.

**K:** Will you and Naomi be doing this level of safer sex with each other?

**R:** While she was here we did, and since we're not living together now we will be doing safer sex when we see each other. I think that when we start living together, we'll both get tested. Presuming that we both are HIV negative, then we will not use latex with each other, but will do so with any other lovers that we have.

**K:** How are you different in a relationship with a woman than a man?

**R:** I always want to say that I'm not different, but I am. One thing that's definitely different is that when I'm with women we do a lot of role playing, because I tend to like butch girls. I don't do that with men. I can't imagine doing it with men; it would be too weird.

I treat my women lovers better than I treat my men lovers. I have a lot of anger against men. I think that every woman in her right mind has a lot of anger against men.

With Jordan, whom I'm very comfortable with and I trust, it's easy for me to use him as a whipping post for men in the universal sense of the word. I have done that, definitely, and we've talked about it. I feel that using him that way is not the best thing in the world for me to be doing, but at the same time I think that it's really under-standable. I think that men who want to be with strong, feminist women should get used to it.

I like the complexity of being with a woman. I like women's bodies. Biologically, men aren't as complex as women, and it's just not nearly as interesting as far as I'm concerned. Being with women is much more intense and much more in depth, much more complex and much more demanding.

It's still groundbreaking for a woman to be in a loving sexual relationship with a woman. We are inventing a new kind of relation-ship as we go along. It takes a lot more concentration. For me, the connection has been on so many more levels with women, and I don't see that changing. The more connections that you have, the more demanding the relationship is, and for me it then becomes a much more fulfilling relationship.

**K:** How is it for you dealing with the lesbian community as a bisexual woman?

**R:** The community as a whole has not accepted bi women yet. I think because of fear regarding their own sexuality. It's like straight people who hate dykes and gay men. We in the queer community see that as the fear that they'll find that potentially gay facet inside of themselves. I think a lot of lesbians are afraid they'll find bisexuality inside of themselves.

If you come out as bi, you're not coming out into a niche. You're coming out into a big, watery, nebulous mass where it may very well be that there is no one social group or even social situation where you feel entirely accepted and comfortable. If you're a lesbian and you live somewhere where there's a large and vocal lesbian community, you can probably find a social situation where you feel comfortable. The only place that I can find that feeling with is with other bi women. Even then, sometimes it needs to be more specific than that, because it's often hard for me to be with very straight-identified women who are bi.

**K:** How is it for you dealing with the straight world?

**R:** I don't hang out with very many straight people at all, because they're not that interesting to me. I am very "out." What that means to me is that I never switch pronouns when I talk about my lovers. So in the lesbian community I do not say "she" if I mean "he." And I do not say "he" if I mean "she" in the straight community. Anybody who asks me what my sexuality is will immediately be told. Anybody who talks to me for any length of time about my personal life is going to find out about my sexuality, and what community I identify with, because it's not any kind of real relationship unless I'm "out."

**K:** How is it for you relating to gay men as a bisexual woman?

**R:** I do fine with gay men. Gay men are very insulated in their gay male community, and because I'm a woman it doesn't matter that I'm bi. They can identify with me, because I'm very queer-identified, and queens like me, because I'm a queen, too, even though I happen to be a biological girl. So it's not an issue. I don't have many gay male friends, though. I wish that I had more, but there's a limit on time and energy in terms of who I relate to right now.

**K:** How is it for you in the bi community?

**R:** Most of my friends are bi women, but they're bi women who really identify with the dyke community.

**K:** How is it for you being around other bi women who relate to the dyke community?

**R:** I love them. They're the most meaningful people in my life. They're my grounding. They're the women that I can sit around with and talk about everything, and it's okay for me to be me. That's the bottom line.

To a large extent I also feel fine with dykes who accept bi women. All of my housemates identify as lesbians; I love them all, and they all love me.

In fact, I have internalized biphobia to the point where I was squeamish about having Jordan over to my house. Even though I moved in with them as a dyke-identified bi woman and told them, "I have a male lover. He comes over. This needs to be okay. If it is not going to be okay with somebody to have a man in this house, then you need to tell me, and I won't move in." Nobody objected. But I used to feel weird about his being there, even though he isn't there much.

All my housemates just laughed at me about this, and said, "Honey, we love Jordan. We're so glad he's here. It's fine." So, I feel great with them, and the fact that they only sleep with women is incidental. We're all queer women.

**K:** Give me a definition of queer women.

**R:** Queer women identify primarily with women, make women the center of their universe and work for women's rights and liberation. I identify as queer. Meaning not like other people, not mainstream or conventional. Also meaning that I sleep with people of my own gender, and I identify with other people, male or female, who are not bound to heterosexuality.

Labels are really important. The only people that I've met who feel fine being unlabeled on a sexual identity level are heterosexual people. If you're not heterosexual, labels become very useful, because you need to know who stands with you, and you need to have a community that you identify with. I need to have a community that I identify with, and it's important to me that there are other people who identify as part of that community.

**K:** Do you think that bisexuality has political implications?

**R:** Yes, I think it's very political; I think it's about being free. I think that in a free world most of us would be bi. Of course there will always be people who only relate to the opposite gender on the sexual level, or to the same gender on a sexual level, and that's fine. I do think, though, that bisexuality is about freedom, and freedom is a very political concept.

**K:** In what way would you say that bisexual people are free that people who are either gay or straight aren't?

**R:** You're free, because you're accepting your sexuality even though it's the most closeted and shitted-upon sexuality that still exists. To have the courage to be bi helps to move the world a step forward out of dichotomies. Bisexuality is anti-dichotomous. It accepts the complexity of reality; it's not black and white, and neither is anything else. I changed so much when I came out bi.

**K:** How did you change?

**R:** I stopped being able to say some of the things that I used to say. I used to make categorical generalizations about men or women. I stopped being able to do that, because it felt wrong to me.

I became uncomfortable in many of the situations that I had been completely comfortable in before. I became uncomfortable with conversations that I would have joined in with and thought nothing of six months ago—that all men are like this, and all women are like that, and straight people are like this.

All of my former categorizing and stereotyping and judging of people who are different from me became more difficult. I have become much less inclined to categorize people.

# 18 ▼ Diana

*Diana is a 30-year-old research scientist who lives in San Francisco. Her family background is white Southern working class. She began this interview by talking about her coming-out experience.*

**D:** There are a lot of lesbian pulp novels out that tell a woman's coming-out story, and in those novels the coming out always goes hand in hand with being in an actual relationship with a woman. So the characters in the story don't think of themselves as lesbian until they're involved with someone. But my experience has been first discovering and acknowledging that I had feelings for women, then dealing with my internalized homophobia, and finally getting to a point of pride and becoming active in the queer community before I ever had sex with a woman. At that point I was ready to have relationships with women, and basically sex was the same as with men, and relationships were not so different.

**K:** Tell me about this process.

**D:** For a long time I thought that my feelings for women weren't real. I just assumed that everyone had sexual fantasies about women, and it probably was the result of women being so sexually objectified in our culture. The fact that I had fantasies about women certainly didn't mean I was gay. I had a lot of fear and doubt and shame about actually applying that label to myself. I would have to identify as "queer"—that horrible thing that people had called me all through junior high school. So I squelched the feelings, and they went underground for awhile.

They started to come out again when I realized there was a woman I was in love with. She led me on without ever following through, because she just wasn't ready to come out herself. But in talking to her about how I felt, all the shame and internalized homophobia came up. I said, "I feel like I'm dirty and disgusting for having these lesbian feelings for you, and that there's something really wrong with me."

She was great, because she said, "You're not disgusting, and just because we're not involved right now doesn't mean that those feelings aren't real and that they're not special." So even though she wasn't ready to reciprocate my feelings, she helped wipe away the shame.

It was a couple of years later, while I was in a very serious relationship with a man, that I began to say, "I am bisexual. These feelings for women are real. This is not going to go away." At that point I began to tell friends of mine. That was the beginning of my coming out.

K: How was it for you to tell people?

D: It felt good. I've never run into any bad reaction from people that I've told.

My first coming-out experience to people I wasn't close to was when I was living in a group house and one of my housemates made a homophobic joke. A few days later we were having a house meeting, and I mentioned the joke and said, "I'm bisexual; that offended me, and I would appreciate it if, at least when I'm around, people in this household wouldn't make homophobic jokes." The man who made the joke was really very sorry, and it never happened again. They were all very supportive. One of my housemates years later said to me, "That was a real courageous thing to do. I always admired you for doing that."

K: How did your male partner feel about your being bisexual?

D: He felt threatened by it, because he assumed it meant that I wanted to be unfaithful to him. At the same time he was envious, because it was part of his ideology that one should be open enough that gender shouldn't make a difference; he wished that he could be that open, but in fact he simply wasn't bisexual, and obviously his orientation is not something he has control over. So he had mixed reactions.

After the relationship with that man split up, I was in a situation where I identified as bisexual, and now it was time to do something about it. But I was not part of a gay or bisexual community, so I wasn't meeting a lot of other queer women. On the other hand, I was meeting a lot of heterosexual men.

That's just the way the world is structured. If you're a bisexual woman your available partners are heterosexual and bisexual men, and lesbian and bisexual women. There are lots of heterosexual and bisexual men, and there are a smaller amount of lesbian and bisexual women. If you just randomly go through life, you're going to encounter more potential male partners than potential female partners. It always seemed like I was open to either, but I kept meeting men I was interested in. In getting involved with them I was missing out on getting involved with women.

So I was "out" to friends. I was "out" to housemates, but I still didn't really identify with the gay community. There was a political consciousness to it that hadn't hit me yet: the realization of how oppressed someone can be by being in a same-sex relationship and not being able to talk about their partner at work, or not being able to hold hands in public. That hadn't come home to me yet, because I had always been in safe, heterosexual relationships; even though a couple of them had been with bisexual men, they were closeted bisexual men.

It was obvious that I wasn't meeting many queer women so I needed to seek them out in order to find female partners. So when I moved to another community, I began going to gay bars.

The first time I walked into a gay bar I cried. I felt like I was coming home. It was wonderful to be in a space where same-sex couples were holding each other and being openly affectionate with no shame, just complete openness. I've never enjoyed being in a straight bar since.

That was when I first began dating women. Going to public gay places where I would be identified as gay just for being there, and dating women in the same way that I dated men, marked my transition from shame to pride. This happened over that one-year period in that new community.

After living there for a while, I moved to San Francisco partly because I knew that San Francisco was large enough to have a bisexual community within the gay community. I knew that I would be able to meet other bisexual people like myself here easily.

The final coming-out step was meeting other people in San Francisco's bi community, looking at them and saying, "All these people are bisexual. They seem to be dealing with it just fine. They're not all weird. They're not suffering from cases of arrested development as so many people in the gay community try to tell us. They're all just living their lives and doing their thing. So I can too."

All of this transpired before I ever had sex with a woman, though not before I had ever dated a woman, or flirted with a woman, or attempted to initiate a relationship with a woman. By becoming part of the bi community in San Francisco I met lots of other bi women, so I had potential partners to become involved with.

I finally experienced sex with another woman and it was just as natural and wonderful as I thought it would be. There was a feeling of relief, "I really did like that. I really am bisexual. I didn't go through all of this pain and trouble of coming out for nothing."

But it wasn't like when you read lesbian experiences of the first time they had sex with a woman or gay men's experiences of the first time they had sex with a man. That's often described as this feeling of just total opening up, of, "I can experience this kind of passion and this kind of arousal with a person of the same sex that I never felt with an opposite sex partner."

I certainly didn't experience that. Sex was exactly the same except for the plumbing—two people giving pleasure to each other. Because the plumbing's different, the actual activities are different, but the process of intimacy is the same, or it felt that way to me. Then I became involved with a bisexual man for a while, but an out-of-the-closet bisexual man.

**K:** Was this the first out-of-the-closet bisexual man you'd been involved with?

**D:** Yes, and both of us being out of the closet made a big difference, because it never felt like a heterosexual relationship. Not that it didn't have a lot of similarities—certain kinds of power inbalances were still there, but we could share the experience of being queer together; we did a lot of political activities in the gay community together. However, it was my umpteenth relationship with a man.

Being part of the bi community in San Francisco, marching in the gay freedom day parade, being active in various bi groups, I devoted my whole life and a lot of energy to being bisexual. All the people I was meeting were people that I didn't have anything in common with except for the fact that we were bisexual. After I felt that I was really out and comfortable, I began to realize it's not enough to have that one thing in common with someone.

So I began to look at all the other parts of my identity: my profession, my spirituality, my politics, all the things that I have chosen for myself. I began to say, "Being bisexual is a fact about me, but it's not as central as the fact that I'm a scientist, or that I have this particular kind of spirituality, or that I'm an environmentalist. Those things are all much more central and much more important facts about me." If I walked up to someone and listed those facts about me, they would learn much more about me than by merely learning that I'm bisexual, which doesn't really tell them that much about me.

I had been putting all this energy into this one part of my character, being bisexual. I thought, I really need to integrate this into my life somehow, so that I'm living it and it's just part of me. It doesn't have to be this big, central thing that I pour a lot of my time and psychic energy into; I don't want to forget the other parts of myself as well. That's when I realized that you can only integrate it by being open to relationships with both men and women and making the transitions between them. I hadn't integrated it yet, because I hadn't had a long term-relationship with a woman yet.

I don't like to use the word "bisexual" to people who aren't bi themselves. I just say, "Sometimes the person I fall in love with is a man. Sometimes the person I fall in love with is a woman. People are people to me." But my actual real-life experience has been different than that. When I wasn't a part of the gay or bi community, I didn't meet that many other queer women.

Plus it is so much easier to get involved in relationships with men, because if a man's attracted to you he'll usually let you know. He'll be assertive about what he wants, and it removes a lot of uncertainty and insecurity, because you can rely on him to make the first move.

When two women are trying to get involved with each other there's this whole process of each waiting for the other to make the first move, particularly if you're used to relationships with men. You're not getting the same kind of signals from a woman, so it's much harder to initiate a relationship between two women. There are a lot of jokes in the queer women's community about this.

I have set up my life now so that I meet mostly women. I'm in a lot of women's groups. I work in an office with a lot of gay men and women. So the men I'm meeting are not eligible partners and the women are. I've constructed my social world so that I'm much more likely to meet women who are potential partners than I am likely to meet a man who is a potential partner.

I'm still bisexual. I still find men attractive and were an attractive male to happen my way I think it would be stupid for me to deny my feelings. It would almost be missing the whole point of being bisexual, which is loving who you want to love and being in touch with your own true feelings and desires. But I would prefer it if the fates just happened to throw a woman in my path.

As a matter of fact, they have thrown several wonderful women in my path in the last few months. I'm courting three different women right now. I'm not in a relationship with any of them yet. I didn't ask for these three very attractive women to all come into my life at the same time, but here they are, and they're all lesbians, not bisexual women. They all seem interested.

I'm confident that within the next few months I will be starting a long-term relationship with a woman. I think once I've done that-—whether it lasts for the rest of my life or not—I will be able to live an integrated bi life, in that sometimes the person I have a relationship with is a man, and sometimes the person I have a relationship with is a woman, and people are people.

**K:** Do any of these lesbians have any issues with your being bisexual?

**D:** No, none of them do. In fact I have never yet met a lesbian who has any issues with me about being a bisexual woman. I have met gay men who have problems with it, but not lesbians. I know that they exist, because I hear stories from other women, and I see their letters in the *Bay Times* [San Francisco's Gay/Bi/Lesbian paper], but I haven't experienced it personally. I guess I've just been lucky.

The way I think of it is that anyone who has an issue with bisexuality is someone who's not comfortable with their own sexuality, so they find it threatening. I have had the good fortune of meeting lesbians who are very comfortable and secure with their lesbian identity; they aren't threatened by people who are different, or people who are similar, but a little bit different.

I did date bisexual women for a while after getting out of the relationship with the bisexual man. Here's a controversial and bi-phobic thing to say: I would much prefer to date lesbians. I trust them more. I know that they're serious about women.

I guess it's not so much that I would rather date lesbians; I would rather date women who are woman-identified, who are serious about women. There is a certain kind of bisexual woman who does find men more compelling than women. All the political rhetoric about that is they want to keep their heterosexual privilege; that it's safer and more comfortable to be with a man.

My experience in meeting women like this is that there's something deeper and more psychodynamic going on. Probably something having to do with their relationships with their fathers, where the need for approval and validation from men is so strong and so over-whelming at a subconscious level that getting that validation in a relationship with a man is always going to be more compelling than getting it in a relationship with a woman. So it's not something they have any control over. They simply find men more compelling. I had the misfortune of dating some bisexual women like that.

**K:** Give me your definition of "woman-identified."

**D:** Someone for whom the opinions of women are at least as important and as valuable as the opinions of men. Someone for whom the company of women is at least as enjoyable as the company of men. Someone for whom relationships with women are as important as relationships with men. A woman-identified woman is someone who lacks the dynamic of desperately needing approval and validation from men; women who need that I call "male-identified." Again it's not a political statement—it's a psychological statement.

Because it takes a while to know with a bisexual woman whether she has that dynamic or not, and because there is the potential that she might, I feel safer with lesbians, because I know that they won't have that dynamic. That's my sure-to-be controversial statement of why I would rather date lesbians than bisexual women.

With men, I would rather be involved with bisexual men than straight men, simply because we can share the experience of being queer. Although there's always the potential with a bisexual man that relationships with men would be more important to him than relationships with women. But I'll take that risk, because it seems very important to share being queer and having had to come out with my partner.

**K:** Are you monogamous or nonmonogamous?

**D:** It depends on whether I'm with a man or a woman. I don't think I could have a monogamous relationship with a man at this time. I've had so many relationships with men, and I've not had so many with women. I feel that there's still so much to explore sexually and emotionally with women that I cannot see myself giving that up. Maybe I would fall enough in love with a man that I would find that I was willing to, but from my perspective right now I can't see that happening. That's another reason why if I were with a man I would like him to be a bisexual man—I think he would be more understanding about my wanting to be with women.

In my relationship with the out bisexual man we had an arrangement where he slept with other men, but not other women; and I could see other women, but not other men. That worked quite well.

But if I were in a relationship with a woman, I would go out of my mind if she slept with another woman or with another man. And I can't imagine feeling any need to be involved with a man while I was involved with a woman, because I've been there, done that. I know what relationships with men are like. I know what sex with men is like. There's nothing new and interesting there to explore. So I feel like a woman could probably give me everything I needed.

**K:** Do you practice safe sex?

**D:** Since 1987 I have always had safe sex. It's a habit. I never break it. I'm very informed about it, and I'm very assertive about it.

**K:** What is your definition of safe sex?

**D:** No mingling of body fluids. I'm mindful of open cuts, so I'm careful about getting any sexual fluids in an open cut. No unprotected intercourse of any kind, always using condoms. So far I've avoided oral sex with a woman. I've chosen to do other things, using gloves. I don't feel like avoiding oral sex has to be a permanent choice, but I would use a barrier. If I were in a monogamous relationship with a woman and after six months together we both tested negative for HIV, I would be open to doing oral sex without a barrier, because oral sex between women does appear to be a low risk behavior.

With a man it probably would be a long time before I would trust a negative HIV test, because male to female transmission is very likely if the male is infected. So I'd have to have many years of monogamy and negative test results before I would have unprotected intercourse with him.

**K:** Do your parents know that you're bisexual?

**D:** Yes. I was afraid to come out to them, but they were great. My father's response was, "I'm surprised, and I admit I don't really understand it, but of course I love you and I don't think any differently about you. If it makes you happy, I'm happy." My mother's response was, "I'm not surprised. Clearly it makes you happy to be here in San Francisco and finding relationships with people you feel compatible with, so I'm happy for you."

**K:** Do you have other family members?

**D:** Yes, a brother, and he doesn't have any problems with it.

**K:** Do you have any children?

**D:** No.

**K:** Do you want to have children?

**D:** Yes.

**K:** How do you envision doing that?

**D:** It depends on whether my long-term mate ends up being a man or a woman. If it's a man, we'd have to either eventually get to the point of having unprotected intercourse or do artificial insemination. Then do the standard heterosexual having-kids-and-raising-them-together kind of thing. But then I'd have to deal with coming out to my kids, and I have no idea how I would handle that.

If I were in a long-term partnership with a woman, it'd be more complicated. I know from research that there is a difference in how people react to their biological children and to their stepchildren. Much as they might not want there to be a difference, people favor their biological children. So I would find it important with a female partner for us to have children that we were both biologically related to.

One way that could happen is to get sperm donated from a male relative of the nonbiological mother, so that we'd both have some biological part in the child. The other way of solving the problem is simply for me to have one child and her to have one child, so that we'd each have had the experience of a child that we're genetically related to. If I wasn't going to get sperm from a male relative of my female partner, I would then look for a gay male who is interested in co-parenting and get sperm from him.

I don't understand bisexual women who say they want to be involved with a man so that they can have children. Sperm are not in short supply. A sperm bank is always an option.

**K:** Is your goal to be in a long-term, committed relationship?

**D:** It depends on how I end up conceiving a child. If I'm in a relationship with a man, and we decide to have children, then he's my romantic partner and the father of my child. So I would want that to be a long enough relationship to raise the children. I'd prefer the same kind of stability for the child if I were in a relationship with a woman, so that the two mothers would be there for the duration of raising the child. However, if I had a child with a gay male friend who wanted to co-parent, it would be important that he and I cooperate in the raising of the child, and that would be independent from how long term my relationship with my partner would be. I'd prefer to rear children with a long-term, life partner, but it doesn't always work out that way.

**K:** When you're involved only with a man, what do you miss sexually and/or emotionally that you get from a woman?

**D:** Men cannot deal with emotions. That's what I miss most. A lot of men don't seem to understand that when you cry, you cry; you get over it, and it blows away. It's not a big trauma. You just have to express your feeling in the moment and then you move on. Women understand that, whereas men usually get very flipped out by women's negative emotions.

Also, there's a difference in how men and women react to anger. A lot of men can't handle a woman being angry; it's as if it's a challenge to their authority.

**K:** When you're involved with a woman, what do you miss sexually and/or emotionally that you get from a man?

**D:** A sense of being protected. It's not even as specific as being physically protected. Just the sense that there's this big, strong person that I can get comfort and protection from. Not that I necessarily get that from men, though sometimes I do.

**K:** How is it for you dealing with the straight world as a bisexual woman?

**D:** I haven't had much contact with the straight world for quite a while. I'm about to again, because I'm about to change jobs. I'm at a place now where I can be very out at work. It's going to be difficult at my new job. But I've never gotten any hassles from any of my straight friends about being bisexual. I always anticipate that if I'm close enough to a straight person they're going to be understanding.

**K:** Do you think that you have a contribution to make to the world as a bisexual woman?

**D:** The contribution I have to make to the world as a bisexual and the contribution I have to make to the world as a woman are two separate things. As a woman, I see my contribution to the world is to be a role model for other women as I go about having a professional career and achieving a certain amount of success as a scientist.

As a bisexual, I see my contribution is to open up people's definitions of what it is to love. I hope my life can be a living example of being free to love whomever you want, and being able to freely choose to express your passion and your emotion however you want. If people can see bisexual people living and loving, then maybe they can begin to realize that it's not just some sick perversion, that fundamentally it has to do with being open to loving all people.

**K:** Is there anything else that you want to say?

**D:** I want to emphasize that my story is unique. I am speaking for myself in this interview, not for bisexual women in general who, in my experience, have a tremendously diverse array of feelings and desires and values.

**Postscript:** Since this interview I have become involved in a long-term relationship with a lesbian woman, as I predicted. She's butch, so I feeling like I'm get the best of both masculine and feminine. I now identify as a dyke. Not a lesbian, but a bisexual dyke. I feel very connected to both the bi community and the lesbian community.

# A

# Safer Sex
## How to Protect Yourself

## by Rowan Frost

The following information focuses primarily on HIV (Human Immunodeficiency Virus), but HIV is only one of several incurable infections that can be transmitted through sexual contact or blood exchange. Hepatitis B and C (which cause liver damage), herpes, and genital warts (human papilloma virus) are transmitted in the same ways as HIV, and can also have serious health consequences. The risk of contracting any of these viruses, and all of the other sexually transmitted diseases, can be greatly reduced by using sexual barriers and by not sharing needles.

HIV is not as easy to get as other viruses, but the consequences of infection are usually eventually fatal. HIV gets inside our infection-fighting white blood cells in order to reproduce itself, and in the process destroys those cells. Although our bodies produce more cells, long-term HIV infection eventually wears down our immune system. AIDS (Acquired Immune Deficiency Syndrome) is what we call the result of long-term HIV infection: there are so few fighting cells left in our body that our immune system collapses and we become ill with infections that a healthy person can easily fight off. It takes two to 20 years from the time of infection with HIV for most people to develop AIDS.

HIV is transmitted through a few human bodily fluids: blood, semen, and vaginal secretions. There's not enough virus present in other fluids to pass HIV on, with one exception: nursing babies can contract the virus through their consumption of breast milk.* If we aren't nursed, never have sex and never get anyone else's blood into our bodies, we're not going to get HIV. But we're human and we all get into risky situations from time to time. Your risks of getting any sexually transmitted disease are higher if you've known your partner for less than six months, or if you or your partner have sex with other people. You can reduce your risk by following a few guidelines.

*If you have sex . . .*

Unprotected anal intercourse with a man is the highest risk sex for the receptive partner, that is the partner being penetrated. HIV wants to be in your blood, and the structure of the anus makes it easy for the virus to get there. Unprotected vaginal sex with a man is also extremely high risk for women. The structures of our vaginas make HIV transmission from a man to a woman ten times more likely than transmission from a woman to a man. Infections, possibly including HIV, can also be passed between women who rub vulvas together or use their hands to pass fluids from one vagina to another. Unprotected oral sex with men or women is lower risk, but oral transmission to and from male and female partners has occurred. It is very important to avoid giving unprotected oral sex if you have bleeding gums. It is also important to not let a man come to orgasm in your face or on any broken skin; HIV can be transmitted if you get blood, semen, or vaginal fluids in your eyes or on an open wound.

Deep kissing, if blood is present, can transmit HIV; but deep kissing between people whose gums are healthy and who haven't had recent oral surgery is very low risk. Fingering, fisting (insertion of the hand vaginally or anally), and mutual masturbation are also very low risk: but if there is any broken skin on your hands, you may want to use latex gloves to be absolutely safe. You can check yourself for small cuts or hang nails by immersing your hands in lemon juice, vinegar, or alcohol. Any places HIV could enter will sting.

Sexually transmitted diseases may also be transmitted by sharing sex toys. Clean them with soap and water between uses; if washing up isn't

---

* HIV can also be transmitted to a baby in utero or during delivery. Women with HIV who are pregnant need special care to protect their health as well as their baby's. Proper medical procedures may greatly reduce the risk that a baby will contract HIV.

feasible, put condoms on them and change them between users to help reduce risk.

You can reduce the risk of any kind of sexual activity by using barriers. Sexual barriers for intercourse include latex or polyethylene condoms that cover a penis during sex, and female condoms which are inserted into the vagina. Male condoms can also be used as a barrier for oral sex with men. Barriers for oral sex with women include "dental dams" which are sheets of thin latex sold specifically for sexual use, or plastic food wrap. These can also be used for rimming (oral stimulation of the anus). Using these barriers will keep fluids from being exchanged that can transmit diseases. That sounds pretty easy, but in the heat of the moment, it's not so simple. Using barriers requires that you have several skills: the ability to purchase them, the ability to talk about using them with your partner, and the ability to in fact effectively use them.

Latex condoms are the cheapest and most common kind of condom. They're widely available in drugstores, grocery stores, and adult stores (where you'll find the widest selection of colors and textures). Some people are allergic to latex; the polyethylene condoms (Avanti brand) are a safe alternative. Don't use the "natural" or skin condoms; viruses can pass through the pores. Female condoms (also made of polyethylene) are useful for women whose male partners refuse to wear a condom or can't maintain an erection. "Dental dams" thin enough for sex are usually available in adult stores, but plastic food wrap, although more fragile, makes a good alternative. If you are too uncomfortable to buy barriers at the drugstore or adult store, look into mail order sources. Most sex toy catalogs also carry barriers. Medical supply stores carry latex gloves.

Lubricants are essential if you use barriers; they cut down on friction (reducing breakage), and they make everything feel better. But choosing a lubricant is important: oil-based lubes (any kitchen or bathroom lubes, including lotion, Vaseline, baby oil, and shortening) will weaken latex and cause breakage. Flavored lubes that contain sugar or saccharine can cause vaginal infections. Lubes containing nonoxynol-9 can cause irritation to sensitive vaginal structures and may actually facilitate infection with sexually transmitted diseases. Try experimenting with plain water-based lubes (marketed as "personal lubricants"); find one that feels and smells good to you. Use a drop in the top of a condom before applying it to make it feel better; put lube on the outside of condoms and latex gloves; and apply to the side of "dental dams" that goes against the skin. If you are using plastic wrap, apply lubricant to the vulva, then use your fingers to smooth the plastic into the folds of the vulva.

Practice using barriers and lube before you'll need them. Take the barriers out of the package, figure out how they'll fit, and get used to how they feel and taste. Put some lube on them, and on yourself. This will make it easier for you to bring them out and use them when you're with someone.

### If you hope you might have sex with someone . . .

Make sure you'll have access to barriers and lube. Make it clear that you intend to use barriers. If they object, reconsider whether you want to have sex with someone who doesn't mind putting you or themselves at risk. Remember, there are a lot of sexual things you can do that don't involve exchanging bodily fluids (masturbation, telling sex stories, rubbing on parts of the body away from the genitals . . .)

### If you have trouble protecting yourself . . .

Alcohol and drugs don't cause sexually transmitted infection, but being drunk or high may increase your risk for several reasons: protected sex may seem less important at the time; men may not be able to maintain the erection necessary for condom use; and you may not have the coordination necessary to handle slippery little pieces of latex. Set limits for yourself and keep them. You might also try the "buddy system": when you go out partying stick with a friend who understands your commitment to safer sex, and who will be able to talk you out of getting into a possibly risky situation.

People in abusive relationships may not have the option of insisting on protected sex. The threat of infection can become one more tool an abuser uses to keep control over their partner. If you think you might be involved with an abuser, there are people who can help you. Contact a hotline or domestic violence program. (See page 247).

Low self-esteem or embarrassment around sex can lead us to put ourselves in risky situations. If you find yourself unwilling or unable to avoid doing things that put you at risk, consider talking to a counselor to find out how you can learn the skills that will help you protect yourself.

*If you want to stop using barriers . . .*

Like every issue in a relationship, the question of using or not using barriers depends on honest communication between partners. Some people have negotiated the issue by agreeing that they will be sexually exclusive with each other, and will use barriers for a period of time (usually the first six months), and then get tested for HIV and other infections. If the tests are positive, they will continue using barriers. If the tests are negative, they will stop using barriers. If a partner has sex with someone else, they will use barriers in that encounter. If a "slip-up" happens, the partners agree to discuss it and resume using barriers. The partners will also need to discuss how they will handle the revelation of sex outside the relationship. If infidelity is intolerable to a partner, honesty may mean the end of the relationship. In that situation, the partners might consider the continuous use of barriers.

*If you use injection drugs . . .*

In the United States, most women with HIV contracted it through sharing injection drug needles or through heterosexual sex with injection drug users (IDUs). If you are an IDU, use a new needle whenever possible. Don't let anyone else use your needle. If there's a chance someone else may have used your rig, or if you have to share (even with your best friends or partner), clean the rig thoroughly before using it. Pull clean water all the way into the syringe and flush it out three times; repeat with fresh bleach; then rinse it with clean water. Don't share rinse water, cookers, or cottons; hepatitis and HIV can be passed through them. If one needle is used to measure or share the drugs, make sure it's sterile before it touches the cooker.

*If your partner uses injection drugs . . .*

You may not know that your partner is an IDU. Many people lie about their past or present use, and some are very good at "covering their tracks." It may be months or years before you're aware of their use. If you use barriers with all partners for at least six months, and practice open communication, you'll reduce your chances of having high-risk sex with an IDU.

When your partner does discuss their drug use with you, ask a lot of questions. If you're respectful and nonjudgmental, you'll probably get honest answers. How do they clean their syringe? Do they ever share needles, cottons (the filter through which the drug solution is drawn), cookers (the container in which the drugs are mixed), or rinse water (used to flush out the syringe and prevent clogging)? All of these are potentially risky. Understand that IDUs may try very hard to be careful, but if the only way to get a hit is from someone else's needle, almost all IDUs will share. To protect yourself, consider using barriers with an injection-drug-using partner as long as the relationship lasts, or until they have stopped using drugs for several years.

### If you want to get tested for HIV . . .

The "traditional" HIV test looks at a blood sample. A newer version of the test uses a swab taken from the mouth (great for needle-phobes). Two kinds of testing are available: confidential and anonymous. Confidential means that the test will be recorded in your medical chart. Anyone who can get access to your records (including insurance companies) will know that you've had a test, and its results. If you test positive, your name will be reported to the state health department, and your sexual partners may be contacted. Most HIV educators recommend an anonymous test. The test itself is the same, but it is usually administered by a county health department. Your name never goes with your sample. You're usually assigned a number which you bring back to the test site for your results.

It's important to understand how an HIV test works in order to understand what negative and positive results mean. The HIV test looks for the antibodies your body produces after HIV infection, not for the presence of the virus itself. A person can be infected with the virus for up to six months before an HIV test will be positive. Recent studies indicate that people infected with HIV but not yet producing antibodies are very infectious; in fact, there are suggestions that up to 80% of all new infections occur in that "window period" between infection and antibody production.

In other words, a person can test negative but still be infected and pass the virus to other people if they have had sex or shared needles within the last six months. That's why it's so important to use barriers with people you've known for less than six months.

Test results may be positive, negative, or indeterminate. An indeterminate test result means that the test couldn't be read accurately, and that you should retake the test within two months. A positive test result means that you have HIV. This is a life-changing, but not life-ending, event. If you test positive, you need as much information as you can get, and you need to receive it in a supportive and caring environment. If you sense any judgment from a health care provider, stop seeing them and find someone who will help you take care of yourself. Remember that the field of HIV is new and constantly changing, and that both western medicine and "alternative" treatments can help people with HIV live well for a long time.

## Some Useful Resources

National AIDS Hotline (800) 342-2437; TTY (800) 243-7889
National Sexually Transmitted Diseases Hotline (800) 227-8922
National Domestic Violence Hotline (800) 799-7233; TTY (800) 787-3224

*Rowan Frost, the author of this appendix, is a health educator and outreach worker living in Tucson, Arizona. For the last three years she has been working in the fields of HIV education and harm reduction. She is currently employed by the University of Arizona's COPASA (Community Outreach Partnership for AIDS in Southern Arizona) program as an interventionist, giving support to women to help them reduce their risk of contracting HIV, and presenting HIV and sexuality information to the staff and clients of other social service agencies.*

# B

# Resources for Bisexual Women

## by Robyn Ochs

Just a decade ago there were few resources for bisexual women, now there are many. Some are targeted solely for bi women, others are for all bisexually identified people. The following is a tour through some of these resources, focusing on English-language resources for bi women. For *much* greater detail get hold of a copy of *The Bisexual Resource Guide 2000* (1999), Robyn Ochs, ed. Cambridge, MA: Bisexual Resource Center ($12.95, BRC, POB 400639, Cambridge, MA 02140). This is simply the best place to begin. It contains information about organizations, web sites, books, films and academic articles about bisexuality, as well as quotes, photos, and informational articles. The *Guide* is updated every two years so information contained therein is relatively "fresh."

**The Bisexual Resource Center**, which publishes the *Bisexual Resource Guide 2000*, also serves as an international clearing house for information about bisexuality and maintains an archives. Their address is above, and those who have Internet access should check out their web site (www.biresource.org).

**BiNet USA** is a membership organization that seeks to give bisexual people a voice in the national debate about bisexuality. Organized from the bottom up, BiNet has representatives from every region in the United States. Everyone is welcome to join, and doing so gets you a subscription to the quarterly *BiNet News* as well as the opportunity to get as involved as you like, and to know that you are doing your part to make sure that bisexual interests are represented. BiNet can be reached at PO Box 73272, Langley Park, MD 20787-7327, USA and on the web at www.binetusa.org.

There are a few web sites that are great starting points. One is the web site of the Bisexual Resource Center www.biresource.org. Another one is www.bi.org, located in the United Kingdom. A third good place to start is www.bisexual.org. All of these web sites are loaded with links to *other* great resource. Of course, you could always do a search for the word "bisexual" and see what you come up with.

There are a few e-mail lists that are targeted specifically to women: Bifem-l is a rather busy list for bi women. For info send an e-mail to listserve@brownvm.brown.edu with "info bifem-l" in the body. Disabled-bi: open to anyone who defines themselves as disabled. To subscribe send e-mail to: majordomo@queernet.org with "subscribe disabled-bi" in the body. Rubifruit is a moderated list for bi women only. Write to majordomo@queernet.org with "info rubifruit" in the body. BiW-MP is a list for bi women in relationships with men. Write: majordomo@bi.org, with "subscribe biw-mp" in the body. And Wombat is another list for bi women. Write to wombat-request@listserve.aol.com. There are many more Internet resources, but these should be sufficient to get you started.

# Selected Bi-Bibliography:

## Nonfiction

Bi Academic Intervention (Phoebe Davidson, Jo Eadie, Clare Hemmings, Ann Kaloski, & Merle Storr). (Eds.). (1997). *The Bisexual Imaginary: Representation, identity, and desire.* London: Cassell. For the academically minded, an excellent anthology of essays theorizing bisexuality.

Bisexual Anthology Collective (Leela Acharya, Nancy Chater, Dionne Falconer, Sharon Lewis, & Leanna McLannan, Susan Nosov) (Eds.). (1995). *Plural desires: Writing bisexual women's realities.* (w) Toronto: Sister Vision Black Women & Women of Colour Press. The voices of many women, mostly Canadian and of diverse ethnic backgrounds, discussing their bisexual identities.

Firestein, Beth A. (Ed.). (1996). *Bisexuality: The psychology and politics of an invisible minority.* Thousand Oaks, CA: Sage. Includes chapters by Beth Firestein, Paula Rust, Robyn Ochs, Loraine Hutchins. Carol Queen and Margo Rila, about bisexual identity and politics.

Garber, Marjorie. (1995). *Vice versa: Bisexuality & the eroticism of everyday life.* New York: Simon & SchusterGeorge, Sue. (1993). *Women & bisexuality.* London: Scarlet Press. If you like literary criticism, cultural studies and word play, this book is for you.

Hutchins, Lorraine, & Lani Ka'ahumanu. (Eds.). (1991). *Bi any other name: Bisexual people speak out.* Boston: Alyson. Sometimes referred to as the "Bible," this is a great starting point. Contains 77 essays by women and men, mostly women.

Rose, Sharon, Cris Stevens. & The Off-Pink Collective. (eds.). (1996). *Bisexual horizons: Politics, histories, lives.* London: Lawrence & Wishart. This is the UK version of *Bi Any Other Name.* Contains some excellent essays, from the personal to the political.

Tucker, Naomi, with Liz Highleyman & Rebecca Kaplan. (eds.). (1995). *Bisexual politics: Theories, queeries, & visions.* New York: Harrington Park Press. (Order info: 1-800-342-9678). This is an excellent anthology, with contributions by many key bisexual activists. For the seasoned activist, but also for those who are wondering what a bisexual politic might be.

Weise, Elizabeth R. (ed.). (1992). *Closer to home: Bisexuality & feminism.* Seattle: Seal Press. 18 women discuss, from a feminist perspective, their bisexual identities. Essays range from coming out narratives to the highly theoretical.

## Fiction

Lisa Alther, *Bedrock.* NY: Ivy Books, 1990. Two married women, who have been best friends for many years, come to realize that they are in love with one another. One has a good, loving relationship with her husband, the other doesn't. Most of Alther's books can be read as having bisexual content.

Carol Anshaw, *Aquamarine.* NY: Washington Square Press, 1992. Interesting and thought-provoking novel about a swimmer in the 1968 Olympics. The book is divided into three novellas, each one projecting her life 20 years into the future, and each with a different outcome, based on decisions which she made shortly after the Olympics. In each of her equally possible futures she has married or remained single, loved a woman or a man, moved to NYC or stayed in her Missouri hometown.

Carol Guess, *Seeing Dell.* Pittsburgh: Cleis Press, 1995. Dell, a taxi driver, has died suddenly, leaving behind two lovers, one male, one female. One knows about the other, the other doesn't. Refreshing novel about working class people.

Erica Lopez, *Flaming Iguanas: An Illustrated All Girl Road Novel Thing.* NY: Simon & Schuster, 1997. Quirky, entertaining book, a novel that resembles a comic book. Two twenty-something Puerto Rican take off on a journey across the United States on newly acquired motorcycles. Tomato Rodriguez, the narrator, is trying to figure out whether she is bisexual.

Marge Piercy, *Summer People.* NY: Fawcett Crest, 1989. Two women and a man are in a triad relationship. Most of Piercy's novels have characters that may be bisexual.

May Sarton, *Mrs. Stevens Hears the Mermaids Singing.* NY: W.W. Norton and Co., 1965. A woman looks back over her long life and recalls her past loves, male and female, trying to understand their relationship to the development of her poetry and herself. Sarton herself self-identified, at various times in her life, as lesbian and bisexual.

Starhawk, *The Fifth Sacred Thing.* NY: Bantam Books, 1993. Futuristic utopian novel with two competing cultures: one egalitarian in which bisexuality is taken for granted, the other oppressive and authoritarian. Incidentally, science fiction is a great vehicle for bisexuality. Other sci-fi authors to check out include Gael Baudino, Diane Duane, Ursula LeGuin, Melissa Scott.

Alice Walker, *The Color Purple.* NY: Harcourt Brace Janovitch, 1982. Shug, one of the major characters, is bisexual. If you want to follow the love story, read the book—it is practically erased in the film version.

Jeanette Winterson, *Written on the Body.* NY: Random House, 1992. Set in the present, a tale of love between the narrator and a married woman. The name and the sex of the narrator, who talks of past relationships with men and women, is never stated. A fascinating and unsettling experience. Also check out Winterson's other books, as they too have bisexual characters.

## Periodicals

*Anything That Moves.* 2261 Market Street #496, San Francisco CA 94114-1600. For people of all genders. 64 pages, glossy cover. Published 3-4 times/year. $18 for a 4-issue subscription. Web page: www.anythingthatmoves.com.

*Bi Women.* PO Box 400639, Cambridge MA 02140, USA. While the focus of the calendar is primarily in the Massachusetts area, it's readership is international. Subscription: sliding scale $20-30 +/-. Bi-monthly, 12-16 pages. Submissions of poetry, letters, news articles, opinion pieces, cartoons etc. from women welcome. Write for a sample copy.

*North Bi Northwest.* PO Box 30645 Greenwood Station, Seattle WA 98103-0645. Another bi-monthly newsletter similar to *Bi Women.*

*Bi Lines.* Wellington Bisexual Women's Group, Box 5145, Wellington, New Zealand.

# C

## Other Resources

*Loving More Magazine* is a quarterly publication whose mission is to support the right of consenting adults to be in relationship with whomever and however they choose. The magazine provides information for people who are interested in evolving new relationship options and affirms that loving more than one person can be a natural expression of health, exuberance, joy, and intimacy. Address: P.O. Box 4358, Boulder CO 80306. Phone: (303) 543-7540. http://www.lovemore.com

**Sacred Space Institute** offers workshops, books, tapes, and individual coaching on issues dealing with nonmonogamy, sexuality, and community. Contact: Dr. Deborah M. Anapole, P.O. Box 4322, San Rafael CA 94913. Phone: (415) 507-1739. http://www.lovewithoutlimits.com